CODEBREAKER
GIRLS

To my parents, the Silent Generation of the Second World War, their families and all future generations.

What would it be like to keep a secret for fifty years...; never tell your parents or your children; never even tell your husband?
Steve Goss, WABE, NPR, Atlanta,
November 2012

I had to work out what was different – it was all gibberish to me.
Daisy Evelyn Lawrence, London,
July 2005

CODEBREAKER GIRLS

A SECRET LIFE AT BLETCHLEY PARK

WITH A FOREWORD BY SIR DERMOT TURING

JAN SLIMMING

Pen & Sword
MILITARY

AN IMPRINT OF PEN & SWORD BOOKS LTD.
YORKSHIRE – PHILADELPHIA

First published in Great Britain in 2021 by
PEN AND SWORD MILITARY
An imprint of
Pen & Sword Books Ltd
Yorkshire - Philadelphia

Copyright © Jan Slimming, 2021

ISBN 978 1 52678 411 7

Typeset in Times New Roman 11.5/14 by
SJmagic DESIGN SERVICES, India.
Printed and bound in the UK by TJ Books, Padstow, Cornwall.

Pen & Sword Books Ltd incorporates the Imprints of Pen & Sword Archaeology, Atlas, Aviation, Battleground, Discovery, Family History, History, Maritime, Military, Naval, Politics, Railways, Select, Transport, True Crime, Fiction, Frontline Books, Leo Cooper, Praetorian Press, Seaforth Publishing, Wharncliffe and White Owl.

For a complete list of Pen & Sword titles please contact

PEN & SWORD BOOKS LIMITED
47 Church Street, Barnsley, South Yorkshire, S70 2AS, England
E-mail: enquiries@pen-and-sword.co.uk
Website: www.pen-and-sword.co.uk

or

PEN AND SWORD BOOKS
1950 Lawrence Rd, Havertown, PA 19083, USA
E-mail: uspen-and-sword@casematepublishers.com
Website: www.penandswordbooks.com

Contents

Foreword   vii
Prologue   viii
Introduction   x

Part I – Early Days

Chapter 1   Tooting SW17   2
Chapter 2   War   18
Chapter 3   'Manoeuvres'   33
Chapter 4   Bon Voyage   38
Chapter 5   Wartime Volunteer?   42
Chapter 6   A Letter and a Telegram   44
Chapter 7   Chosen   53
Chapter 8   Departing   60

Part II – War Secrets

Chapter 9   Arriving at Bletchley   64
Chapter 10   New Surroundings and a Friendly Face   68
Chapter 11   Room 40   74
Chapter 12   Enigma and the Polish Bomba   80
Chapter 13   Bletchley Park, the Prime Minister and a Letter   88
Chapter 14   Living in Digs   97
Chapter 15   The Workings of Bletchley Park   103
Chapter 16   Working and Waiting   126
Chapter 17   Intelligence Triumphs   132
Chapter 18   Rationing and Writing   140
Chapter 19   From SW17 to PO Box 111   146

Chapter 20   Block E, Typex Communications   151
Chapter 21   Culture or Intellect?   154
Chapter 22   Wrens   159
Chapter 23   The Listeners   163
Chapter 24   Speaking of Japanese   174
Chapter 25   Hut 7 and Top Secret Ultra   180
Chapter 26   Lonely Girl   191
Chapter 27   Fun and Games   197
Chapter 28   Lead up to D-Day   206
Chapter 29   Letters from Home   209
Chapter 30   Winter of 1944   218
Chapter 31   War's End   223
Chapter 32   'We Also Served'   231
Chapter 33   Rain of Ruin, Rain of Tears   234

Part III – Secret Burden

Chapter 34   After the War   244
Chapter 35   Memory   249
Chapter 36   Bletchley Park   253
Chapter 37   Hospital   257
Chapter 38   Mental Health   265
Chapter 39   Believe   270
Chapter 40   Recovery   275
Chapter 41   The Seventies   279
Chapter 42   Reunion and the Sales Time   288
Chapter 43   Still No Recognition   294
Chapter 44   Conclusion   298

              Epilogue   307
              Acknowledgements   312
              List of Names   314
              Abbreviations   318
              Endnotes   321
              Index   335

Foreword
by Sir John Dermot Turing

Since the news first broke in the mid-1970s, the once-secret story of Bletchley Park and its astonishing achievements which assisted the Allied victory in World War II has become well known. More recently, authors have focused on the people who worked there, and in particular the women who largely worked in mundane but equally vital roles alongside the supposedly more glamorous codebreakers. In 1945, more than three-quarters of the Bletchley Park staff were women. What, until now, has been less clear, is that there was an immense variety of roles which women could carry out at Bletchley Park: by no means were they all WRNS operating Bombe machines. *Codebreaker Girls: A Secret Life at Bletchley Park* looks at the diverse roles of the women at Bletchley, while providing proper context and a wealth of incidental and interesting detail which emphasises the trying conditions of the war.

What makes *Codebreaker Girls* special, though, is the personal element. The principal character is Daisy Lawrence, and it is through her eyes that we see Bletchley Park. This approach, richly coloured with Daisy's own archival material, allows us to see directly what the experience of a young woman at Bletchley was like. And, tellingly, it allows us a glimpse at the hidden tensions created by the contrasting war stories of Daisy and her fiancé Stan. Jan Slimming writes with a clear and engaging style. It is a commendable book: enjoy it.

Prologue

'I'll be back in an hour.' Her supervisor's voice reverberated around the cavernous room as the door slammed. 'Right you are,' said Daisy.

A warm summer breeze wafted through the open window as she gave her usual response. The echoing words trailed off in the ensuing silence as she turned to the task in hand. This was one of those solitary shifts. Her wooden desk and chair were of wartime utility type, comfort was considered unnecessary. She began to remove the secret message slips from the special tube and as she did the delicate paper crackled.

Her supervisor would return in an hour; she was always punctual. Daisy was aware of the urgency and importance of her job even though she was just one small link in a long chain of people working toward victory. They had to win this war. She had been at Bletchley Park for eighteen months, but the war had dragged on for five years; German U-boat attacks in the Atlantic, aerial bombings, Japanese attacks on British and American soil, huge loss of life. It had to stop. At first, she hadn't realised how crucial her role was, as she and many others secretly worked together to outwit the enemy. She also needed to find her fiancé, believed captured by the Japanese.

Daisy knew she was looking at intercepted enemy messages. Some came via teleprinter, others by dispatch rider. Her long slim fingers carefully unrolled the several strips of paper to reveal foot-long lines of typed letters on the desk in front of her. Sometimes the messages were numeric. Today was the usual concoction of gobbledygook letters that made no sense whatsoever. She stared at the blackish type on the yellowing paper. It was her job to analyse the secret quarry; look for errors, divide letters into groups of five, mark with a pencil. The second and third strips lay parallel to the others but still did not provide an obvious solution to the puzzle. She tried to pick out letter patterns; read between the lines, identify unusual features.

PROLOGUE

The fourth strip proved more fruitful as a pattern began to appear. This time it was the double letter 'P'. She continued to set out more strips until the tube was empty. She confirmed her analysis and would pass the information on to her supervisor. Sometimes she indexed the information on various cards and filed them into small boxes. Other times she used the overhead conveyor to relay the messages. The vacuum-operated contraption pierced the calm of her empty room, with its weird cranking and whooshing noises, as secret messages rattled overhead to another office. Her supervisor would be pleased with this batch. She was not to speak about her work to anyone except other decoders. It was Work of National Importance. She must work with diligence and speed.

The messages Daisy Lawrence handled originated from Axis powers. Enciphered by special machines, they were part of the enemy's larger plan. British, American or other Allied coastal listening stations had intercepted the messages and swiftly sent them via teleprinter, wireless communications or motorcycle in a secured tube to Bletchley Park. This is her Second World War story, and beyond.

Introduction

Daisy Lawrence was my mother.
I was six the first time she told me about Bletchley Park;
we went there, Mum, Dad, Jill and I
but it would be four decades later before I returned.

London 2006

'What's that?' Neither of us had seen the small bundle before. As Jill proceeded to remove the ribbon from the delicately tied package, we both realised we were holding our breath in anticipation of a surprise inside. We weren't disappointed. The flimsy treasures revealed well preserved papers belonging to our mother: Second World War call-up papers, newspaper cuttings, correspondence from the Foreign Office, old letters and telegrams from my father, communications from other family members, pay stubs and photos.

White sharp fold lines contrasted with dark ink dust shadows. The old newspaper cuttings were so frail and crisp to touch, we were afraid they might break. Folded for six decades, yellowed with age, the documents lay hidden in her blanket box. Most faces in the photographs were unfamiliar, few were annotated. Jill, my twin, agreed to store our find until we had time to properly ponder the contents – I would study them in detail on my next trip home to England. We knew the papers referred to Bletchley Park, but what was this secretive world of our mother. Who were the people she worked with? Why was she chosen?

* * *

When we were younger our parents told funny stories of their childhood, but when it came to adult life and the Second World War, we never knew the extent of their involvement. On Sunday afternoons, Dad watched dreary black and white war films that were often violent and sad – unsuitable for little girls to see, so we left him to watch them and played outside while Mum baked cakes. At times we heard relatives talk about the war, especially with Dad, but then conversations were curtailed with the usual words, 'Well, it was a long time ago, and you don't need to worry about that.' They rarely divulged details and therefore we never knew they were part of important moments in history, not until much later. Only when we were older and studying history at school did we inquire more about what they did in the war.

Dad's answers were more revealing; his war seemed brutal and sad. Mum said she worked in an office at Bletchley Park. We were never encouraged to converse or ask further questions and it wasn't until the 1970s, when Second World War information was declassified, that we became more inquisitive. Alan Turing, labelled the Enigma codebreaking genius and Bombe inventor, was international news again. My mother said she knew him from a distance, 'the shy one at Bletchley'. By now everyone knew why the maths genius was chosen to work there, but we didn't know the answers to our questions. How did she fit into this?

'You were a spy!' I once asked her, incredulously. 'No,' she laughed, 'Of course not!' Her answers were always the same: 'I never knew why,' and 'the work was always boring'. She was young in 1943, just 26, Daisy Evelyn Lawrence, a working-class girl from Tooting, South West London; nobody special. Would we ever find answers to our questions?

* * *

In 1938 the political situation in Europe was uncomfortable and war with Germany again was imminent. Britain needed a smart plan to be on top of its enemy's intentions. After capture of a German codebook during the First World War, Winston Churchill was aware of British Foreign Office success in decoding enemy messages. He also knew of advances made in breaking codes of a German enciphering device called Enigma.

During the early years between the wars, the British government's codebreaking department of the Foreign Office was located within London's Admiralty. Known as Room 40, the section had first become successful under the Director of Naval Intelligence (DNI), Admiral Reginald 'Blinker' Hall. But after his retirement in 1919, it was decided to combine methods of all military forces. Each had their own ways of collecting intelligence, but now it was time to consolidate; consistent and collective use of information was imperative for future operations. The Navy, Secret Intelligence Service (SIS) and MI6, which included the intelligence corps of the Army and Air Force, reluctantly merged and between them, the process of reading enemy messages improved.

The resulting classified information was then shared between the sections and assessed at higher government levels. As another war loomed and message interception increased, faster codebreaking was needed. However, the offices in London were inadequate and a safer location was sought to accommodate the growing combined intelligence section now called the Government Code & Cypher School (GC&CS).

It was then that a group of senior government officials – mostly military representatives from GC&CS – inspected a deteriorating Victorian estate for sale in the middle of the British countryside. Orchestrated by Admiral Hugh Sinclair, head of SIS and MI6, they went under-cover as 'Captain Ridley's Shooting Party'. The backwater location was considered perfect for their proposed staff, had rail connections to London and the north and south of the England, including Oxford and Cambridge universities. But before commuting concerns there was also another key reason for its suitability, less than a mile away – the telephone booster station at Fenny Stratford. Wiring for the London to North of England trunk line 'repeater' unit could easily be extended to Bletchley Park. The purchase went ahead and over the next few months, 150 Foreign Office employees arrived to develop the government's new and secret war station. Two senior naval commanders then set about employing other trustworthy and intelligent people, many of whom had excellent maths and logic skills for codebreaking. However, these were not the only skills needed.

At the outbreak of war in September 1939, the extended specialist team of men and women descended on Bletchley Park. All had to comply with the government's Official Secrets Act. Their most important task was to break the enemy codes, one of which was the now well-known German cipher – Enigma. But there was also another secret cipher to be broken carrying the high diplomatic messages of the Japanese and German governments – Lorenz. The tasks of the codebreakers to collectively read enemy messages was considered 'Work of National Importance' and known to those involved to be equivalent to National Service. GC&CS was the British government's premier agency for secret intelligence during the Second World War. It was codebreaking on an industrial scale and many of the messages, once translated, analysed and formed into outgoing 'Special Intelligence' reports, became known as Top Secret Ultra. Over 10,000 employees around Britain, including London, Bletchley, British outposts abroad and eventually Washington DC, were trained in both manual and mechanical codebreaking to read enemy messages by collectively solving what some thought were 'unbreakable' codes.

The work of Bletchley Park and its satellite stations was said to be the best-kept secret of the Second World War, after the atom bomb. Some historians calculated that the intelligence gathered, assessed and disseminated there, helped win and curtail the war by at least two years, saving countless lives. But it was not only military generals, servicemen, servicewomen, government ministers and senior intelligence officers who adhered to the rules of the Official Secrets Act, but perfectly ordinary civilians whose families were totally unaware of their wartime duties. The success in keeping this secret work hidden for many decades is almost unbelievable. The Second World War was a pivotal time for many young adults from varying backgrounds, and in this secret environment of impermeable intelligence departments, new skills were learnt and lasting friendships made. All their tasks were cocooned in secrecy and only now, as the blanket ban of silence is lifted and further information is declassified, can surviving codebreakers reflect on their work and the best time of their lives.

Part I
Early Days

Chapter 1

Tooting SW17

Daisy Lawrence was a bubbly child, born on 7 January 1917 during the First World War, the Great War, the war to end all wars, a time of unprecedented death and destruction in Europe. The war with Germany started in 1914 and by 1917 many had lost loved ones – husbands, fathers, brothers, sons – over one and a half million. Wounded soldiers returned in horse-drawn carriages, hansom cabs or trains to South London. Nurses with brown flowing capes helped families reunite. Young men, returning from the front, cried out in pain as they manoeuvred wooden crutches across the steps of their mothers' terraced houses. Daisy's mother, Annie watched sympathetically from an upstairs parlour window.

In the smog-filled air, a distant blue-grey circle indicated a brighter orb of sun that hung magically over the railway track; hope of a better afternoon. She could hear the cackle of chickens in the henhouse at the bottom of their small garden, next to the railway-crossing. Steam trains heading for Tooting Junction or Merton Abbey often trundled by, but they no longer stopped. The level-crossing was closed. After feeding the chickens, Oswald Lawrence leaned on the fence to puff on his tobacco-filled white clay pipe, waiting for another train to pass. Deep in thought, he smiled as scenes of bygone years came to mind and the time he worked on the railway. Now the gates at Kenlor Road were shut and had been for some time, but he well remembered the hustle and bustle of horses, coaches and carts as they crossed over the tracks.

At the time Daisy was born he had moved on to work as a general painter and decorator. He'd learned new paint techniques for wood, a fashionable skill and far superior to that of just a brush hand. When that work dried up, he took other work as a night watchman or general labourer. It was hard and monotonous, but it paid the bills and provided food for his family. The drudge of his non-working days was often lifted by the friendly cries of the Cockney delivery lads as they cycled by.

Old Tooting – The Broadway. (Paul McCue)

'Morning Mister! Cheers, Mister!', they cried, 'Keep y'er pecker up.' He was a friendly man, always ready to have a laugh and joke. Everyone called him 'Mr'.

* * *

Annie Lawrence's children were born at home in their rented flat. Daisy was her third. Her older children, Harry (10) and Ciss (9), often played outside, especially after the railway crossing closed. Their road had instantly become a cul-de-sac and provided the perfect playground. After school and at weekends they would bundle up with thick cardigans and coats to play outside their cramped flat in all weathers. The black iron cemetery railings on one side of the road were great for climbing and the tall green trees growing majestically behind provided plenty of shade in the summer. They played hopscotch, football or cricket and when it was time for tea, Annie lifted her parlour window to call in her children. Summer evenings often seemed very still; a pungent aroma of hay-perfumed horse manure was sometimes accentuated by a light breeze. Opposite the graveyard, on the corner of Kenlor Road, SW17, Daisy Evelyn Lawrence's home was happy. Annie hummed an old song everyone sang or whistled; a catchy tune from the early 1900s.

3

Daisy Bell sheet music by Harry Dacre. (Author)

The music hall singer, Katie Lawrence was no relation as far as Annie knew, but her song 'Daisy Bell' was still popular – how lucky, she was to have a second chance to call her new baby Daisy, after that sweet song.

Early Years in Kenlor Road

We wonder if there were other pregnancies between Daisy and her older sister, Ciss. Nine years was a long time without other children. Perhaps Annie and her husband used early forms of birth control such as olive oil and sponges, the withdrawal method, or maybe he worked elsewhere. There are no records to support this, but a 1920 photograph reveals he helped build tramlines and it's possible he travelled to other areas for this type of work. Breadwinners needed to find employment for their families to survive. There was no social security or unemployment benefit in England then.

Mr., building Tooting's tramlines (far right). (Daisy Lawrence Archive)

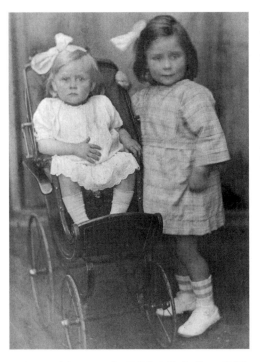

Daisy and her cousin Edith Mitchell, c.1918. (Daisy Lawrence Archive)

The acrid smell of boiling washing on the stove made their noses wrinkle. Traditional washing days in Tooting were Monday and Friday, when a caustic aroma of boiling water, bleach, soap powder and linens bubbled together in a large iron pot in the scullery; it smelled like fish. But the damp atmosphere of wash days was comforting for the Lawrence family in the upstairs flat they called home. As hot steam vapours hit the cold windows, the Lawrence children drew pictures on the glass with their fingers – matchstick-men, a round cat with whisker, or a rabbit – simple and fun distractions from the rain. Or perhaps they would read a book or work on a difficult maths problem. In July 1919, Walter Oswald Lawrence arrived. Daisy giggled with delight to see her new brother. She was two-and-a-half years old. Ciss, was almost 11 and well-versed in childcare as she whisked the new baby off to the kitchen table to change his nappy (everything was done on the table), and later finished the washing. She played the role of the 'little mother'. Their real mother had returned to work cleaning somebody else's house.

Annie and Oswald Lawrence worked hard to feed their family in less than glamorous jobs, but their children were happy, especially as their extended family of joke-telling aunts, uncles and cousins lived close by. Together they enjoyed summer trips to the seaside, Christmas and birthday parties, or 'any-excuse-for-a-knees-up', when all the family would gather around the upright piano to sing old London songs, drink tea or beer, tell funny stories and play hilarious party games. Daisy loved to join in and by the time she was five, she would happily flick her blonde curly hair and flutter her blue eyes at the thought of what was to come. One game was Animal, Mineral, Vegetable, another was Kiss the Blarney Stone, blindfolded. Between her father, aunts, uncles, cousins and her brothers and sister, there was always family leg-pulling going on somewhere. She learned at an early age to be smarter and deal with their wisecracks.

She liked to play the mind-stretching games the adults produced which also included Pelmanism and Tell Me. Harry, her older brother, helped with new words using his Oxford English Dictionary. She remembered 'mineral' was one: *obtained by mining; (belonging to) any of the species into which inorganic substances are classified*. 'Minerals are in rocks,' he explained, 'You know, things that come out of the ground like tin, coal, gold, silver, and … diamonds!' His eyes sparkled and Daisy scanned the entry for a word that could have been 'diamonds', but he slammed the book shut just missing her nose. However, she just noticed the words 'ginger beer' at the bottom of the page, next to 'mineral water,' and she ran to the scullery to find a refreshing cup of home-made ginger beer.

* * *

Small things pleased, and every penny earned was a blessing; life was simple. Daisy loved to learn from Harry, who was a salesman at the Co-op. She played with her little brother and copied her older sister. Ciss, whose real name was Ann, earned her nickname from Harry and was quite happy to be called something different from her mother, Annie. At 13 she had also just started work at the Co-op. On summer afternoons their mother sat outside their front door in the sunshine to watch her younger children play. Sometimes they climbed on the iron fence opposite, but that soon stopped when young Daisy's head became stuck between the cemetery railings. The fire brigade was called to free her.

Despite Daisy's brush with the graveyard pailings, a year later she was left in charge of Walter, who for some unknown reason was now called Bill. Her parents and older siblings had gone to an aunt's funeral in Somerset, a two-day trip. Six-year-old Daisy and four-year-old Bill stayed with Mrs Apps next door, but they were allowed to play in their own back garden, feed the chickens and collect the eggs.

The trains at the bottom of the garden were always of interest and as Daisy tended the chickens, four-year-old Bill ran around, but he also loved to climb. Daisy didn't notice him move an old chair to ascend the drainpipe next to their father's greenhouse where he grew tomatoes. The first she heard was crashing glass and Bill screaming among the plants, his legs covered in blood. The chickens clucked noisily aware of danger, but Daisy acted quickly, shouted for Mrs Apps, and pressed on the wound firmly with her handkerchief and skirt. She had just learned First Aid in Brownies. Mrs Apps heard the crash and Daisy's calls but couldn't climb over the fence. Instead she ran out of her front door, around the corner and into the Lawrence's back garden, where together they managed to slow the flow of blood, and calm Bill down. 'What on earth happened?' scolded Mrs Apps. 'Why was he on the roof?' Daisy couldn't answer. Quickly, they ran to the doctor with him draped across a pushchair where a nurse stitched together the gash in his right thigh. He was lucky the wound was not more serious or life-threatening. All he had wanted was to watch the trains from the roof.

* * *

Records indicate that Daisy's ancestors were once poor west country agricultural workers from Winfrith-Newburg and Tolpuddle, Dorset. They had travelled north to London via Reading, Berkshire looking for work. Now, in south London, the family were fortunate to have four rooms upstairs in a terraced home. Most of the small London houses in Tooting, close to Colliers Wood and Wimbledon, were built in the nineteenth century by farm and industry landowners: textile printers, paper mill owners, railway companies, daffodil and lavender farmers. The dwellings had two levels, upstairs and downstairs, and often provided homes for two large families. Inside was dark with only windows at the front and the back, but the Lawrence's flat on the end of the terrace enjoyed extra daylight through its side windows. One room was a combined dining and sitting room, where a fire often blazed in a cast iron grate. A mid-sized settee, on newly polished floorboards, filled a third of the living space and a small dark-wooden dining table stood on a multi-coloured rug. When the family gathered every Sunday for lunch, the table was extended and pulled into the middle. Four spindle chairs accommodated most, but one person always had to sit on the wobbly three-legged stool.

Over lunch on weekdays – called 'dinner time'– they discussed the news. Daisy and Bill nearly always ran home for lunch from school, while Harry and Ciss came home from work. Their parents were not always there because they worked at different times. Harry, now 16, usually bought a newspaper which he read while he waited for Ciss to serve his lunch. He was a junior assistant in the Co-op's china department, but their conversations often centred around the news and fashion. Ciss worked in the fashion department at the Co-op. Coco Chanel was in vogue and her knitted twin sets and hats sold well. As an avid knitter, however, Ciss knew she could create something equally pleasing for far less money.

Daisy wished she could have a hat like Chanel and made a mental note to add this to her Christmas list. Harry continued to read the newspaper. Working class females were expected to do most of the cooking and household chores then and were often subservient to older males in the house. Daisy was still too young to cook so Ciss or her mother made the meals, but she sometimes helped mix the Coleman's mustard.

The other three rooms on the same level were bedrooms. Daisy shared hers with Ciss. Harry had his own, and young Bill slept in a small bed in his parent's room. The two girls had a wooden commode between their beds, which held a lilac-flowered china bowl and matching jug of icy water to wash in private. A strip wash was often best with a flannel and a clean rough towel for drying. A matching chamber pot was in the small cupboard underneath, just in case nature called during the night, one could relieve oneself in the potty, sometimes called the 'guzunder' (goes under the bed). The pot would be emptied in the downstairs WC in the morning. A small wardrobe held their clothes, and Mister added extra clothes hooks to the wall above two wooden chairs. A fireplace provided warmth in the winter, and colourful handwoven rugs of linen scraps on the damp floorboards, either side of their beds, helped make getting up less shocking on cold mornings. The toilet, WC or water closet, was in the shed outside under the fire-escape. They shared it with the family downstairs. Here Harry's newspaper from the day before came in handy for toilet paper as well as a relaxing read.

The black iron stairs also led down to their enclosed garden through the door of the scullery. This small anteroom contained a large porcelain butler sink for washing dishes and clothes, with just enough room for a new gas-burning stove and oven to cook the Sunday roast and heat pots of water. Once a week, the tin bath was brought up from the garden shed and placed in the middle of the living room. Multiple buckets of hot water were boiled on the stove and the living room fire to fill the tub. Their father was usually first in, modestly protected from female and children's eyes by a wooden clotheshorse draped with sheets. On Friday evenings he would bathe and spruce himself up for a weekend of social intercourse and church on Sunday. Tooting SW17 was a working man's haven among the Victorian suburbs of the landed gentry in Clapham, Streatham and Wimbledon, South London. This was home.

Life in Tooting

Daisy remembered visiting Harry at work at the Royal Arsenal Co-operative Society one rainy day before Christmas. It was a large new emporium between Tooting Broadway and Tooting Bec. She was in awe of the vast staircases, huge windows and different floors with multiple sales counters. There was a distinctive smell too, which reminded her of Bazooka bubble gum – a sweet and sickly smell. The cause of the nose-wrinkling distraction was probably the dim burning gas lamps. Harry doted on his little sister and often brought her presents from the store.

The Tooting Branch of The Royal Arsenal Co-operative Society opened in 1923; its merchandise was inexpensive and employees were paid a fair wage. There was also opportunity for employee promotion. Harry became an expert in the china and glass department and enjoyed serving everyone, including the well-to-do ladies of Tooting Bec and Streatham Common who frequented the store. Their husbands were businessmen in the growing middle classes, but not as rich as the landed gentry of the London's elite, who lived in larger houses. 'Nobs' was a favourite term given to most of the higher classes by working class Londoners.

* * *

In the busy centre of Tooting Broadway, market boys with barrows appeared from all directions, shouting 'Mind'ja backs, mind'ja backs', as they hurried to their stalls. Their large wooden flat-bed carts were painted red and green and loaded with rustic crates of fruit, vegetables, sad-looking fish, live turkeys and chickens screeching as if they knew their destiny. Merchant lorries and steam trains from central London's Smithfield and Covent Garden markets brought fresh goods to the suburbs for distribution and consumption. Fresh milk from the dairy was delivered by milkmen who pulled milk prams, some with the help of a horse. They used jugs or large tin cups to serve the milk, but glass milk bottles were becoming popular.

David Greggs' or J. Sainsbury's sold fresh meat, cheese and eggs, but the new Co-op had a grocery department too, offering interesting foods from other countries. Back then, meat and cheese counters were built from cold slabs of marble and tile, erected on beds of ice in wooden crates – an early form of refrigeration. Today we would call this a delicatessen. Families bought fresh food daily, except Sunday when all the shops and markets were closed. The Lawrence family carried their own supplies home, but richer families paid extra for a delivery. The young, fit, delivery boys transported huge baskets filled with orders to local homes on black bicycles. They were knights of their profession.

The area between the Broadway and the Lawrence's home culminated in a bus terminus at Longley Road. In rush hour it was a hive of activity, packed with people running and dodging carriages, carts, tramcars, trolley buses and new Ford Model Ts. Shoppers and workers walked or hopped on trams or buses to go about their business. Sometimes they travelled by the new and rapidly expanding underground railway, known as the Tube – the underground station at Tooting Broadway had opened in September 1926. Its Northern Line was becoming a great social leveller providing a direct route for bankers and stockbrokers to the City of London, as well as for general workers and regular civilians. With the benefit of this transport alternative the Victorian and Edwardian suburbs rapidly became an important pathway in Greater London's post-war expansion.

School and Work

Some of the Lawrences' neighbours were poorer than they were, noticeable by their unhealthy pallor, tatty clothes and long socks that crumpled around their ankles. Perished garters meant winter months with cold legs resembling corned beef; some children seemed not to have washed for a week. Despite this, Sellincourt Road School, a fifteen-minute walk from Kenlor Road was considered the best for the Lawrence children. Daisy walked there with her sister and when older she led her younger brother Bill to the classroom. On the way they played games;

hopping, skipping, jumping over puddles, trying not to step on cracks or joints in the pavement. At school they huddled in the playground with friends, before the bell rang indicating the start of lessons, glad of the collective warmth. Primary, junior and secondary were all on one site in the two Victorian soot-stained buildings of yellow-sandstone brick that dominated the small playground. Morning classes seemed to go on forever and despite cold temperatures, the pupils could not wait to be outside again. At the sound of the morning-break bell, the children burst through the double doors to continue their games. They were heard but not seen – safe from the road and hidden by high walls, iron railings and gates – until the school bell rang again for classes to resume. Swiftly they filed back in line, ascending the concrete steps, to the corridors of white tile and the lofty classrooms inside. One building accommodated the youngest children, the other junior and secondary students. Older girls and boys had to climb wider and steeper staircases, to the upper floors and separate classrooms.

Daisy in her neatly pressed school uniform c.1927. (Daisy Lawrence Archive)

From 5 to 13 years, school was an important time in Daisy's life. Education by now was freely available to all, but success came in varying degrees depending on your financial circumstances and ambition in life. Her mother was a cook 'in-service' as many of her relatives before, and her father worked night shifts when available, but Annie Lawrence had a different plan for her children.

After the First World War working class families started to think differently. They were 'allowed' to have ideas, and young families felt less restricted by the expected paths of their ancestors. Loss of men in the war meant more women found their voice in the workplace too, traditionally the hierarchy of men. The way forward was to excel at school, secure a well-paid job, become a manager in a big new department store, or in an office. Methods were changing in mechanisation, merchandising and business generally; new skills were offered. Innovative machines produced goods more efficiently at affordable prices and increased availability. American 'inventions for success' were constantly advertised in newspapers and soon their ideas were replicated in London and around the British Isles.

Stores had become bigger and better, and so did everything else, including, unfortunately, traffic jams, despite the new underground railway. Now the safety of pedestrians and drivers was a major problem, as reported:

> 'The traffic boom in London over the past month has resulted in more than three hundred and nine automobile deaths; the total of deaths so far this year is already eight hundred and twenty-seven. A government White Paper looked into the crashes; most it seems were careless driver error.'

More rules were needed with legislation for drivers – lessons and qualified drivers' permits seemed promising ideas. Daisy and Bill's route to school, away from the Tube and the terminus, was safe by comparison. Longley Road was lined with tall silver birches and genteel Victorian houses, some three or four stories high. The front garden terraces were narrow, perhaps 12ft by 5ft wide, with low brick walls to contain a tidy flower bed or shrubbery. Some were built in rows of terraces, others stood detached and double fronted, with outside steps leading to a basement flat for a maid. A small path led to the front door. The middle classes lived in these and Mister didn't miss the opportunity to offer his painting and decorating services between periods of night watchman duties and unemployment.

* * *

Daisy's mother often walked part of the way to school with her children, en route to her job as housekeeper and cook at Waterfall House on the corner of the High Street and Longley Road. On those days she wouldn't see them again until teatime at 4pm. As they went their separate ways

Daisy often asked: 'What's for tea?' To which her mother replied: 'Bread-and-pullit.' Bill soon cottoned on that although 'pullit' sounded chewy, it wasn't food at all. He couldn't imagine just having bread… though sometimes, especially on Thursdays, this could be the case since pay day was not until Friday. Treats were rare, but occasionally ice cream from the corner shop was possible, otherwise it was usually Bird's Eye fish fingers with Peterkin peas, freshly baked bread with butter.

School for Daisy was a delight. As a junior, she wore her navy-blue tunic uniform with pride, over a carefully ironed white shirt, neatly belted at the waist. Beneath she wore warm cotton underwear and thick navy woollen stockings held up with elastic. Her sturdy shoes and lined raincoat – discounted from the Co-op – kept out the chills. After ironing her uniform every night, she always completed her homework, then securely retied her schoolbooks with a wide leather strap. She was good at most classes but didn't boast. The only lessons she disliked were Latin and French, which sadly affected her view of all foreign languages. With homework finished Daisy, sketched and wrote proverbs in her autograph book in her spare time, as well as reading, sewing and weaving. In the springtime she liked to create intricate miniature gardens using red Oxo tins given to her by the lady in the corner shop. The small square tins were filled with black soil from her father's vegetable garden and decorated with pebbles to resemble pathways edged with tiny plants and flowers. Sometimes a piece of broken mirror represented a pond or a lake. Often her artistic arrangements won prizes at the school's summer fayre. She was always delighted, but when it came to music, she could not excel like Ciss, who played the piano well. She liked to sing, but musical instruments were not her forte.

Daisy was never in trouble at school, except for one disastrous and unforgettable occasion when she was 11. 'It was awful,' she recalled. As head monitor, she was trusted to be in the juniors' classroom during breaktime on her own. She was handing out marked homework during the afternoon playtime, concentrating to ensure everybody received the correct exercise book, when someone banged on one of the high windows from the outside playground. Startled, she quickly turned around, and a few exercise books slid off the pile she was holding. It was a boy. How he climbed up there, she didn't know. Somewhat shocked by the intrusion into her quiet but important world of monitor, Daisy bent down precariously to retrieve the books and as she did her bottom hit the single pedestal next to the teacher's desk. As it wobbled, she couldn't decide whether to drop the remaining books or stop the column from falling. In the end she tried both, but it was too late and the bust of Blighty, that sat on top of the column, crashed to the floor with the rest of the books. 'Blighty' was the nickname given to the sculpted bust of either Queen Victoria, or Boadicea. Daisy couldn't remember which. The noise was deafening.

She couldn't do anything to hide and stood with her hands on her head thinking, now what? And as she looked in the mirror on the wall in front of her, there in the reflection, she saw the boy looking through the window behind, pointing and

Daisy Senior School c.1930 (Daisy Lawrence Archive)

sniggering at the accident he had just caused. By then her headmistress had rushed into the room and was not amused to see one of the school's icons destroyed. Daisy was beside herself with fear. Her teacher also ran in, first checking on Daisy, to make sure she wasn't hurt for by now she was sobbing uncontrollably. Owning up to the accident she told the teacher about the boy who banged on the window. After several nose blows into her handkerchief and some sweet tea to calm her down she recovered from the shock. It was probably the only time she was ever in trouble. She couldn't remember the boy's name, but thought he received several days of writing lines after school as punishment.

Without further incident Daisy continued to excel at arithmetic, and her cursive writing was well practised and perfect. She was always one of the top students, passing all her exams, and she liked to read. Her favourite titles around this time were *Gulliver's Travels*, *Black Beauty*, *Oliver Twist* and *What Katy Did*. *Alice in Wonderland* was also on her reading list. She studied hard and was awarded a copy of *A pair of Red Polls: A Book for Girls* by Mabel Quiller Couch to acknowledge her results. Short in stature, she disliked participating in sports such as swimming or high jump but played hockey and rounders instead. She also became a proficient cyclist on her trusty 'steed', the black Daisy Bell bicycle.

* * *

When it was Daisy's turn to go out into the world, ten years after her sister, she was easily embraced by the Co-op department store, a popular employer. Harry was now a manager and Ciss continued to enjoy her sales assistant job in fashions. Through her older siblings the family came highly recommended as hard working and trustworthy.

Her first days at the Co-op in 1931 were in haberdashery when Daisy was 14. 'Miss Lawrence' measured beautiful coloured ribbon and helped sell hats. 'We tried them on when no one was looking,' she laughed. She sewed her own clothes for work, a skill learned from her mother and Ciss at an early age, and she enjoyed making garments for others too. Selling Indian cottons, wool and fine silks, her duties as shop girl were easy, but she was only in haberdashery for about a month. She liked the job, but as she was good at figures and showed an aptitude for organising money and accurate book-keeping records, she was quickly moved upstairs to the accounts office. 'One day I was in hats, the next I was a clerk upstairs with the money and new punched card accounting machines,' she mused. Still very young, she did not challenge this position; it was after all a good move and she wanted to impress her managers. This rapid elevation was wonderful progress in the eyes of her family and friends; she was set for life. Several years later she was promoted to run the store's growing travel department, where she booked travel for her customers on trains, buses and cruise ships.

As a teenager Daisy was shy and preferred to be part of a group. Socialising and attending local dances was a key part of growing up. She was taught how to ballroom dance by her older brother, Harry, when she accompanied him and his girlfriend to Co-op dances. Sometimes they would go to Wimbledon Palais where big band musicians blasted out popular dance tunes of the era. The Palais was exciting, with Dance Marathons – a craze started in America – and, because she was with her older brother, she could stay until ten o'clock.

By the time Daisy was 15 her family had a wireless. The Marconi invention had been around for a while and by now most families had one.

Previously they listened to music using a friend's gramophone, where music and singing came from black shellac vinyl disks turning at around 78rpm. Now they could hear 'live' voices projected from a wooden box without disks. Since the twenties, when the BBC first broadcast, a thirst for the latest sounds had gathered momentum and Harry saved to buy a wireless set from the Co-op for his mother's birthday. It was expensive and he and his friends joked that the Co-op's name, RACS, stood for 'Robbing All Customers Slowly!' Daisy thought this rather harsh since everyone went to their store for bargains and fair prices. But now they could listen to music and the voices of news reporters and famous people only seen in newspapers before, including the BBC's new Empire Service introduced by King George V, the first monarch to broadcast live.

Despite the music, Daisy liked to read. She loved mysteries by Agatha Christie, and romances such as *Lorna Doone* by R.D. Blackmore. She also enjoyed time spent with Ciss and her friends when they attended Tooting's opulent picture palace. Everyone was in awe of the local gem and the black and white films offered. The cinema's grand interior was art deco in design with an ostentatious Modern Italianate style of art, shining marble pillars, red velvet seats and glittering golden mirrors. Among the grandeur, its silver screen came to life with magical music from a magnificent Wurlitzer that rose through the stage floor, as its energetic organist dramatically played the film's score. The amazing instrument is still the centrepiece of the Corinthian style building, the first cinema in the world to be Grade I listed.

Chapter 2

War

Daisy was 16 when she met her future fiancé, Stan. He was a year older and they met in the staff cafeteria at the Co-op. 'He was with everyone else, just there, part of our crowd,' she recalled. Stan was born in Camberwell, the youngest of three from Walworth, London, SE17. His father and aunts ran a second-hand furniture emporium in Trafalgar Street – a junk shop – which today would be labelled an antiques store. He helped with furniture, fixing broken table legs and such like, and attended to the horse kept in the back courtyard. Old Ned pulled a flat-bed cart for furniture collections and deliveries. From an early age Stan and his older brother Frank, helped their father load and unload goods, but Stan also had the glorious task of walking behind the horse with a bucket and spade to scoop up manure. As a result, his father was well known in the area for delicious home-grown tomatoes.

During the late 1920s his family moved south for a healthier lifestyle to Mitcham, on the edge of London in the rolling countryside of Surrey. Stan went to Graveney School, named after the river which flowed into the larger River Wandle. The rivers that bordered the towns of Tooting and Mitcham, rippled over dark luminous soil and sandstone rocks as they merged and flowed gently into the River Thames. For many Londoners the rural smallholding setting, away from city stench and smoke, was an appealing prospect. New houses were being built with government money, borrowed from America post-war, but Stan's family rented a comfortable older-style home close to Figges Marsh, in Edenvale Road.

His full name was Stanley Albert William Moore: S.A.W. Moore, an acronym that would serve him well in future years. When his older brother Frank and sister Doris left home, Stan had his own room at the top of the house, with southerly views over rooftops toward the green hills of the North Downs. The air was clear and his panorama cradled a beautiful patchwork of trees, fields and small farms spanning the horizon. Flower fields of many hues produced multiple strains of apothecaries' herbs, including the fragrant lavender of Potter and Moore and Black Mitcham Mint. Through the centuries the county of Surrey was a preferred country retreat for London's nobility including Lord Nelson and Emma Hamilton. Today, Mitcham retains much of its historical landmarks: historic homes and inns, portraying former royal and rustic life. It is also home to one of the oldest cricket clubs in the country, Mitcham Cricket Club established in 1883.

Stan's father, Frank Moore, retired from his junk shop business when they moved to Mitcham, but his mother, Emma Moore, continued as a seamstress. Her Singer sewing machine was her pride and joy and a valuable tool for the family's finances. Stan was 13 when he moved to Daisy's area. But Mitcham was on the other side of the railway tracks to Tooting and the reason why he attended a different school. At weekends he started at the Co-op delivering groceries to the 'hoi polloi' of South London – the wealthy 'nobs' of Balham, Tooting Bec and Streatham Hill. He loved the freedom of this part time job, riding his black delivery bike with the heavy Co-op grocery basket attached to the front. The young delivery boys were very fit for such arduous work, especially when there was a steep hill to ascend.

Graveney school held few memories for Stan. He liked to sketch and create with his hands, but arithmetic and spelling were not his best subjects. He was glad to start full-time work when he was 14. At the time he and Daisy met, Stan was approaching 16. He was also quite shy, but eligible, with dark hair and tanned skin. Daisy thought he was handsome, especially when he later sported a small moustache and wore his hair greased back Hollywood-style to resemble Clark Gable. Stan had progressed from deliveries to grocery and provisions assistant in the meat and cheese delicatessen, and began to converse more with Daisy and her friends during their Co-op lunch breaks. Her long wavy blonde hair was attractive – also like a film star – and she was clever too. But it was a while before he plucked up courage to ask her out.

His promotion gave him the opportunity to join the Co-op Cycle Club with his friend Bill Morris. They enjoyed cycling the Surrey hills or the towpaths of the Thames, and sometimes they would undertake more challenging journeys to the beach, near Brighton, 'less than fifty miles, as the crow flies,' he said. They were all very fit, and Stan was a good swimmer and diver. Eventually, the cycle club and Daisy's group began to enjoy cycling weekends too, building new adventures. Stan eventually saved enough money to buy a motorcycle, and sometimes they went further to the south western beaches, where the weather seemed warmer, the air fresher and the sun sparkled on the sea. Distance for them wasn't too much of a problem and they enjoyed their trips. Sometimes the two groups camped overnight. The weekend sojourns were exhilarating. However, extra time from work was not always possible, meaning their Sunday evening journey home was long, and great control was needed to resist a stop at more than one of the many pubs along the way. Their first goal was at least to reach the Wheatsheaf, Esher, for a refreshing pint of beer before the downhill stretch to London's sprawling suburbs of slate-grey roofs and smoke-filled chimneys.

* * *

Once a week, the Co-op friends attended the works' dance on the top floor of the store. After one of these evenings in 1933 Stan plucked up courage to ask Daisy if he could take her home. Daisy's Co-op friend, Peggy Johnson was there with her boyfriend Ralph Skinner. Daisy checked with her to see if she should. 'Why not?' came Peggy's reply, 'He seems nice enough.'

Stan smiled from ear to ear when she said yes. He had wanted to ask for a while, after all Daisy and he had worked together at the Co-op for a year and they had become friends. But the stars were not aligned that night due to an unfortunate mishap. It wasn't serious, just extremely annoying for Stan after he'd found the courage to ask, and because his cherished second-hand motorbike and sidecar was dented.

The recent addition of a sidecar consolidated his plan to ask, since Daisy had previously indicated she 'would never be seen dead on the back of a motorbike!' That night they danced to the waltz and quickstep, enjoying each other's company. When they left at 9.30pm, it was drizzling but Daisy was happy to be sheltered from the rain. Her small slender body fitted perfectly into the sidecar for the five-minute journey. In the darkness, they stopped at the red light on the crossroads of Tooting High Street and Longley Road. Stan signalled with his arm to turn right into Blackshaw Road when the traffic-light changed to green for him to make the turn, but the driver in an on-coming taxi did not notice his light was red and failed to stop. The crash seemed slow to Daisy as she watched the taxi drive into her. Shocked and open-mouthed, she tried to scream. Fortunately, he braked, but the slow impact was enough to dent the sidecar and scare the young friends. Daisy emerged, shaken, from the flimsy cover saying she was fine, with just a bump on her head. As she was not hurt there was nothing else to do and no doctor's check. She didn't know until much later that the small incident could be blamed for other medical problems.

* * *

As the years rolled by their tight-knit group of Co-op friends continued to blend work with play. Stan also owned a tandem – a bicycle made for two – perfect for lunchtime picnics by the river or at a local park, sometimes just with Daisy. They went to many places. For longer

Stan (right) promenading at the beach. c.1936. (Daisy Lawrence Archive)

journeys, they rode his motorcycle combination through the beautiful southern countryside to the chalky seaside cliffs and beaches of the English Channel. Peggy and Ralph often went with them. Team spirited, their pre-war years were fun and carefree, with happy joyrides, events and memories sometimes captured by a box-brownie camera. A bicycle trip was often arduous, but a journey to the edge of the British Isles was exhilarating, especially if your friend had a motorcycle. 'Feel the wind in your hair,' laughed Daisy, as they sped through the countryside to the sea. By now she had plucked up courage to sit on the back. Everything seemed so easy then.

Europe Heads for War

By 1935 the friends couldn't avoid noticing the turmoil growing in Europe and the complex decisions their country might have to take. Events had escalated in Europe and Asia. Totalitarianism – full government political power over public and private life – became a form of communist government in the USSR under Joseph Stalin, while Spain and Italy followed fascist ideals, similar to those brewing in Adolf Hitler's Germany. There was also a move toward fascism in Japan, where the creation of Manchukuo, Japan's puppet government in Manchuria, started war with China.

Conflict in Europe meant Britain's future was uncertain. In a world-wide economic depression, as Franco led a right-wing revolution in Spain, Italy's Benito Mussolini supported Hitler's ideals, and Germany controlled the Rhineland in their intended expansion of Europe. America stood on the sidelines. The Neutrality Act amendment in 1935 spurred strong American isolationist policies and non-interventionist feelings. The memory of their expensive involvement in the First World War was all too raw. Nearly two decades later America's allies still owed huge sums of money; the debts seemed impossible to repay. The American people were reluctant to fall foul again by getting involved.[1] In 1937, however, another amendment was passed to allowed provision of any item, except arms, to other warring nations, including belligerents.

The British Parliament formally recognised Franco in a vote of 344 to 137. This caused ugly scenes in the House of Commons. General Franco had gained control of Barcelona and Madrid early in 1939, aided by Italian Air Force bombers, which resulted in many deaths and extreme starvation for civilians hiding underground. The Catalans, after patchy resistance, either surrendered to Nationalist troops or escaped to the borders of southern France. Connecting the decision to Hitler, the UK's opposition government shouted, 'Heil Chamberlain' and 'Now the Vulture', but Prime Minister Chamberlain justified the recognition stating that Franco possessed most of Spain and nobody knew where the losing Republican government was or how many were left. In truth, the few remaining had fled to the northern Spanish mountain area of Figueras.

Meanwhile, Britain's Royal Air Force (RAF) enlarged its stock of air power four-fold and elevated the importance of its pilot training programmes. Germany increased their aircraft arsenal by six. On 15 March, Hitler reneged on the Munich Agreement and invaded Czechoslovakia. Six months earlier the Nazi leader had lied when he announced: 'Germany had no other claims to territory in Europe.' As Czechoslovakians were forced to salute their Nazi invaders, Chamberlain pledged to defend Poland and Britain braced itself for the reality of conflict. The Home Office started to provide free corrugated steel bomb shelters to British low-income families who earned less than £250 per year. The domed panelled structures, 6ft 6ins by 4ft wide, were easy to erect. Soil and grass covered the shelters for extra protection. Large families were given extended versions, and twenty-eight London districts likely to be bombed were given priority. Plans were made to provide gas masks and evacuate 2.5 million children. Further, the British government, including the Foreign Office and the military, were pressed to make difficult decisions, when conscription of young men aged 20 instead of 21 was reluctantly endorsed by the House of Commons. Soon they would complete six months intensive training before deployment to other territories.[2]

* * *

Across the Atlantic, isolationist policies still gripped the American people: Nazi Germany was 4,000 miles across the ocean, why should they be involved, have heavy losses of human life and more unpaid European debt? By August 1939 Mussolini had joined Hitler in a fascist alliance, and a proposed collaboration between Britain, France and Russia faltered when Stalin agreed a non-aggression pact with Germany instead. The Western Powers were surprised and shocked.

The settlement, inevitably, meant war was imminent. As dark shadows loomed over Europe, America's congress re-considered its position but for now stayed on the sidelines, offering safe havens for migrants and partial help.

War UK

Daisy and Stan's lives changed as the atmosphere over Europe became serious. In the uncertainty, their cinema evenings and fun excursions were affected and often curtailed. The growing spat between Chamberlain and Hitler reached its climax when Germany invaded Poland on 1 September 1939. If it wasn't clear before, it was now patently obvious that Hitler intended to spread his empire across all of Europe and perhaps beyond the Atlantic – an Aryan Race with utopian values. His dictatorship capitalised on economic worries, popular discontent and political infighting. People in Poland were slaughtered, and rumours of persecution against Jewish populations and other dissenters in Germany were at a critical stage.

Families kept abreast of the news as events unfolded, and Harry with his newspapers was always ready for any discussion. He had also managed to obtain another wireless set from the Co-op for his sister's family. Ciss had met and married a dashing young Royal Navy officer destined to be chief petty officer, and by 1939, she and Ernie Collingridge had three young children, Pamela, Patricia and Ronald. On 2 September all the family gathered around the wireless at their house in Blackshaw Road, just around the corner from Kenlor. The Prime Minister was about to speak.

Daisy sat with her family in the small dark dining room – Harry, Bill, Mister, Annie, Ciss, Ernie and the three children. In the silence, the children wondered what could possibly be so important. Apart from a child's odd murmur the atmosphere was tense. Daisy opened a large sash window to allow a degree of fresh air and warmth from the sunny afternoon and a gentle breeze ruffled the long net curtain. With a crack and a whistle, the announcement came:

> *I am speaking to you from the Cabinet Room of 10 Downing Street. This morning the British Ambassador in Berlin handed the German government a final note, stating that*

unless we heard from them by 11 o'clock that they were prepared at once to withdraw their troops from Poland, a state of war would exist between us. I have to tell you now that no such undertaking has been received and that consequently, this country is at war with Germany....

Daisy's parents lowered their heads. It was happening again. The Great War was supposed to be the war to end all wars. What now? More destruction and lives lost. Wasn't it bad enough before; were there no lessons learned? Another lost generation, this time it could be their family, Harry and Bill. The silence ensued for what seemed an age but was only seconds. Daisy jumped as Mister stood suddenly and deliberately kicked the bucket near the door. It was half full of water and still held a mop which slopped over the linoleum. He lit a cigarette and walked outside to the small garden. Everything seemed to echo and move in slow motion as Daisy turned her gaze to the open window, and watched her father come into view. The orange marigolds in the garden seemed peaceful against the long green grass. He slumped down on the old wooden chair where Ciss usually peeled potatoes and, with head in hands, he wept. She watched as curls of smoke drifted from the cigarette held in his nicotine-stained fingers. He reached for his handkerchief to blow his nose. Daisy didn't know how long she sat with a knot in her stomach watching her father weep, but she was jolted back to reality when Bill closed the window sharply; the air raid sirens had started. Many years later, she wrote about that day in a letter to her grandson:

In our house we went around closing the windows as the air raid siren was sounding, and we thought that Hitler would be sending his planes over England dropping a poison gas. This was a very frightening time as we didn't know what to expect. The Barrage Balloons were raised all over London from their moorings. These were to impede the enemy aircraft. We didn't see any aircraft and the all clear eventually sounded.[3]

After the 'all clear' siren, Daisy rushed to Stan's house; she knew he would soon be called up, it was just a matter of when. Everyone was skittish at first; waiting for a real attack. But after a while life seemed to go on as usual. When air raid sirens wailed a certain amount of resourcefulness and calmness remained, and people carried on with their normal business. Headlines on 7 September 1939 read 'London Keeps Calm'. Gas masks were issued to all, for fear of poisonous gas. At work Daisy and her Co-op friends questioned and speculated; they didn't know what would happen next or how they would be involved. Air raids came and went but fortunately, no bombs dropped close to Tooting then.

* * *

After four months everybody talked about the effects of the war with restrictions on food, clothes, petrol, transport and freedom. Life was no longer the same. The family had also moved to the ground floor apartment at 111 Kenlor Road, as Annie wanted to be closer to her neighbour's air raid shelter. Daisy wasn't sure why her parents didn't have one. On rationing the government would soon completely control livestock, but initially families didn't need coupons for such items as offal, rabbit, poultry, game or fish, nor brawn, sausages, pies or pasties. Other meat was rationed based on value. Their ration coupons were torn from small government-issue booklets and handed to the grocer who controlled quantities: butter 4 ounces, sugar 12, uncooked ham or bacon 4. Cloth and linens were also rationed, but coupon books were not yet used in restaurants.

Public talk now was not only who was going off to war and where, but sad tales of families losing loved ones in enemy attacks. In February, the government, intent on stopping people's chatter and to build an air of caution toward gossip, started a poster ad campaign: *'Like Dad – Keep Mum!' or 'Careless Talk Costs Lives!'*

The posters were comical and colourful, but with a serious message. Cartoons showed scenes of Hitler and his friends, eavesdropping at the back of local a bus or hiding under a restaurant seat. The implication was you could never be sure who might be listening, so keep quiet – keep 'mum'. Don't let the enemy know.

Called Up

When the blackout was in full force, ready for enemy air attacks, 'Turn out that Light!' was a familiar cry in the streets around Britain.

Night wardens hid in the shadows and offenders rarely escaped. If you lit a cigarette outside it was a major *faux pas*. Streetlights and headlights were unlit or dimmed, with only shaded lights of double-decker buses gliding eerily around London, resembling the drooping yellow eyes from a darkened puppet theatre. Blackout rules, however, suited Daisy and Stan as they became romantically entwined. But young men had started to receive their call-up papers for conscription and Stan received his within six months.

In April 1940 he joined the army and attested to the 18th Division of the Royal Army Service Corps (RASC). At first it was a challenge not to confuse the initials with his work at the Royal Arsenal Co-operative Society (RACS). Daisy thought he looked dashing in his army uniform and even more like Clark Gable. He told her he trained as a driver and had a revolver, though he was never taught how to use it, he later admitted. He had also earned an official car drivers' licence, a step-up from motor-cycle proficiency. He and 'the boys in the army' were on their war-effort adventure. East Anglia, Scotland, Wales and Droitwich were some of the training venues. There were many rules to follow, sergeant major inspections and marches two or three times a day. As military personnel he was automatically required to adhere to a certain amount of secrecy. But even with arduous tasks and serious regimental duties, there were good times, especially when the concert party troops turned up, ENSA (Entertainments National Service Association). Daisy remembered the first variety radio concerts were in October 1939 where the BBC broadcast to the British Empire and local networks from RAF Hendon, North London. Stan mused to Daisy:

> 'Those were great nights! We saw all sorts of stars and the boys had a lot of fun, somehow we managed to get at least one beer at the local pub. We couldn't have too many, of course. There was Mantovani and others, including the melodious singer Gracie Fields and the comedian, George Formby. Most of the time it was very enjoyable and got us all into fighting spirit, not to mention life-long camaraderie.'[4]

ENSA was created in 1939 to provide live and uplifting entertainment for British armed forces, in a combined effort by the Army, Navy, and Air Force. They also performed short versions of Shakespeare's plays.

Many talented entertainers served through the entertainment association – movie stars, past, present and future – but, the organisation was spread thin over a vast area and many shows were substandard. Eventually, the acronym ENSA became known as *'Every Night Something Awful!'*

* * *

The first eight months of war reflected a long period of military inactivity after the 1939 invasion of Poland. There was a marked lack of major Allied land operations on Germany's Western Front, and US Senator William Borah's comments in September 1939 seemed to stick when he said, 'There is something phoney about this war.'

Poland was overrun in five weeks during the German and Soviet invasion and the Western Allies did nothing, despite promises. No Western power was committed to a significant land offensive. This contravened the terms of the Anglo-Polish and Franco-Polish military alliances, where Britain and France were obliged to assist Poland. The period of inactivity was punctuated with small actions on both sides. When Germany launched attacks against British aircraft carriers and destroyers, sinking several with the loss of 518 lives, there was defensive air force reaction, but with little effect. It was known as 'Twilight War, the Sitzkrieg, 'the sitting war', a word-play on *blitzkrieg* by the British Press, and the 'Bore War', reminiscent of the Boer Wars. In France *drôle de guerre* meant 'funny' or 'strange' war; in Poland, *Dziwna Wojna* translated to 'strange war'. Planned Allied campaigns were delayed or cancelled, while other Scandinavia countries were threatened by the enemy.

* * *

The Phoney War came to an end with Germany's successful invasion of Belgium, Luxembourg and the Netherlands on 10 May 1940, the day on which Prime Minister Neville Chamberlain resigned. Discredited through bungled campaigns costing many lives, the British people lost faith in his ability to lead and felt a mounting military catastrophe. Winston Churchill was chosen to pull together an emergency coalition government. 'He would tell the truth.'

Thousands of British, Belgian and French troops were cut off and surrounded by the German army. As Churchill put it the 'whole root, core and brain of the British Army', were stranded at Dunkirk and seemed about to perish or be captured. Instead the rescue, code-named Operation Dynamo, was hailed as a 'miracle of deliverance'. Between 26 May and 4 June, over 338,000 Allied soldiers were saved from Dunkirk harbour and beaches in northern France by fleets of small boats, many owned by local fisherman. But despite this the 'Miracle of Dunkirk' was a disaster with 68,000 of the British Expeditionary Force (BEF) either dead, wounded or captured. However, Churchill was quick to say the 'miraculous evacuation' was not to be celebrated as a victory, 'Wars are not won by evacuations.' The British Channel Islands, however, were a casualty of the Fall of France, when the government demilitarized the area and evacuated many families to England and Scotland. German troops landed on British soil June 1940.

More than the 'blood, toil, tears and sweat' that he promised would be needed. He knew another kind of war was required for his country to survive, one far different from any before. It would be a war fought with intelligence and science more than vessels and gun powder, a strategy to which he later referred to as a 'Wizard War'. The whole country was mobilised as the new Prime Minister took stock of the manpower needed to defend the nation. Meanwhile the Luftwaffe continued bombing Britain.

* * *

Churchill fostered good relations with America, especially as his mother was American; the country to him was family. Secretly, a plan for America to help Britain's war was hatched, and on 8 July Lord Lothian, Britain's Ambassador in Washington DC, was directed to make an offer to Roosevelt to reveal secret technical information about England's latest developments in radar and other scientific fields. Churchill had highly confidential information in his grasp and believed America was behind. He hoped this would help secure their assistance. Two days later the offer was formalised by Lothian to Roosevelt:

> *Should you approve the exchange of information, it has been*
> *suggested by my Government that, in order to avoid any*
> *risk of the information reaching our enemy, a small secret*

*British mission consisting of two or three service officers
and civilian scientists should be dispatched immediately to
this country to enter into discussions with Army and Navy
experts.*

The letter went on to suggest compensation for such secret information:

*His Majesty's Government would greatly appreciate it, if the
United States Government, having been given full details of
any British equipment and devices, would reciprocate by
discussing certain secret information of a technical nature,
which our technical experts are anxious to have.*

Roosevelt brushed aside dissension from high-ranking military officers
including General Marshall, and provided resources for Sir Henry
Tizard, a chemist, to visit America in September as adviser of Britain's
Ministry of Aircraft Production. In his briefcase were MOST SECRET
details on radar and radio interception. But one special intelligence
report remained under wraps, TOP SECRET ULTRA – the confidential
key to Britain's survival, and their most important intelligence secret
of all.[5]

* * *

The daily news was paralysing at times. While the number of deaths
at Dunkirk dismayed Daisy, frightening air attacks often caused major
timetable delays in between. She was home one morning when the
sirens sounded, and she took cover in her neighbour's Anderson shelter
in the back garden. Emerging from the dirt at the 'all clear' siren, she
was surprised by the influx of people and unprecedented rush-hour
traffic jams. Her journey to work was usually by tram, but on this day,
all were full. She heard that trains going to Waterloo were already
packed at earlier South London stations – Surbiton and Worcester
Park – and further down the line. Stations such as Wimbledon, Collier's
Wood and Tooting had queues for tickets stretching along the road for
more than 100 yards. Hundreds were stranded on platforms as trains
departed late. Sixteen people crushed into small carriages meant for
eight, first class as well as third. Guards' vans were crammed, and

some travelled in the rear drivers' cab, which was unheard of. Rail employees couldn't cope, resulting in major confusion for several hours. Daisy decided to walk.

* * *

The Battle of Britain was a pivotal moment for Harry, Daisy's brother, when he joined the Royal Air Force. Nearly 3,000 were to serve in Fighter Command as London's population took shelter and watched air fights from below. The RAF deployed 640 planes and increased further aircraft production, while the Luftwaffe battled with 2,600 fighters and bombers. It was unnerving to hear the average age of an allied pilot was only 20 years old; many came from the British Dominions, occupied Europe or neutral countries. As pilots and crews waited, they chain-smoked and downed stiff whiskies, knowing this might be their last. The front and rear gunners, the navigator, the pilot; there was a strong chance none would survive this next assignment. 1,023 RAF planes were shot down throughout the on-going battle. The Luftwaffe lost 1,887. Loss of military and civilian life from bombing was over 40,000, with London taking half the fatalities.

After training, Harry's unit soon left for a mission overseas. He couldn't tell his family where, but rumours suggested the Middle East. Daisy and Ciss organised a Co-op farewell party for him inviting friends and family. His departure was tearful. Like many others, he didn't know when he would return. Several months later Annie Lawrence heard he was in Tel Aviv, Palestine.

America Inches Forward

After Henry Tizard's September visit to Washington DC, Churchill learned an American secret; they had been able to break a high-level Japanese diplomatic code. He was impressed and considered revealing Britain's own intelligence methods but needed to wait until Roosevelt was re-elected for a third term. On 5 November 1940 Churchill wrote to the victorious president. *'...I prayed for your success.... We are entering a sombre phase of what must inevitably be a protracted and broadening war....'*

The president didn't respond, but subtly engaged in preparing America for the possibility of future entry into the conflict. Four days later, on 9 November 1940, Neville Chamberlain died of cancer. He was 71. Though haunted by his appeasement policies of the 1938 Munich Agreement, his country and world leaders paid tribute to a great patriot, a devoted servant of the nation, and his struggle to preserve freedom and world peace. His words, 'Peace for Our Time', still resonate. It just wasn't to be in his.

Chapter 3

'Manoeuvres'

Stan, Bill and Harry had already left for training, related skills or placement. Daisy's aunt, uncle and cousins fled to the countryside, and her nieces and nephew would soon be evacuated to some far-off place. Ciss's husband, Ernie, had also boarded his Royal Navy ship in Portsmouth, leaving his wife and young family behind. Families were ripped apart, some forever. But Daisy, her parents and sister were determined to stay.

When Harry left, Daisy moved into his room. He gave her his dark-brown wooden trunk which she decided would be perfect for her needlework and keepsakes. Mister painted her new bedroom a fresh coat of green, her favourite colour. A large window at the side of the house provided extra light and with a few yards of green jacquard fabric she made new curtains. The black iron fireplace contrasted well with her choice of colour. On top of the mantle she propped a small china vase and letters from Stan. He had been gone for several months but was still in northern England as far as she knew. Army manoeuvres sounded tedious, but he would soon be home on leave.

During the winter, on most Friday evenings, Daisy hauled coal and wood into her little room for a fire in the grate. This was her weekend treat. As dawn began to break, she rose to relight the fire and rushed back to the comfort of her bed for additional sleep on her two days off from the Co-op. There were no bedroom fires on weekdays, not unless there was snow on the ground. On these autumnal mornings, she dressed in bed. Sometimes, the morning frosts were almost too cold to poke her nose out from under the covers, so arm by arm, leg by leg, she would slowly don freshly laundered clothes. Gradually the cold garments were warmed by her body heat which made getting up less shocking. Washing on chilly days was also an issue, the water in the china bowl on her washstand stung her fingers as she tried to break the ice. Grabbing her scarf and cardigan, she moved quickly to the heat of the kitchen stove to prepare toast, then a visit to the WC. By now, in the small brick-built water closet there was a new white porcelain toilet which flushed efficiently. After a light breakfast of toast and marmalade, Daisy gulped down a cup of tea, then brushed her teeth in the kitchen sink. With her morning routine complete, she pulled on her coat and boots and left to catch the tram for work, hoping there wouldn't be an air raid on the way.

Proposal

As 1940 ended, Stan planned to propose to Daisy. He would soon be posted but didn't know where. His embarkation leave from secret training at Christmas was perfect timing and with six days in hand, he travelled home to Mitcham. His parents were overjoyed to see him, and later that evening he spent time with Daisy. The next day while she was at work, he drove his motorbike five miles east to visit his brother in Croydon. Frank had married a lively young lass a few years before, Violet Hale, who preferred to be called Molly; they had a seven-year-old daughter, Valerie. Frank was free for a couple of lunchtime beers, and several Senior Service cigarettes, while Stan announced his intention to marry Daisy. His brother, who was in the Home Guard, was delighted. Before the sun set on the North Downs, with his brother's approval (and a small cash loan), Stan had purchased a single diamond ring from Croydon's E.G. Routley, Goldsmith, Jeweller and Watchmaker.

On Christmas Eve, a light-hearted jovial dinner took place at Ciss's home. The food preparation was much the same as any other Christmas, but with fewer people and an air of 'enjoy it now, because it might not be here next year' – even more reason for Stan to ask Daisy, to be positive about coming home. He quietly asked Daisy's father for her hand in marriage before they ate. Mister couldn't contain his joy and beamed throughout the meal and Annie sensed what was happening and beamed too. After dessert of mince pie and custard, Stan suggested they take a short stroll in the cool evening air, away from the heat and family. As the moon shone bright over Lambeth Cemetery Stan proposed on the corner of Kenlor and Blackshaw Roads. Daisy gave an immediate 'yes', followed by a passionate kiss. They planned to marry when Stan left the army. Their families were delighted to hear the news, of course,

Above left and above right: Engagement photos Daisy Lawrence and Stanley Moore 1941. (Daisy Lawrence Archive)

but nobody would have guessed then that the following Christmas Stan would be on the high seas off the coast of a faraway land.

* * *

Churchill, relieved by Roosevelt's re-election and his Arsenal of Democracy broadcast, hoped the president would expand military hardware and shipping to Britain without monetary payment. He was right. Roosevelt persuaded American citizens and Congress that repayment for this costly service would instead take the form of defending the US in the Lend Lease programme, 'Destroyers for Bases'. In the early months of 1941 American, British and Canadian military staff held secret talks in Washington DC with a brief to agree a basic outline for military co-ordination, should America enter the war. The Lend Lease scheme was formally settled on 11 March 1941 under the 'Act to Promote the Defense of the United States' which supplied Free France, Britain and the Republic of China with food, oil and matériel.[1] Their talks also included sharing intelligence.

Four weeks before, on 6 February 1941, important American personnel had arrived at a naval seaport in Scapa Flow, Scotland, for their first official journey to Britain. HMS *King George V* anchored in a heavy snowstorm that afternoon, and its guests swiftly transferred with luggage and special crates to a cruiser destined for London's Thames estuary. As they sailed the North Sea down the east coast of Scotland and England, the reality of war came close to the Americans when they experienced a German bomber attack. They were terrified but not hit; however, as missiles landed, explosions lifted their vessel to an alarming height. Their crates were peppered with fallout, but they survived. They also saw sunken ships abandoned in shallow waters from other attacks, their funnels and masts still visible. One could say these special visitors had a difficult journey.

They were safely met at a London dockside by Deputy Commander Edward Travis, a Foreign Office official who took charge of their luggage and the crates, one of which contained a strange machine and highly classified papers. Their mission was to exchange secret techniques and information with the British government under veils of strict confidentiality. The men were Abraham Sinkov, a mathematical cryptanalyst, Leo Rosen of USA Secret Intelligence Service and officers Lieutenant Prescott Currier and Lieutenant Robert Weeks from the US Navy's OP-20-G. From London they travelled to a dimly lit mansion house in the countryside. There, over a glass or two of sherry – a typically British, but odd thing for American whiskey drinkers to experience – they settled in and were introduced to another senior British commander and his staff. It was the beginning of a renewed trust between Britain and America.

As the Luftwaffe continued to bomb Britain, Hitler's Panzer divisions attacked Russia, contrary to the promise of non-aggression made to Stalin two years before. On 22 June the town of Minsk, located halfway to Moscow, fell and tank battles took place near Kiev in Ukraine. Germany had amassed over a hundred armies, using Finnish and Rumanian allies. Russian Commissar for Foreign Affairs, Vyacheslav Molotov, broadcast to his people that the action was 'an unheard-of attack on his country, which is without example in the history of civilised nations'. Stalin set up a committee of defence to run the Russian war effort during July and retaliated by bombing Finland, East Prussia and Danube oil ports.

* * *

On 20 July 1941 Daisy and Ciss stayed up to hear the launch of Churchill's V-sign Campaign via the BBC. Part, unusually, was in Morse code. The telegraph code system was familiar to Daisy, after she learned the signals from Harry, an ex-Boy Scout, and Ciss recognised the V-sign tones as the opening notes of Beethoven's Fifth symphony. The musical notes were played repetitively to support troops and friends in occupied countries and to annoy Hitler. Everyone joined in and the V-sign and Union Jack campaign became widespread; they were even printed on milk bottle tops. While the BBC played the V-sign tune in Morse code, a contrary campaign of German propaganda was broadcast, in clear English to Britain and the United States. The Irishman William Joyce, known as Lord Haw-Haw, always opened his programme with the words, 'Germany calling, Germany calling'. His aim was to instil disillusion and discouragement into all who listened, especially troops far from home.

Chapter 4

Bon Voyage

In October 1941 Daisy was shocked to hear Stan would leave England in four days. After eighteen months of training at various locations, his army unit would soon board a ship in Liverpool. The dockyard had been badly bombed, but the port was still in use. Things were far more serious now; Liverpool, London and Coventry had all been affected. Devastation in the cities was far and wide with over 46,000 people killed. Stan's destination could not be revealed.

For the 18th Division, it was a time of bravery and resourcefulness – worrying and exciting at the same time. Some said they would be dispatched to Singapore, some said Egypt. They didn't know what lay ahead. What had been the Phoney War was now very real with constant German air raids and attacks on shipping in the Atlantic. Lives across the country, and those of men at sea, were at considerable risk every day. Stan was allowed three days Soldier's Embarkation Leave. It was hard for him, as it was for so many. His last hours were spent with his family and Daisy. She was just 24 and he was a year older.

T/170638 Driver S. A. W. Moore of the Royal Army Service Corps 18th Division. 1941. (Daisy Lawrence Archive)

Their last days together seemed too short as they silently hoped this would not be their last. Stan was excited about travelling and his familiar words of 'Chin up!' soon meant it was time to go. His father put on a brave face, but his mother shed a silent tear. He knew she would worry because he, their youngest, was leaving. Earlier he and Daisy had walked together in the park close to his home, discussing plans for when he returned, but the time finally came for them to part. Their hearts were heavy in that final hour, as they stepped into darkness outside Daisy's home to say goodbye. After holding her for a while Stan kick-started his motorbike and turned full throttle. She ran the short distance with him to the end of Kenlor to stand on the corner, where he saluted as she waved and shouted goodbye. His bike roared along Blackshaw Road to the distant traffic light that had just turned red and she watched the dark shadow of his body turn to wave and salute her again. She imagined his captivating smile, but then the light turned green and all she heard was the echo of his motorbike as the sound bounced off the houses in Longley Road. He was gone.

Crossing the Atlantic

Pulling herself together the next day, Daisy lived with her faith for Stan's safety; he said he would write when he could. Apart from understanding his departure was from Liverpool, she didn't know where he was going and wondered when she would find out. Nobody knew the destination of the 18th Division, except the military commanders and the surveillance departments of Britain's intelligence services. The orders were secret and communication was limited. Only the captains of war knew Stan's ship, and its protective convoy, were due to sail across the Atlantic to Halifax, Nova Scotia.

On 30 October 1941 two vessels packed with army personnel quietly set sail in the dead of night. In strict secrecy Stan's division was assigned to a Royal Mail ship converted to a troop carrier. Within hours of leaving Liverpool, they slowly fell into formation with twenty other eerie silhouettes as they approached the dark horizon. The armed convoy, HS-124, was ready to escort them across the ocean. German U-boats, called Wolfpacks, were their main concern and Stan's ship HMS *Andes*, part of a convoy carrying troops and supplies, was at risk.

The Battle of the Atlantic was being fought, as German submarines hunted allied vessels zigzagging across the ocean. Many lives were lost when enemy torpedoes successfully hit their targets, but miraculously, Stan's convoy crossed safely to Halifax. Allied protection enabled British troops to be placed in strategic positions, with necessary food supplies and, eventually, munitions to be delivered to Britain. Stan and Daisy's families did not know of the danger he was in, not until many years later.

For two months Daisy wondered. No news was considered good news. She wrote regularly with local bulletins, to a BFPO Box number (British Fleet Post Office) and eventually letters or postcards were received from Stan. He was unable to reveal his mission or location, but one letter mentioned he enjoyed being on board and eating American chocolate. Rationing in the UK made chocolate a sought-after luxury and tasting the treat again 'made us troops feel we were in heaven'. In fact, for much of their trip they really were in paradise. He had changed ships and could tell Daisy he was on the USS *Wakefield*. He was unable to say it was a converted luxury ocean liner built in New York, originally called the SS *Manhattan*, nor could he reveal his destination, but a later letter described life on board with views of luscious green vegetation, a hot climate and beautiful sunny skies – a stark contrast to London's winter.

Stan's unit was anchored off Port of Spain, Trinidad, for three days awaiting orders. The troops were forbidden to leave the ship, with only the division's postal unit having access to onshore mail and telegraph facilities. They enjoyed the sunshine, but it was frustrating for Stan who loved to swim in the sea, however, the rule proved useful since he later discovered the waters were shark infested.

* * *

The young British soldiers were eager to fight for 'king and country' and enjoyed the camaraderie of their Top Secret mission, disembarking from one vessel to another, ready for a different adventure. En route the troops trained for seaworthiness and later, land combat. But they wondered why they were on an American ship with the US Coast Guard. America was not yet at war. Canada had offered Britain help with military protection of merchant shipping lines as their vessels were also threatened, but the US had continued to aid only at arms-length, and within the Neutrality Acts. Only Canada, and other European Allied military vessels protected the convoys as they weaved across the Atlantic. Now their voyage stayed close to the American coastline, their destination still classified – the

Philippines through the Panama Canal? North Africa, Middle East, the Far East? They were not told. Meanwhile, America maintained an 'armed neutrality' from the sidelines.

* * *

On 6 December 1941, Japan's attack on the US Pacific Fleet tipped the balance. Now America was officially in the war and all scepticism faded. Three thousand naval servicemen lost their lives the night Japanese aircraft bombed Pearl Harbor on the island of Oahu, Hawaii. America declared war on Japan and Germany declared war on the USA. Immediately US military manpower, fighting ships and weapons were provided to Britain and the Allied forces, who struggled to keep Hitler at bay, but all were ambivalent to the threat of a Japanese invasion in the Far East, which included the British colonies of Hong Kong, Malaysia and Singapore. Instead their main defence strategy was to protect Britain and Europe.

Some went as far to say that after the Pearl Harbor attack, Churchill's first thought in anticipation of US help was: 'We have won the war!' But the Prime Minister's subsequent discussions with Roosevelt went on to refine the Atlantic Charter and the strategy for Europe with little regard for the Far East. Meanwhile, Hong Kong fell to the Japanese on 25 December after a seven-day battle.

On New Year's Day, 1942, twenty-six countries gathered in Washington DC, to affirm their opposition to the Axis Powers of Germany, Italy and Japan. The first four major participants to sign the Declaration of the United Nations were America, Britain, USSR and China. Other representatives of a further twenty-two countries signed the next day, including Australia, Belgium, Canada, Czechoslovakia, El Salvador, Greece, India, Netherlands, and New Zealand.

Chapter 5

Wartime Volunteer?

Daisy knew at some point she would be involved as she saw more young men go off to war. Women were needed to work instead, but many thought a woman's place was 'in the home'. War was radically changing how females were seen in the workplace, but factory industry trade unions were reluctant to let women enter the traditional domain of men, even for a small 'fair' wage. Women already worked hard through volunteer programmes and were not to be dismissed. Government propaganda posters were widespread and reports of her 'patriotic duty' etc. started to take effect. The posters tried to eliminate conflicts between personal and political roles to create heroines out of women.

Daisy could see herself a heroine but didn't want to work in a factory. Perhaps she wouldn't have a choice. With her promise to Stan to await his return she would decide on the right type of war-work for her. Many women were in the same position, committed to a relationship and not quite ready to sign up because they might be sent overseas. Consequently, the government had difficulty in immediately gaining women's support for the forces. Often, women were responsible for managing the home as well as working for their family. Daisy stayed at the Co-op to fill the gaps left by male staff who had already gone to war.

However, industrial employment, in various forms, eventually raised women's self-esteem in all classes, giving them a significant leap to their full potential while doing their part to defeat Hitler. Compulsory conscription in Britain started in 1939 for men of a certain age, who then registered for the Army, Navy, Air Force, or other defence work. Eventually this created severe labour shortages in towns and the countryside. With men fighting overseas, it became necessary for the British government to pass the National Service Act on 18 December 1941 for women to make up the emergency shortages at home and sometimes abroad. This enforced all unmarried women between the ages of 20 and 30 to sign-up.

Daisy knew she could join one of the auxiliary services, such as the ATS (Auxiliary Territorial Service), the Wrens (WRNS Women's Royal Naval Service), the WAAF (Women's Auxiliary Air Force), or the WTS (Women's Transport Service), known as 'mobile women'. When Stan left for training, she became a volunteer fire-fighter in the Women's Voluntary Service (WVS). Later, when the government set objectives for Civil Defence, being with the WVS equated to automatic enrolment for Air Raid Precaution services of local authorities (ARP), so Daisy stayed with the new combined group.

Sometimes known as the RVS (Royal Voluntary Service), WVS was founded in 1938 by Stella Isaacs, Marchioness of Reading, Berkshire, as a women's organisation to aid civilians and as another option to supplement in-town emergency services at home. The Women's Land Army was similar, helping in the countryside and on the farms, where many young women enjoyed escaping from the confines of their stultified, middle and upper class lives. It was their time for adventure. FANY (First Aid Nursing Yeomanry) was another service which cared for the injured in bombed areas and where many met their future husbands. The women were trained to drive ambulances, but also drove for other services. Some also worked in Signals.

Daisy was trained and well-practised in firefighting drills. Her uniform included a khaki skirt and jacket, with a red fire-fighting armband, a tin hat and whistle. She had to know how to locate water, treat burned and injured people, how to fit gas masks for herself, other adults and children. The mask was kept in a khaki canvas pack worn across her chest and was always to be carried outside of the home. The coarse jacket she wore was scratchy against her skin, but when it was her turn for duty, she would wear the lined skirt of her uniform to bed, in case she was called in emergency. Air raids were usually at night, so her jacket, leather belt and shoes were nearby and instantly available when needed. She was happy to be a part-time fire-fighter and glad she could stay at the Co-op. Now she was a bookkeeper in the dividends office – affectionately known as 'the Divvy.' The war and the Blitz were of grave concern, but Daisy was happy to be doing her bit locally.

Chapter 6

A Letter and a Telegram

Daisy had not heard from Stan since his letter just after Christmas. Surprisingly, this correspondence had come from Bombay. Stan's whereabouts was always a good topic of conversation, but they had no idea of where he would go next, they could only speculate. When Daisy heard of the British Forces' embarrassing capitulation to the Imperial Japanese Army in Singapore, she hoped his unit was not involved.

The impregnable fortress of Singapore had been a British naval-base stronghold for many years, but Daisy knew little of the island, a small dot at the end of Malaysia. Newspapers gave incomplete news of a negotiated truce indicating that Japanese forces had taken thousands of Commonwealth soldiers as prisoners. Stricken families read ranting reports of the unprecedented surrender to Japan in February 1942. Churchill called the Fall of Singapore, the 'worst disaster and largest capitulation in British military history'. The cost to the nation was more than £50 million. Was Stan's unit there? It was devastating and worrying to think he might be part of this military defeat; a major national controversy.

Journalists had reported the Battle of Singapore lasted eight days. As news filtered through, everyone was shocked, but there were few details regarding survivors. The tropical area was often called the 'Gibraltar of the East', and the island sounded delightful, but the distance was unimaginable as they tried not to think of bodies being sent home, or worse, never coming home. Their darkest thoughts led to horrific places and distressing scenes. Nobody knew the fate of the soldiers and government officials were unable to formally advise where Stan's unit was. Was he still alive? A prisoner of war? The family was in despair.

* * *

For two long painful months there was little or no news about the troops in Malaya. But one evening, on her way home after work, Daisy had a distinct feeling of happiness as she ran to catch the tram. In the crisp April air, she had sensed something good was about to happen and was not surprised to see a blue airmail letter on the hall shelf when she opened the front door. Her mother looked on and smiled, 'It's from Stan.'

She grabbed the letter opener and sat down. The postmark said Malaya, though confusingly, the print on the letter said INDIA, but that had been crossed through. It was his handwriting and that was the main thing – at last, some form of communication. Within seconds the flimsy airmail folder was sliced open. She couldn't wait to read it.

Now she knew he must be in Singapore. Stan and his family always called her Pat. She preferred that name to Daisy. But something else was odd, and her mother started to question when it was written. Daisy carefully folded back the thin blue paper along the fold lines and cast her eye to the top of the first page – 6 February 1942 – in the middle of the Japanese attack and nine days before the capitulation. It was a very matter of fact letter and Stan had given no indication of trouble. She understood he could not write about military orders, but wished there was more information, and maybe even more emotion. With still no news if he was alive, she felt sick and helpless and took the letter to Stan's parents,

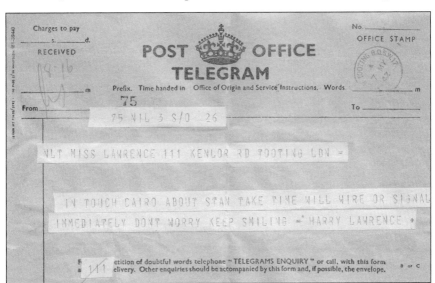

Telegram from Harry Lawrence, 7 May 1942. (Daisy Lawrence Archive)

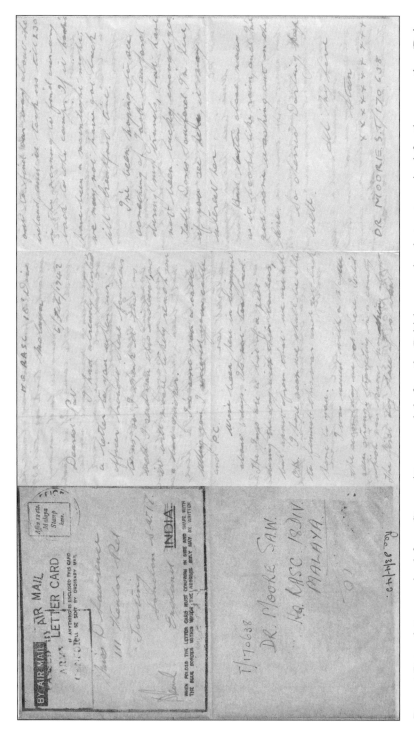

Dearest Pat..., letter received from Stan written a week before the British surrender, but not received for three months. (Daisy Lawrence Archive)

where they consoled each other. They had also received similar mail from before the capture. Were these his last letters? Ultimately the news was bad, Malaya was now in Japanese hands. Was he still there? Did he escape? Surely, they should have heard something by now.

Two weeks later she received a telegram from her brother, Harry, via Cairo. He'd heard from Ciss, about the distress and anguish the families were going through. On 7 May 1942 he cabled news of his help.

News?

The government gave nothing away about the situation in the Far East, only journalists indicated thousands of unaccounted people were held captive in Japanese prisoner of war camps, more than 85,000 British, Australian, Indian, American and Dutch. Daisy hoped Stan was there, but then she heard humiliating stories of British prisoners forced to pull Japanese officers through streets in rickshaws, and beheadings. These reports were later denied when Australian prisoners' letters managed to reach the Australian press, but now she didn't know if the stories were true or not. Official PoW camp sources believed Australian humane treatment toward Malay civilian internees influenced the Japanese to treat Prisoners of War properly, under the humanitarian laws of armed conflict. Daisy wished this was true but remained sceptical and hoped to wake from the nightmare soon.

Brief information was published by journalist, Murray Edwards under the headline of 'News of Malaya Lost.' At last information was beginning to trickle through about the fate of servicemen and civilians captured by the Japanese in Malaya and Hong Kong.

* * *

Stan's mother showed Daisy other clippings from the *Daily Mail*: '3 Letters A Year'. Together they collected as many as possible to try to understand Stan's situation. An International Red Cross delegate arriving in Melbourne, indicated food rations and bedding allowances, and that prisoners of war were paid. This seemed odd to Daisy, but they had no other way of knowing what was really going on. Also, three letters a year was few, but then she remembered several had not received

Newspaper cuttings. (Daisy Lawrence Archive)

any letters; if one came it would be better than none. She hoped the British government would soon confirm the information they all needed. Newspaper reports were just hearsay. When would they know the truth?

A British Prisoners of War Relatives Association news sheet was issued. *'No Red Cross or next-of-kin parcels were getting through as Japanese officials refused to allow relief ships into their captured harbours.'* The rumours and reports were frustrating for the family. All they wanted to hear was that Stan was alive. But the troubles in the world were unprecedented. Daisy read other reports to keep her mind off Stan's situation for a while such as 'WILL KICK HITLER OUT.' Or on the back she read lighter subjects: 'Child Harvesters get £2', where at the National Association of Teachers' London conference, affiliated Labour parties were opposed to the exploitation of child harvesters – 'Wooden-soled shoes were considered a necessity not a fashion item,' and: 'If a child of twelve earned 35 shillings or £2 a week it was a dangerous economic experiment.' Daisy laughed and wondered if clogs hurt. She was glad to be a town girl.

* * *

Months passed before an official explanation of the capitulation was published. Daisy read Reuters' headlines: 'I NEVER HAD A CHANCE', said Lieutenant General Arthur Percival, the former General Officer Commanding (Malaya). On the reverse of the cutting was lighter reading: 'The Amazing Mrs Holliday', a popular (u) rated film. Clearly life was going on as normal despite the bombings and uncertainties. The day before she had gone to the library to find an atlas. She was unable to take one home, but could at least trace a map of the Far East on a sheet of greaseproof paper. She continued to read old news.

In December 1941, the Japanese 25th Army under the command of Lieutenant General Tomoyuki Yamashita had launched an amphibious assault on the Malay Peninsula, one hour (local time) before the attack on Pearl Harbor. Any discrepancy in the timing was because both places lie on opposite sides of the International Date Line. The first Japanese invasion force arrived at Kota Bharu on Malaya's eastern coast, but this was a diversionary tactic since the main landings took place the next day further north at Singora and Pattani on the coast of Thailand (still part of the Malay Peninsula). There Japanese troops rapidly deployed across the northern border of Malaya with little detection. On 10 December

Lieutenant General Percival issued a stirring, if ultimately ineffective, Special Order of the Day:

> *In this hour of trial, General Officer Command calls upon all ranks in Malaya Command for a determined and sustained effort to safeguard Malaya and the adjoining British territories. The eyes of the Empire are upon us. Our whole position in the Far East is at stake. The struggle may be long and grim but let us all resolve to stand fast, come what may, and to prove ourselves worthy of the great trust which has been placed in us.*

But the Japanese had advanced rapidly using bicycles as transport, and on 27 January 1942, Percival ordered a general retreat across the Johor Strait, and the main causeway to the island was destroyed. Buying time, he had organised a defence along the island's 70-mile coastline. But the Japanese did not dawdle and landed on Singapore's northwest corner on 8 February. After a week of fighting, Percival held his final command conference at 9am on 15 February at command headquarters. The Japanese now occupied half of Singapore and it was clear the island would soon fall. Ammunition and water supplies were destroyed in the fight and would be depleted by the following day; Percival agreed to surrender. At the time, he did not know the Japanese were also running dangerously low on artillery shells.

Daisy held her breath as she finished reading the article. Did this include Stan's 18th Infantry Division? The articles were not at all comforting, but now at least she knew more.

* * *

It was many months later that Daisy saw the chilling newspaper photograph of Lieutenant General Percival surrendering to Japanese officers, a white flag raised as he and his officers marched along the Bukit Timah Road to the Old Ford Motor Factory, ready to negotiate terms. A tired Percival insisted the British keep 1,000 men under arms in Singapore to preserve order; General Yamashita finally conceded. At 6.10pm on 15 February British Empire troops had laid down their arms and ceased fighting at 8.30pm. Through this action many lives were saved in spite of Prime Minister Churchill's unpreparedness, lack of weaponry and instructions for prolonged resistance.

But none of this provided precise information about Stan. His mother, Emma Moore, was strong but she too was worried a telegram would arrive with bad news. The daunting sickness they all felt continued. Was no news really good news? Sadly, they weren't alone. As everyone tried to piece the puzzle together, it was little comfort to know that thousands of families also waited for news of loved ones. In August a rumour fermented: the 18th Division had moved to Formosa, an island off the east coast of China. Was he there? Newspapers also reported that Arthur Percival was now on the island of Formosa,[1] detained in barracks described by Japanese as 'spacious' with other high-ranking British, American and Dutch officers. 'He spent much time tending a small garden, reading and re-reading books he brought with him and is allowed the *Japanese Times*' – aka the Jap Foreign Office mouthpiece, a propaganda tool.

The island was not traced by Daisy on her map, but she had discovered that Formosa was Portuguese for 'beautiful island'. Support came from family and friends, and Co-op management was sympathetic to her plight and that of others in a similar state of hell. She missed him desperately, but life carried on and Daisy was moved to the Co-op Travel Department. With her new knowledge of global affairs, it was a good move for her situation and her mind. The summer came and went, noticeably slower than previous years. Spare weekends were filled with excursions to the coast, usually Southend or Margate, accompanied by the friends who were still around. Her best friend, and long-time Co-op colleague was Peggy Johnson. Daisy loved her company and was grateful for her support. Peggy knew where Ralph was, but Daisy had no idea what had happened to her fiancé. Another Co-op friend, Dorothy Edney from Colliers Wood, also helped her pass the time.

All expected mandatory call-up papers soon. As Daisy began to consider another service – WRNS, WAAF, ATS – other young women disappeared from work and parents waved goodbye to their daughters, ignorant of where they were going or what they would do in the war.

In mid-May, Daisy read another newspaper article regarding Far Eastern prisoners of war:

> *'Food Plentiful, Treatment Good.' Relatives of local Streatham men, taken prisoner in Hong Kong and Singapore, would be interested in the report from Kent's Red Cross committee. The information was passed to the newspaper, not by the government or Red Cross, but by a Streatham*

Dorothy Edney, Peggy Johnson and other Co-op friends help Daisy enjoy day trips to the beach. (Daisy Lawrence Archive)

man whose brother was in the Far East at the time of the invasion. The report read: 'The Prisoners of War are now in Changi Barracks.'

Daisy wondered if Stan's name was listed. She prayed it was. The last line of the article read: *'Treatment of prisoners is good and improving in Hong Kong. No further atrocities.'*

Atrocities – the word made her shiver. The family, however, believed him captive on Formosa, but information for his division was unavailable.

Chapter 7

Chosen

November 1942 and Daisy's call-up papers had not arrived. Thoughts of another miserable week weighed heavy on her mind as she pulled her coat from the hook and fumbled for the plastic rain hat in the pocket. Feeling sick, she realised she'd forgotten to have breakfast. Her days were always mixed up and if it wasn't for her mother and Ciss, she probably would never eat. The combination of rationing and worry about Stan, left her weight low, at six and a half stone. Seven months had passed since she'd heard from him; nine months since the capitulation. Running back to the kitchen she grabbed a packet of biscuits from the larder. As she passed by the table, she collected a cutting from Saturday's newspaper and ran to the front door, stuffing the article into her pocket and remembering to take her umbrella as she went out into heavy rain. The tram stop was five minutes away on the High Street.

Daisy and the tram arrived at the stop simultaneously. She stepped up onto the small wooden platform and quickly found a seat near the front, the narrow carriage was steamy and full of silent commuters. Nearly all wore thick black coats and hats of grey or maroon felt that shielded their faces as well as their hair. The autumnal stench of damp woollen overcoats was overpowering. Once seated, she removed the newspaper article from her pocket, trying not to tear the thin paper. The six stops on the tram would only take ten minutes. She just had time to re-read the information and absorb how to write to prisoners in Japan. A new method had been announced by the GPO on how to address letters to prisoners where the camp address was unknown. There were two options and she decided to write to both. When would Stan's survival (or demise) be confirmed? What was the British government doing? Soon it would be Christmas; if only they could receive good news.

Newspaper cuttings. (Daisy Lawrence Archive)

CHOSEN

One of the most costly battles against Germany had taken place on the northern coast of France on 19 August 1942 – the Dieppe Raid (also known as the Battle of Dieppe, Operation Rutter and Operation Jubilee). Churchill had been urged to open a second front in north-west Europe (to relieve pressure on Russia) and some said this would be a test by Allied forces to see how the German military would react to a major sea-port battle – providing crucial intelligence information on the way and a practice for a future beach landing. The 'hit and run' operation went ahead, but few objectives were met due to inadequate co-ordination of Allied support. A chance off-shore encounter in darkness between Commandos tasked with silencing an important enemy artillery battery and a German coastal convoy had a serious effect on the operation. Heavy fire commenced at 11am and lasted three hours. Almost 1,000 lost their lives while others were wounded or captured. Men were either trapped on the beaches or came under German fire and drowned in the English Channel. Canadian troops suffered heavy losses with 1,946 taken prisoner and 916 killed. Over 6,000 allied soldiers took part in one of the worst tactical blunders and senseless slaughters of the war.

A call went out for more men and women to join the war effort. Now the Allied forces prepared for another, hopefully successful battle. By the end of the year 'joining up' was mandatory for certain categories. When the National Service Act was signed in parliament, women objected to the summons for service, on moral grounds. A third of the Conscientious Objectors List were women. Many were prosecuted under the Act, as threatened in their call-up letters, and some were sent to prison. However, ninety per cent of women in Britain did their part for the war effort. They were barred from battle, but due to the shortage of men, were often placed in support roles such as radio and radar operators (interceptors), anti-aircraft operators and military police. Their jobs were risky, and women died in these roles. Famous ATS members were Mary Churchill, daughter of Prime Minister Winston Churchill and Princess Elizabeth, the future Queen of England who trained as a mechanic and truck driver. Meanwhile, as Daisy considered her options, she read more about Far Eastern PoWs in the lengthy, and sometimes helpful, columns of Garry Allighan, a writer for the *Daily Mirror.*

* * *

Christmas Day 1942 – the second without Stan and still no news. Ciss's children were excited to receive gifts from Father Christmas and everyone did their best to make the day less morbid. The distractions of innocent children helped clear minds for a while, as adults joined the cheerful façade – brave faces in a numb void of nothing. Christmas Eve and Christmas morning services at St Nicholas' Church were joyful, but songs of the seasons brought tears to Daisy's eyes. She hoped Stan could hear them; perhaps through a radio. Maybe he was singing too; joining in, alone, miles from home. She couldn't wait to return to work to occupy her mind.

Daisy's call-up papers eventually arrived in early January 1943. At the Tooting Labour Exchange, she was told to attend an interview on the 6th Floor of Devonshire House, Piccadilly, London. She went the next day and answered a few easy questions. They said she would be contacted. Daisy didn't know her friend Dot Edney had been interviewed there too and already had two letters. One from the Ministry of Labour and National Service, the other from the Establishment and Finance Department of the Foreign Office, Devonshire House. Both instructed her to catch the 10.40am train from Euston on 29 December 1942 for employment at the Foreign Office Bletchley, Bucks., as clerk, TwCIII, Salary 51/- pw + OT (overtime). Dot had already left.

On 16 January an identical letter arrived informing Daisy to catch the same 10.40am train, from Euston to Bletchley on Monday, where she would be met 'by transport'. She was to tell no one where she was going or why, but she would soon be able to send a cable to her mother indicating PO Box and phone number for emergency contact. She wondered why she was chosen for this job. Was it her performance at school or was she just lucky? At the heart of everything she guessed they needed trustworthy and reliable girls and she was both. Her Co-op boss would have given her good reference, but Daisy was not aware her credentials were also vetted through unsuspecting neighbours, family and friends by SIS – the British Secret Intelligence Service.

* * *

On Sunday, 17 January Daisy packed her small grey valise. At the bottom she placed the last letter she received from Stan and copies of their engagement photos, protected by a few sheets of tissue paper. On top

MINISTRY OF LABOUR AND NATIONAL SERVICE.

NATIONAL SERVICE ACTS, 1939-1941.

DEAR MADAM,

Under the National Service (No. 2) Act, 1941, you are liable to National Service whether in the Armed Forces of the Crown, in Civil Defence, in industry, or otherwise. In your case it has been decided that you should perform your national service in industrial employment, and the direction below is issued to you accordingly. In the case of women who are in employment to which they have been directed their liability to serve in the Women's Auxiliary Services will not be enforced.

Yours faithfully,

Waterslaw

National Service Officer.

EMERGENCY POWERS (DEFENCE) ACTS, 1939-1941.

DIRECTION ISSUED UNDER REGULATION 58A OF THE DEFENCE (GENERAL) REGULATIONS, 1939.

Note.—Any person failing to comply with a direction under Regulation 58A of the Defence (General) Regulations, 1939, is liable on summary conviction to imprisonment for a term not exceeding three months, or to a fine not exceeding £100 or to both such imprisonment and such fine. Any person failing to comply after such a conviction is liable on a further conviction to a fine not exceeding five pounds for every day on which the failure continues.

To *Miss D. M. Edney*
34 Gamble Rd.
Tooting. SW 17.

Date 29 DEC '42

In pursuance of Regulation 58A of the Defence (General) Regulations, 1939, I, the undersigned, a National Service Officer within the meaning of the said Regulations, do hereby direct you to perform the services specified by the schedule hereto, being services which, in my opinion, you are capable of performing.

If you become subject to the provisions of an Essential Work Order in the employment specified in the Schedule the direction will cease to have effect and your right to leave the employment will be determined under that Order. Otherwise this direction continues in force until withdrawn by a National Service Officer or until the employer specified in the Schedule dispenses with your services.

I hereby withdraw all directions previously issued to you under Regulations 58A of the said Regulations and still in force.

Waterslaw

National Service Officer.

Wt. 16171/1214 250M 6/42 C.N.&Co.Ltd. 749 (7927)

SCHEDULE.

To travel by 10.40am train from Euston on 29.12.42. for employment with Foreign Office Bletchley Bucks. as TwcII. Salary £1/- per to O.T.

E.D. 421.

Dorothy Edney's Ministry of Labour and National Service direction to "industrial employment". (Dorothy Edney Archive)

were a few essentials including a cardigan, small towel, flannel, a pair of shoes and slippers. Her red lipstick and pink hairbrush were already in her handbag, with a sewing kit for unexpected emergencies. Since Daisy did not know when she would return home, she threw in a small bottle of shampoo, in case she was away longer than two weeks, though she could always use soap. A Christmas card from Harry was still on the

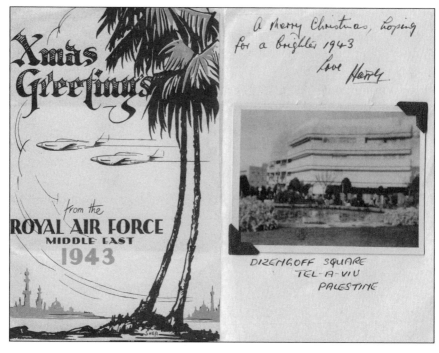

A merry Christmas, hoping
for a brighter 1943
Love Harry

DIZENGOFF SQUARE
TEL-A-VIU
PALESTINE

Harry Lawrence's Christmas and New Year wishes for 1943 from H.M. FORCES MIDDLE EAST, Tel Aviv, Palestine. (Daisy Lawrence Archive)

mantelpiece in her bedroom. She had been surprised to receive the card which doubled as a Happy New Year message from her older brother. He was now in a position to send cards to his family for Christmas 1942. She placed the makeshift war memento back on the shelf; she'd be pleased to see it on her return.

Daisy checked the times of trains from Tooting Junction. There was one to Waterloo that went almost straight through with just one change at Clapham Junction. From there she could catch the tube to Euston in time for the 10.40am train to Bletchley the next day. It was short notice but an adventure, and she was looking forward to her unexpected trip, in a nervous sort of way.

* * *

The next morning her mother and father waited in the kitchen. Daisy told them she was going to Buckinghamshire to work as a clerk.

She didn't mention anything about the Foreign Office. Instinctively her mother knew not to ask questions, this war-time job was different. Periods of awkward silence and stilted conversation prevailed as Daisy clambered into her heavy grey winter coat and slipped on her brown sheepskin-fur boots. As she left, her mother produced a packet of Lyon's Rich Tea biscuits from the larder and pushed them into her daughter's bag. Thankful for the snack and a chance to give them a lasting smile, Daisy said goodbye and hugged both her parents. With butterflies in her stomach, she turned to wave as she reached the door, just in time to see her mother wipe a tear from her eye. Mister's arm was around her mother's shoulders. Daisy was the youngest daughter and last of the Lawrence children to leave.

Ten days before she had turned 26. By now she thought she would be married, but the war had whisked her fiancé away and delayed any ideas of settling down or raising a family. In the meantime, she decided she would work hard to save money and at least they could be together when Stan returned. She shuddered at the thought he might not…. As Daisy carried her suitcase, she considered the many unanswered questions. Nearly a year before, 18th Division families had been promised information from the government, but still there was no news. Eleven months not knowing! She had sent letters, but there were no replies, or bodies – dead or alive. Rumours from the Far East were grim. Apart from escape and his immediate return, the best they could now hope for was his incarceration in a Japanese Prisoner of War camp. Anything else was worse or uncertain.

Chapter 8

Departing

At 6.30am Daisy reached Longley Road. It was early but a typical cold January morning. A dusting of snow covered the icy pavement as she carefully picked her way along the road, trying not to slip. Smoke began to billow from the chimneys as fires inside were stoked. The station entrance was on a small incline which seemed daunting as she approached the icy slope, but then she noticed someone had thrown down ash. It was a task her father would have done; a shovelful of grit to ensure everyone could walk up safely. Gingerly, she made her way to the top; fortunately, she had enough time for delays.

She bought a newspaper from the kiosk and a rail ticket from the ticket office. It was 7.15am. The train arrived at 7.25am and Daisy hauled her suitcase on to the seat beside her; it was too much for her small body to lift it on to the rack. She waited for the train to depart and busied herself with the newspaper crossword. More people got into the carriage. As she chewed the end of her pencil the steam train began to creep slowly down the track and gradually increased speed. After ten minutes they pulled into Clapham Junction where she alighted to catch the Waterloo train.

The connecting train was packed but a young lad offered her his seat and they departed promptly. At Waterloo, she cautiously made her way down to the underground through the crowds. Smoke and steam signalled the arrival of a Northern Line train as it rolled out of the black tunnel into the station. 'Be careful as you step off the train, ladies and gents,' shouted the station boy. There was a large step over a sizeable gap at this station caused by the straight edge of longer carriages that failed to bend to the curve of the platform. Stepping carefully up through the doorway, Daisy pushed herself inside. She was unexpectedly helped by three or four others as they piled in behind to make sure they got on the train.

This was London's rush-hour that Daisy had heard of but never fully experienced. All the tube carriages were crammed. Shop assistants, store managers, bankers, secretaries and office types. She stood most of the way to Euston, clinging to her suitcase and handbag for fear of pickpockets. The throng of passengers thinned at Tottenham Court Road and she sat for the last three stations. Finally, the train clattered into Euston and everyone got off. The worst was over, she thought, as she stood among nimble passengers who seemed to run in all directions. Everyone moved with intent, destinations pre-arranged, but Daisy stood bewildered for a minute until a station guard shouted directions: 'Main Line Trains this way.'

She followed his voice and found herself at the bottom of a wooden moving staircase. It towered above, appearing much larger than the one at Tooting Broadway. She carefully stepped on to the moving steps, leaving a gap between her and the next person for her case, and rested a moment to catch her breath and clutch her handbag. The ride seemed long and far more daunting than the one she was used to at home when, even there, she was frightened of falling backwards. At the top of the escalator daylight came into view as she timed her alighting step perfectly and continued marching to the main station gate to show her ticket to the ticket collector.

Euston station and its vast concourse seemed another world after the cramped conditions of the tube. Steam from distant engines billowed and trains whistled as the muffled hum of passengers moved in theatrical silence toward the underground. She raised her head to breathe the marginally cleaner air and noticed pigeons flying in the metal rafters of the domed glass roof which provided natural light. Like bats, the birds were silhouetted in rays of sunshine that peeked through the clouds. It was 8.55am – plenty of time to find a station guard and check the platform number for the 10.40 train to Bletchley.

Part II

War Secrets

Chapter 9

Arriving at Bletchley

The small tea kiosk on Platform 10 was connected to the waiting room. Daisy bought a cup of tea and a slice of fruitcake instead of eating the biscuits from her mother. She'd save those for later. The tea lady's hair was wrapped in a nylon chiffon headscarf which covered her curlers; a smouldering cigarette hung from her mouth as she poured brown liquid from a large metal pot into a thick railway-issue cup on a chipped saucer. Daisy nodded, smiled and moved away from the kiosk as the curler lady started to comment on the cold weather and enquire about Daisy's journey. She wasn't about to spill the beans of her secret mission to a stranger. She entered the waiting room where, in two trips, she managed to carry her belongings and enjoy her tea and unusual fruitcake breakfast. At 1/6d it was overpriced (around £4 today) the cake was tasty but the strong tea was barely drinkable. With time to spare she completed the crossword and finished reading the news for 18 January 1943.

A few trains came and went before Daisy left the warm waiting room door to an icy blast of cold air to board her train. Immediately she was enveloped in a cloud of steam as the red train halted. The carriage was almost empty. She made herself comfortable with her suitcase next to her on the seat. A ticket collector came by to clip her ticket and the train pulled out of the station. She looked at her wristwatch – 10.40am – on time as instructed, the last leg of her journey.

As the train chugged along Daisy could just make out the houses of North London and the countryside beyond through steamed-up windows. Snow started to fall. She had not been north of London for a long time, at least not for work, and certainly not on her own. She thought of her nieces, Pam and Tricia, and nephew Ron. The children would soon be evacuated to other northern towns for safety. They were so young and would be far from their mother. How distressing not just for her sister, but also the children, but at least they would be safe. Gradually she fell asleep.

She woke with a sudden jolt. It was midday. They had stopped at Leighton Buzzard station, Bletchley was next. The old ticket collector came by again. He probably had seen many young girls like Daisy clutching their life in a suitcase, heading toward Bletchley. After ten more minutes travelling across the snowy countryside of Buckinghamshire and Bedfordshire the train pulled into Bletchley station. She stepped down onto the platform, dragging her suitcase behind her. It was foggy and wet and there was a distinct smell of burning in the air. The aroma was vaguely familiar, but she could not quite place it. She was told somebody would meet her and if she couldn't find the person there was a phone number to call. She looked around and noticed the exit sign on the other side of the tracks. Following other alighting passengers, she walked along the platform toward a Victorian pedestrian bridge. She sighed at the old iron steps in front of her and struggled with her heavy suitcase, up one side and down the other, her feet clunking on the thirty metal steps. Emerging through the exit gate a ticket collector took her ticket, as another middle-aged man wearing a black Trilby and grey belted overcoat approached. Daisy thought he looked sinister and was surprised when he said her name, followed by. 'I'm here from Bletchley Transport. Do you have your papers?'

She confirmed her name and placed her suitcase on the ground to rummage in her bag for the official papers he requested. He took a brief look and handed them back, waiting for her to safely return them to the hidden pocket in her handbag. He smiled and gestured toward the door and the black car waiting outside the station. He didn't seem quite so sinister now, but she thought it odd he hadn't introduced himself. Their journey wasn't long – not even five minutes – before they stopped at a pair of imposing black iron gates; the driver spoke to a man in uniform. The guard saluted, opened the gates, lifted the barrier and on they drove.

Once through the barrier and clearing condensation from the windows with her glove she peered through the mist at her surroundings. The gardens were well-manicured in front of a large house, an outline of which she could just see. She'd never been to a place like this before. Her mother often described opulent mansion houses where she worked in service, and Daisy supposed this might be similar. She wondered which room was hers. As they drove closer to the red-brick house, its strange architecture became clearer. It had an odd assortment of roofs, one of which was green, a large glasshouse, a grand doorway and multiple mullion framed windows. But instead of stopping in front, the man steered toward a long hut at the side, pointed to a small door, and said, 'Wait inside.'

Struggling to get out of the car with her belongings, she made a cumbersome entrance into the hut. It was a waiting room where two smartly dressed women sat on chairs. Each wore a warm-looking grey overcoat, a felt hat and held a handbag, their suitcases neatly on the floor beside them. Daisy did the same and tried to compose herself. There were six chairs and three women, including Daisy. She sat near the middle and smiled; they smiled back. One was blonde, like Daisy, the other brunette. They self-consciously waited together in silence, handbags on their laps, suitcases by their feet. They all knew their assignment was secret and said nothing. One by one they were called to the next room by the secretary, who introduced herself as Miss Abernethy. She explained they were in Hut 9 and this was where Daisy should leave her suitcase before seeing the Commander. She felt intimidated.

Soon it was her turn to go into the Commander's office in the mansion. The large oak-panelled hallway in the house seemed cavernous to her as she followed Miss Abernethy to his office on the ground floor. She could tell the tired interior had once been a magnificent place with gold trim, precious works of art and rich furnishings. The Commander stood by a window looking across the lawns and a lake which Daisy hadn't noticed before in the mist. As she entered, he turned to face her with a grand hand gesture and asked her to sit on the small wooden chair in front of his desk. He sat on a large leather chair with small wheels which he engaged to pull himself forward. Silhouetted in the window, he proceeded to tell Daisy that everything she saw or did at Bletchley Park was Top Secret. A faint smile passed over his lips as he emphasised the rules she was required to follow. If she passed the training, she would be allocated to a specific department. She was now part of the Foreign Office and could not discuss details of her training or the work she was to undertake with anyone outside her allotted department. Daisy jumped when he thumped the desk and shouted, 'Do I make myself clear, young lady!?'

She consented, though she was nervous and could only wring the handkerchief hidden up her sleeve around her fingers. From that moment she was to operate under the Official Secrets Act for the British government on Work of National Importance. The job was highly classified which she couldn't mention to anyone; to do so was treason. She could not tell anyone; not her parents, her siblings, or Stan. Imprisonment or hanging was the usual death penalty for treason, and for a moment, she rapidly blinked to remove an image of herself swinging from a rope. She noticed a gun on his desk. She did not want to be shot either. Quickly she nodded again, shifted in her seat and tried to ignore the cold trickle of sweat running down her back as she tucked her clammy hands and the handkerchief under her legs. The Commander then thrust a form in front of her to read and sign in compliance with the Official Secrets Act. Regaining her composure, Daisy decided that being trustworthy was not difficult. This was important. She would not be a traitor to her country and she would pass the training test. After five minutes reading the document, she signed. The Commander took the form and dismissed her without a further glance. Daisy collected her handbag and left the office as swiftly as she could.

Barbara Abernethy advised Daisy she would work eight-hour shifts at various times after training, which would start the next day. She was to be allocated to a Naval Section, under a department supervisor. For now, she should go to the hostel close by where new recruits lived until a suitable billet was found. The hostel, on Wilton Avenue, just outside the park gates, also housed the canteen. Later Daisy and the two other girls shared the little food they were given and a few snacks left from their journeys. They sat on their beds in the hostel's large dorm and chatted. Peggy was from Barnsley and Mary was from Chesterfield. They talked about home life, schools, families and jobs but by nine o'clock everyone was tired. It had been an exhausting day and Daisy still felt butterflies in her stomach. A good sleep would help her relax.

* * *

Daisy understood that many like her had started in the hostel, a draughty, ramshackle former community hall hurriedly converted to basic sleeping quarters. But sleep was not forthcoming. There was little privacy and far too much noise. She tried to block out sounds of chatter and trains with her pillow. She missed her family and friends but knew she must get used to the new situation and decided she would write a brief letter home in the morning, to let her mother know she was safe. She thought of Stan in a faraway land. There was information in the papers about Australian PoWs and the death of Major General Merton Beckwith-Smith in Formosa. He had commanded the 18th Division of the British Army – Stan's unit. The idea of Stan being there was still a possibility, but nobody knew for sure. She just hoped that somehow, he had managed to escape capture. Then with her pillow pulled tightly around her neck she fell asleep fully clothed. It was too cold to undress.

Chapter 10

New Surroundings and a Friendly Face

As Daisy stirred from interrupted sleep, she started to come to terms with her new situation, remembering her journey the previous day and, now, the different and somewhat uncomfortable, surroundings. She had no idea how long she would be there, but knew she needed to get used to the distant cranking of trains in the nearby shunting yard. Soon the aroma of sizzling bacon wafted in from the other end of the hostel, which helped mask the stark atmosphere and mustiness of the area where she slept. Careful not to wake the girl in the next bed, she rose quietly, slipped on her thick coat and fur boots to visit the communal washroom and toilets outside. She splashed her face with the icy, slightly rusted liquid that spluttered from the tap and patted her skin dry with the small towel she brought with her before returning to the hostel. It had been a while since Daisy enjoyed a hearty fried English breakfast; rationing in London was fierce. Ravenous, her egg, bacon, mushrooms and tomatoes went down quickly with a hot cup of tea.

That day she started her training at GC&CS, Foreign Office Intelligence. At 8am a high-ranking Wren ordered the girls to collect their coats and handbags to prepare for bus transfer to Elmer's School, a former private grammar school for boys. The red brick building on Church Green Road, opposite St Mary's Church and Rectory, was just south-west of the park. It had been requisitioned by the government some years earlier when the Commercial and Diplomatic sections had space constraints at Bletchley Park. In 1942 it became one of GC&CS's training centres. There Daisy learned about call signs, indicators and network identifying discriminants, all of which seemed alien at first. The work was serious and intense, but she was determined to pass. One of their main sources of reference was 'Jane's Fighting Ships'. They also had translation dictionaries: German, Italian and Japanese. The course was seven weeks which, on passing, she would undertake specific secret Work of National Importance.

At eleven o'clock her class took their first refreshment break of the day, and Daisy was surprised and delighted to hear the familiar voice of her friend, Dorothy Edney from the Co-op. Dot, as she always called her, was sitting in the break room drinking tea; she beamed when she saw Daisy. Dot was completing a different training course details of which she could not divulge, but Daisy was pleased to have a friend nearby. They both understood they couldn't speak about their secret war work, so most of their conversation centred round home life in Tooting, SW17. Dot always called Daisy 'Lawrie', derived from her last name, Lawrence. The nickname had stuck at the Co-op and was how she introduced Daisy to her friends at Bletchley. Dot lived in what she called the 'Chalet'. She knew the ropes well and helped Daisy settle in.

* * *

A conference in Casablanca, Morocco code named SYMBOL had taken place earlier in January, between Winston Churchill, Charles de Gaulle, Henri Giraud and Franklin Roosevelt. They discussed future strategies and likely outcomes such as an Italian campaign, a future cross channel invasion, the Axis Powers' declaration of 'unconditional surrender' and unification after a Churchill/Roosevelt invasion of French-controlled Algiers.

War was taking its toll, but all willed Britain to victory to enable peace in Europe. Despite devastation and many deaths, positive spirits came with a 'stiff upper lip'. Only days after Daisy travelled to Bletchley, thirty-eight children between the ages of five and seven were killed in South East London. They had eagerly awaited a performance of *A Midsummer's Night Dream* at Catford Central School for Girls. The German attack was in daylight, and there was no air raid warning or barrage balloons lifted. With fatalities and many injured, frantic parents helped Civil Defence workers in the rescue operation. Daisy was in shock and, as a former volunteer firefighter, thought perhaps she should be there instead.

Over the weeks and months, as well as her work, Daisy learned more of her location while strolling in the grounds either with friends or alone, drawn often to the peacefulness of the deep and dark ornamental lake. In contrast, the mansion was considered an ugly building of many styles, but the gracefulness of the rose garden and lake made up for its ugly design. Follies had been spliced on to the façade in earlier times, creating a mixed concoction of architecture; whims of the previous owner. The 600-acre country estate included small farm buildings, grasslands and, in grander times, lawn tennis courts and a maze of evergreen hedges. The site was owned by Sir Herbert Leon, a wealthy banker and Member of Parliament for North Buckinghamshire, whose wife Fanny, was a strong pillar in the local community. After Fanny died, he sold the property to Captain Faulkner who wanted to tear the building down and erect multiple houses. But instead Admiral Hugh Sinclair, Chief of SIS and MI6, acquired the estate in 1938, for £6,000. Locals were happy the house avoided destruction, but it is unclear whether the government or Sinclair, bought the estate.

Its remote location in the middle of the English countryside, was perfect for clandestine visits of high-ranking government officials, away from London. The esteemed 'hunting' group ruse – as Captain Ridley's Shooting Party – surveyed the estate and before too long it became a relocation site for the British Intelligence department known as Room 40. Over the months Bletchley locals found the strange gatherings rather amusing, but few knew of their activities. They also didn't notice the radio mast installed in the grounds, hidden by a tall tree. It was connected by a wire to one of the top rooms in the mansion and, for a while, was the tenth listening station in a network across the country, Station Ten, often simply written in roman numerals as Station X. But the facility, it is said, was moved from Bletchley just before war was declared. It is believed its positioning might have drawn too much enemy attention to their other work of message processing. The name Station X stuck, but it is incorrect.

Bletchley Park retained its local status as an important official's house for a while, but gradually high fences with barbed-wire and small wooden huts began to appear, followed by factory-like reinforced concrete buildings two-stories high. Captain Faulkner maintained a building interest in the site, and provided the oversized construction, as needed by GC&CS. Eventually this destroyed the ornamental gardens, maze and tennis courts. However, locals didn't question the development because it was wartime and changes were everywhere to support the armed forces. Across the country other large houses were falling into disrepair and government offices, disguised as corporations, were taking over. Bletchley locals seeking employment applied to what they thought was an electrical wiring company. Only suitable candidates were hired and they too, like Daisy, complied with the Official Secrets Act. Bletchley Park's purpose remained secret.

Between 1938 and 1940 the population of Buckinghamshire increased over thirty-five per cent. The sudden influx was caused by the expansion of workers needed for the so-called wiring company at Bletchley Park. Though many had special qualities, the early employees, mostly debutantes, had few of the specialised work requirements for a successful organisation, except perhaps for socialising and foreign languages. The expansion needed professional people with specific and efficient administrative skills at all levels. By 1943 staffing numbers increased again with more civilian recruits, most employed by the Foreign Office (FO), graded from CII to CVI. Some were classed as T/A which was believed to mean Temporary Assistant, including Daisy and Dot, but the acronym could also mean Traffic Analysis, for both graduate and non-graduate personnel. Debutantes, or 'debs,' were often at the same level even though, perhaps, they were less qualified.

Bletchley Park wage slips indicating Daisy's take home pay after deductions. (Daisy Lawrence Archive)

They were a mixed bunch of personalities with varying skills. Daisy's weekly pay started at £2.16s.0d and after insurance deduction of one shilling and seven pence (1/7d), she took home £2.14s.5d on Fridays. By January the following year she'd had a massive overall rise to £4.12s.2d, but after further billeting, transport and income tax deductions she only had two shillings extra at £2.16s.11d. Her travel and rent, however, were now covered.

Some were 'navy types', a term Daisy used for people in uniform. The Wrens seemed to have a higher rank of authority. They were drilled daily and followed regimental rules which as civilians, Daisy and Dot did not need to follow, much to their relief, though they respected the Wrens' position and commitment to duty. The WRNS had expanded considerably since the National Service Act of December 1941 and some were well trained in engineering and radio work where wires and machines filled their daily tasks.

> *They lived two lives. One in the canteen where they would talk about boyfriends, where to buy nylon stockings and trains to London, and then where they worked surrounded by high walls and barbed wire with two naval marine soldiers on guard. Twelve noisy Bombe machines would be working; there was no need to try to speak to anyone over the noise.*

Ruth Henry, Naval recruit, 1943-1945- Bombe Operator[1]

* * *

People congregated for meals in the vast canteen, which some preferred to call the cafeteria or refectory. At its peak it provided thousands of meals each day – 4d for beans on toast, one of Daisy's favourites. She learned the Budd family was central to the catering operation. They had lived at Bletchley for a while. Robert Budd was chief groundsman, driver, quartermaster and head of refreshments in Hut 2. His wife Emma was canteen cook, under the catering manager, Cecil Crawley. A strict schedule for meals was enforced, with only half an hour for lunch. Mrs Budd was a strong and domineering woman with dark hair and a friendly smile. She loved wearing the flowery aprons of the day called 'pinnies' and could be seen up to her arms in flour, baking cakes.

They had four young children: Bobby, twin sisters Jean and Faye (real name Sarah), and baby Neville.

The children were instructed to close their eyes and keep quiet around the people in the secret world of Bletchley Park. They could not converse with anyone. Once, from a tennis court bench, the twins taunted two Americans as they played: 'D'ya 'ave any gum, chum?' They were in serious trouble for days. Their family was supposed to be invisible; not seen and not heard. Later Jean admitted she once took a photograph from her bedroom window in the round tower of the mansion, however, photography was absolutely forbidden. It was of Cottage 2 opposite. She had no idea this was where some of the first codebreakers worked in 1940. She laughed about their upbringing decades later and, returning to the subject of food, she confirmed that despite the rules of rationing, Bletchley's food portions were not meagre. The taste, however, was not always top notch except if you knew, or subscribed to the rumour, of an accomplished chef installed from London's Savoy Hotel. Also, when a sizeable contingent of American military intelligence arrived, many believed Bletchley's food supplies were suddenly in abundance.

Chapter 11

Room 40

Daisy had heard about Room 40 when she first arrived, and discovered this was the name for GC&CS at the Admiralty in London. In the months leading to war, the British government had considered many options for their weapon of expanded 'secret intelligence gathering'. With heightened air power it was certain the enemy would bomb the capital, so their secret human weapon needed additional protection. The general public knew little about 'intelligence gathering, analysis and dissemination'. Indeed, many thought 'intelligence' referred to an intelligent person. Nor did they know much about the Operational Intelligence Centre (OIC), in the newly built bomb-proof Admiralty Citadel, connected to the War Office in Whitehall. Newspapers occasionally referenced 'intelligence' in their reports, but few knew the methods used to collect information, and most certainly did not know about the original small department deep inside the old London buildings of the British Admiralty. The department secretly gathered information on other countries, in a system considered necessary to counter security threats. In times of war it was imperative to know what the enemy was thinking and to gain the upper hand. It was the expansion of this small department, GC&CS, that relocated to Bletchley Park.

Coded secrets, enciphering and deciphering is centuries old, especially between warring factions. There are many books on the subject. However, Britain was not skilful in this area until the First World War. The British Army solved cryptograms in the Boer War and on India's Northwest Frontier, but the navy didn't engage in cryptanalysis until August 1914, when Rear Admiral Henry F. Oliver lunched with Sir Alfred Ewing – a renowned figure in mechanical sciences and the only admiralty person interested in cryptology.

In the early days of the First World War, sunken German transatlantic telegraphic cables were severed in the North Sea, at Emden, on the Dutch coast bordering Germany. The amputated cables were Germany's only link to global connections, and they needed a new way to communicate with their collaborators.

Ewing went on to describe a new deciphering machine to Oliver and outlined modern enciphering methods, including those used by Germany. Oliver was interested and mentioned he had a few messages accumulating on his desk, intercepted by British naval and commercial radio stations. Ewing was interested to help him understand them and when Oliver confirmed the Admiralty had no department to deal with such cryptograms, Ewing said he would help, and they immediately set about breaking codes.

Ewing honed up on ciphers in the British Museum Library, the construction of commercial codes from Lloyds of London and General Post Office files. As director of naval education, he could also enlist the help of others from Dartmouth and Osborne naval colleges. Soon Alastair Denniston, W.H. Anstie, E.J.C. Green and G.L.N. Hope, all proficient in German, squeezed around Ewing's desk to solve the first messages. Denniston, a Scot and son of a medical practitioner, was fortunate to have studied at the universities of Bonn and Paris and, as a German master at Osborne naval college on the Isle of Wight, he was delighted to be promoted. In 1914 this was his chance to be part of a new department in London. Their codebreaking was not an immediate success, however, as belligerents in the Mediterranean were unable to be intercepted. But ant-like progress was made in other ways when they learned to distinguish naval messages from military, discovered that 'call signs' and names of radio stations were different from main text code, and created systems for sorting and filing intercepts methodically – all crucial cryptanalysis skills.

In October they had a lucky break when they acquired a German codebook after the German cruiser SMS *Magdeburg* became stuck in the Baltic Sea. Under threat of capture by Russian vessels the captain arranged for his ship to be blown up, after evacuating most of the crew and important documents. But the detonators were premature and some crew died. Once the ship was safe to board, a Russian first officer found other hidden codebooks. The find held the secret key to Imperial German Navy codes and access to others.

Later (the importance of divers cannot be underestimated), more codebooks were found on the seabed 30ft below. Recognising the value of their discovery, Russia, ally to Britain's naval power at the time, notified them of the hidden cipher. However, they kept the other soggy documents for themselves. In October, in a well-organised and secure plan, the heavily leaded Codebook 151, was safely delivered to Winston Churchill, First Lord of the Admiralty. 'It was a gift more precious than a dozen Fabergé eggs,' the big, blue *Signalbuch der Kaiserlichen Marine.*'

The Admiralty's fledgling agency welcomed the valuable find, which provided the German key to five and three letter groups. This proved useful for weather reports and messages to auxiliary vessels, but the texts in general produced only gibberish. A breakthrough came later when another maritime code book was seized from a merchant ship in Australia, along with a method for disguising the codes' four-letter code words. The *Handelsschiffsverkehrsbuch,* or HVB, replaced other letters in the key. This was an example of superencipherment. It was then that Fleet Paymaster Charles J.E. Rotter joined the group. He had spent many periods of leave in Germany and his German was good. This enabled him to apply local logic to intercepts and deconstruct the superencipherment, fully exposing important messages of the German High Seas Fleet. The breakthrough gave these cryptanalysts plenty to think about and more people were employed, including navy personnel Frank Birch and Frank Adcock. Soon a larger room was needed and Room 40 was selected. The secret expansion of British codebreaking had begun.[1]

The new room in the Admiralty was large enough to accommodate the additional staff; there was even a bedroom for tired codebreakers' respite after long work sessions. The department was officially known as Room 40 OB (Old Building). Its location had the advantage of being separated from mainstream Admiralty traffic, but near enough to the Operational Intelligence Centre[2] which intercepted messages via secret listening stations around the country. Even when a new designation was given to the department, ID25 (Intelligence Division, section 25), and when it eventually moved to another location, the name Room 40 stuck.

Another recruit to the Admiralty, was Dilly Knox. Alfred Dillwyn Knox. Schooled at Eton and King's College, Cambridge, he was a distinguished classicist of Greek papyri. By 1915, he showed a strong aptitude for German naval ciphers and, among many others, broke the German Admiral's cipher. After the First World War it is thought he also worked on Russian and other diplomatic codes. He shared a house with his younger Room 40 colleague Frank Birch, in Edith Grove, Chelsea. Knox was one of three to be promoted to Chief Assistant. During this time, Churchill was keen to be abreast of the new department's results and insisted he see actual decrypts as well as reports. A procedure was devised for a daily selection to be sent to him personally, containing key naval intelligence documents 'in their original form'. They were known as BJ telegrams, or Blue Jackets, simply because their covers were blue.

Nigel de Grey transferred to Room 40 in 1915 after serving briefly in the Navy Volunteer Reserve in Belgium. He complemented the growing unit and when a diplomatic message was intercepted by Admiralty sources, he helped Knox and the Reverend William Montgomery decrypt one of the most important telegrams of the First World War, bringing America into the conflict. It is now simply known as the Zimmermann Telegram. The German foreign secretary, Arthur Zimmermann, had sent a message to Heinrich von Eckardt, Germany's ambassador to Mexico, on 17 January 1917. Zimmermann told him to offer the return of Arizona, Texas and New Mexico to the Mexican government as inducement for them to side with Germany against the USA. Through intelligence, the public disclosure of this proposed pact soon brought America into the war against Germany and, with their military might, a ceasefire was eventually agreed for 11am on 11 November 1918 (Armistice Day).[3]

* * *

The Zimmermann Telegram and Translation. (By kind permission Director GCHQ)

Over a period of time Daisy learned of other key figures previously connected to Room 40 such as Admiral Sir Reginald 'Blinker' Hall and William F. 'Nobby' Clarke. 'Blinker' Hall led Room 40 with Ewing at the start of the First World War. Hall joined the Navy in 1884 aged 14 and trained on HMS *Britannia*. Childhood malnutrition caused him to develop a twitch which resulted in the effect of flashing eyes; a condition today that might be a mild form of dyspraxia; the nickname 'Blinker' stuck. Eight years later he was recommended for a gunnery officer's position which involved training in mathematics at HMS *Excellence*, a shore-based school on Whale Island, Portsmouth. In 1905 he was promoted to captain, in charge of inspecting new engineer cadets, but his sea-going career was curtailed in his forties, due to ill-health, and he found himself with a desk-job. By 1914 he was Director of British Naval Intelligence.

William 'Nobby' Clarke was educated at Harrow and Magdalen College, Oxford. He trained as a lawyer and was admitted to the bar in 1906. Similarly, during the war he was unable to serve in the military because he failed an eye examination. Instead he was commissioned into the navy as paymaster at the age of 32 and allocated to Room 40. There he used his German for information analysis. By 1919, Clarke was head of the department and, along with Frank Birch, commissioned to write the history of Room 40. The report, however, was suppressed.

After the First World War the department merged with the War Office's Cryptographic branch, MI(b). The new combined section was a unified signals intelligence agency linked to the Foreign Office. Rear Admiral Hugh Sinclair was non-operational director in addition to his role as Chief of SIS. Sinclair was known as 'C' in government circles and his department became known as both 'C's organisation and MI(c) (Military Intelligence c), which eventually morphed into MI6. The codebreakers of Room 40 (now NID 25 – Naval Intelligence Department 25), worked beside SIS staff who were responsible for distribution of the intelligence Room 40 deciphered. In return, access to past records held by SIS were available for Room 40's future research. The combined group was transferred from the Navy to the Foreign Office and named the Government Code and Cipher School. Denniston, in 1920, was one of the key figures who recognised the strategic importance of the merger and when Nobby Clarke moved to work on American diplomatic traffic within GC&CS, he became the director.

For several years Frank Adcock and the affable Frank Birch assessed and recruited candidates from both Oxford and Cambridge universities for NID 25. Those selected were highly suitable for special intelligence work. Hugh Foss was one, who joined GC&CS in 1924. Born in 1902 in Kobe, Japan, to missionary parents – his father was Bishop of Osaka – his British education led him through Marlborough College to Cambridge University. The animated red-headed Scot was fluent in Japanese, with a keen interest in cryptology, and these qualities alone opened the door for him to Room 40. He also had knowledge of a new kind of enciphering machine called Enigma, a commercial version of which, according to Foss, Knox bought in Vienna.[4] By 1928 Foss had written a paper solving the non-plug board machine, called 'The Reciprocal Enigma'.

Another Scot, John Tiltman, went to Room 40 between the wars. Tall, dark and handsome, he was born in 1894 to Scottish parents living and working in London. In 1914 he served with the King's Own Scottish Borderers but was wounded in France, for which he received the Military Cross for bravery.[5] He was seconded to MI1 (Army Intelligence) and, after a Russian Language course, he transferred to Indian Army Headquarters in Simla as cryptanalyst, from 1921–1929. The mountainous region 220 miles north of Delhi, was also known as Shimla, the summer capital of British India. Tiltman's new job was to help plough through a backlog of translation work, and with a small group of people, messages were intercepted, ciphers analysed, translated and directed, in a process which became known as 'traffic analysis,' and formed the basis of a system he called Bookbuilding. All Russian diplomatic cipher traffic was read from Moscow to Kabul, Afghanistan to Uzbekistan, and Turkestan.

Tiltman's excellent translation and decoding skills were so successful the War Office loaned him to GC&CS for a year. However, he never returned to conventional army duties, except at the beginning of the Second World War, when was he recalled to active service at Bletchley Park. Tiltman considered himself fortunate to have a varied experience of different languages and branches of signals intelligence. His knowledge of cryptology led him to become one of the finest cryptanalysts on non-machine systems.

Chapter 12

Enigma and the Polish Bomba

With its secret codebreaking operation and advances in reading enemy messages, Britain was confident Germany could be tackled, but only if more staff and faster codebreaking methods could be found. Knowledge and resources were key and eventually Bletchley Park had all. Enigma was one of the first mechanical ciphers to be broken.

* * *

Daisy's initial codebreaking training was elemental, with only a basic knowledge of the encoding machines used by the enemy. However, everyone should have learned that a 'code' meant that each *word* in a message is replaced with a code word or symbol, whereas a 'cipher' is where each *letter* in a message is replaced with a cipher letter or symbol. Generally, though it was accepted that most people tended to say code when they were actually referring to a cipher. While Daisy tackled the maths and logic to analyse codes and ciphers, she did not know the name of the cipher machine, or machines. Back then the word 'enigma' only featured as a solution to one of her crossword clues; it was never part of her codebreaking dialogue. Not until decades later, did she discover that some intercepted messages came from a machine such as Enigma.

Nonetheless, it is pertinent here to give a short history of the Enigma machine which for many at Bletchley Park was central to their challenge. Simply put the Greek word Enigma means 'puzzle'. In the 1920s the encipher machine was used by banks and other commercial businesses to protect telegrams containing businessmen's secrets. Its first public airing of note was during the Congress of the International Postal Union in Bern, Switzerland, but the audience for whom it was intended showed little interest and slated it as 'an expensive piece of puzzling equipment'. Its German inventor, Arthur Scherbius, was dismayed that this version never achieved widespread use. He was the son of a local businessman, born in Frankfurt, in 1878, where his schooling emphasised mathematics, natural sciences and modern languages. From these disciplines he went on to study engineering and electricity at a technical college in Munich where he later matriculated to another college in Hanover. After two years he finished his dissertation, 'Proposal for the Construction of an Indirect Water Turbine Governor', which was accepted, and at the age of 25 he was granted a doctorate in engineering. He worked for several major German electrical companies and a large Swiss electrical firm where he made his first invention: a high-voltage motor drive that handled sudden changes of stress. There he met E. Richard Ritter, a certified engineer, and founded the firm of Scherbius & Ritter.

He became known in the field of inventions, especially asynchronous motors. He wrote and published many articles, but it was during the First World War that he succumbed to the infectious pull of cryptography. His first cryptographic invention aimed to code messages sent via telegraph. Prior to this, thick codebooks were published with thousands of commercial codes for private firms. They represented business and personal phrases such as, 'Do not exceed the limit', which may have translated to JIWUL. The point was to save money on cable fees, but there was an element of secrecy in the same way as other codes. The titles of the messages always included the word 'code' which brought the system into the influence of cryptology. The code words in his system were sometimes taken from other languages, sometimes they were made up, but they always were pronounceable – cable rates were higher for unpronounceable code words and code numbers. Scherbius aimed to maintain this economy while making non-secret messages secret with his new machine.

After the first invention flunked at the Swiss trade fair, Scherbius & Ritter transferred their cipher patent rights to Gewerschaft Securitas an entity which appeared to be a corporation for mining. The rights to a Dutch rotor were also granted and the operation was seen as a funnel for risk capital into cipher machines. In 1923 Securitas founded the *Chiffriermaschinen Aktien-Gesellschaft* (Cipher Machines Stock Corporation) in Berlin, and both Scherbius & Ritter were on the board of directors. By 1924, after modifications and improvements the machine, which looked like a typewriter with lights in a wooden box, was called Enigma. The German post office – *Deutsche Reichspost* – tested the machine and exchanged greetings with delegates of that year's

International Postal Union. As a result, the German government and Naval Command in Berlin, decided to reconsider Scherbius' invention and adapted it for military use, by phasing out the original commercial model and producing a new, smaller, Model C.[1] Scherbius died in 1929, aged 50, never realising the impact of his machine in world conflicts.

The main internal mechanism consisted of three rotors, each with twenty-six electrical contacts around the outer edge, representing a letter of the alphabet. To encode a message the German operator set the rotors in a pre-determined order and position, using the current issue of his printed codebook – the 'settings'. He then typed each letter of his message into the machine. By pressing a key an electrical impulse went through to each rotor and lit up the letter, in code, on a lamp-board which held a series of lights. The operator noted the encoded letter for each letter of the message typed into the machine. When all the letters of the message were encoded, he sent the message via wireless or radio, in Morse code. The message would then be decoded at the other end using the reverse method and settings of the same issue of codebook.

Going deeper into the mechanics of the Enigma machine, as a letter was typed the first rotor moved forward one position, after that rotor had moved a certain number of times, the second rotor would move forward one position. When the second rotor moved a number of times, the third rotor would move forward one position. As a result, the code was constantly changing and the messages scrambled. The German navy then added a plug board which they thought would be more secure and make Enigma unsolvable. But they were wrong.

The Bomba

This early Polish invention was a faster way of unravelling the Enigma cipher but there were setbacks as Germany's Enigma machine became more sophisticated. Eventually a newer version of the original mechanical Bomba became the brainchild of Alan Turing with a slightly different name 'The Bombe'. Daisy knew about the machine at Bletchley Park, and occasionally its problems, but was not permitted to enter the hut where it was kept under high security. Only Wrens and others with special clearance were admitted. However, even those with special passes did not know the history of the Bombe, or the Polish codebreakers who were some of the first to deconstruct the commercial Enigma machine to invent the original Bomba.

According to Polish historians, a German Enigma machine happened to pass through Warsaw Airport in a wrongly addressed German package in 1927.[2] It was intercepted by customs and photographed, which eventually enabled Polish monitoring stations to decipher Enigma-generated enciphered messages. Major Guido Langer, in 1931, was the head of a bureau of Polish intelligence gatherers which was created to catch and collate German cipher changes. A course in cryptology also started at the University of Poznan for twenty advanced students in mathematics who spoke German. As the course concluded, three gifted men excelled at constantly being able to solve the ciphers and were given a small section, within military intelligence, to continue their studies. On the third floor of the north wing of the university's general staff building, Langer's secret university section became a satellite to the cipher bureau, BS4. The men were Marian Rejewski, Henryk Zygalski and Jerzy Różycki. In 1932 Rejewski, the oldest and most skilled was placed in a room alone, where, in great secrecy he received photos of two instructional pamphlets and obsolete key lists acquired by a German spy. His top-secret challenge was to solve the German navy's unsolvable Enigma cipher.

Later that year the three students were able to buy a commercial version of the Enigma machine on the open market, with the German military's plug board addition. Rejewski continued his analysis, following paths that differed fundamentally from earlier cryptanalytic methods, while Poland and France started to share intelligence. With some false starts, and a little help from the French, Rejewski was able to reconstruct the internal workings of Enigma and identify the indicator system used by the German Army.

Meanwhile, Zygalski worked on a manual codebreaking technique using twenty-six perforated paper sheets to determine certain data in a message. With the alphabet duplicated horizontally and vertically in a matrix of 26 x 26, each sheet represented the 676 possible starting positions of the middle and left (slowest moving) Enigma rotors. When the sheets were stacked in a certain order and placed over a light box, the small pinholes revealed a starting position of the daily wheel or ring settings used on the machine. This codebreaking solution was successful for several years, but slow. As German forces networks grew, they considered their Enigma ciphers safe, but that was not so. Their messages were listened to, read and transcribed.

In 1936, however, perhaps there was an inkling of doubt as significant changes were introduced when Germany added new safeguards to their machines and codes became tougher. New methods were needed to hack into the German system. As the likelihood of invasion increased, BS4 transferred its department to a camouflaged high-security headquarters outside Warsaw, in the Kabaty Woods near Pyry. German safeguards on Enigma remained tight, but the Polish team developed a new machine to speed up the codebreaking. They called it 'Bomba' because its components looked like the Italian ice cream, 'bomba'. For a while they were successful, but when the German military introduced two additional wheels to Enigma they struggled.

The German invasion of Czechoslovakia took place in August 1938 and the Poles were now keen to pass on their knowledge to France and Britain. Poland, they felt would be next. A tri-lateral meeting was held in January 1939 which included the three Polish codebreakers, French Captain Gustave Bertrand, Henri Braquenie, and the British delegation of Denniston, Tiltman, Foss and Knox. Unfortunately, however, the rendezvous was considered a waste of time. The Poles were instructed to reveal nothing unless there was something in return. There was nothing and the talks failed.

May approached, and tensions between Poland and Germany reached breaking point. Langer contacted France and Britain again with news of something different. A subsequent meeting took place in Warsaw at the end of July, this time with Sinclair and Commander Humphrey Sandwith, instead of Denniston and Foss. The meeting was successful; mostly because the Poles were in an invidious position and needed to pass on their secrets. When war was declared the Bureau at Pyry closed. By 10 September all evidence of machines was destroyed and all staff evacuated. But ten days later, Bertrand delivered a replica Enigma machine to the head of MI6, Colonel Stewart Menzies in London,[3] a gift from the Poles. Sadly, Admiral Sinclair did not live long enough to see the subsequent fruits of his work since he died of cancer in November 1939.

Combatting Enigma during the Battle of the Atlantic

The Battle of the Atlantic was one of the longest military campaigns in the Second World War. Daisy was aware of the submarine attacks on Allied ships from early British news reports and especially during

1941 when she was concerned for Stan's and her brother's safety as they travelled overseas. What she didn't know, until she arrived at Bletchley, was that German U-boats used encoded ciphers in Morse code to convey their messages. Shark was one. This was a Short Weather Report cipher which condensed meteorological reports into seven-letter messages for re-encoding on Enigma, which was then transmitted to U-boat captains in Morse code. British codebreakers cracked Shark in December 1942, after U-boat 559 was sunk by British aircraft in the Azores in October and the corresponding German key book was recovered. Allied Intelligence continued to listen secretly, but by February 1943 the source diminished with only a smattering of messages on the same wavelength and cipher. Fewer messages meant something had changed, and by early March, Britain's First Sea Lord Albert Dudley Pound – who, like Churchill, had an American mother – advised chief naval staff that U-boat Special Intelligence had received a severe setback. 'Intercepted messages are only valuable if solved within twenty-four hours,' was his view.

It appeared that Germany had replaced the Short Weather Report Cipher with a new edition. In somewhat of a void, the codebreakers needed to re-group and return to original codebreaking techniques looking for clues or prompts in 'cribs' and 'kisses'. Intercepts, for example, would often have a standard phrase in code in the preamble, such as *Wetterbericht*, German for 'weather report'. Usually, this clue could be understood quickly, and the main message decoded using the same methods. Most other messages for that day could also be read, until the code changed at midnight. Other easy and useful prompts from German operators were at the end of the message, such as Heil Hitler or *Nieder mit die Englander* ('Down with the English'). Clues or prompts to the code – standard title names or sign-off phrases – were known as 'cribs' or 'kisses'.

As Shark dried up in the first quarter of 1943, First Sea Lord Pound was too pessimistic, since Bletchley's Hut 8 had another codebook key retrieved from U-559. It had seemed less important before, but the revisit to the Short Signals key showed the new cipher had three rotors instead of two.[4] British codebreakers became successful once more in reading messages on a daily basis. At the same time, a profile index on behaviour procedures of individual submarines and their skippers was built and maintained. Almost every piece of information, boring as it may have been, eventually provided more solutions. From March to June a further ninety Shark keys were broken, which helped Allied Atlantic convoys reroute to avoid dangerous German U-boats, and saved many lives.

But then Germany brought in a fourth rotor, Enigma model M4. However, Hut 8 was not deterred for long and reconstructed the wiring within a few days. They also learned the rotor selection for the machine was made on the first day of each month. This type of regularity simplified the codebreakers' tasks once more. At the same time a new department in Washington DC was developed with British help, where they exploited cribs and kisses in the new M4 cipher. With three wheels the German operator could choose from six possible configurations, now he had an increased choice of possible configurations making codebreaking more difficult. The new code was still called Shark, but Germany called it Triton. New versions of the Bombe machine were also installed in America, but British codebreakers continued to work on three-rotor Enigma intercepts which generally contained orders to German land forces and shore stations as well as selected messages via M4. Bletchley provided longer and more reliable cribs but these took longer to test on the older British bombe machines. Washington was almost a mirror-image of Bletchley's intelligence and codebreaking procedures, but with updated technology in a safer land.

As personnel on both sides of the Atlantic diligently worked together but separately through their codebreaking and command centres, they flagged enemy radio transmitter positions. Location and directions of enemy craft, air, land or sea were carefully recorded and transferred to grids or plotting maps to provide a clear picture of the aggressor and his potential victim. Mapping was a crucial visual reference to illuminate the enemy. Convoys escaped, but when the supply of signals again began to wane, the codebreakers returned to the drawing board to solve a new version. A fifth rotor had been introduced to Enigma. Now a billion more hurdles had been created instead of just a few million. Germany had also increased the number of plug-board connections to ten; encryption possibilities were now 159,000,000,000,000,000,000.[5]

***

'It was a tonnage war,' a term coined by German Captain Admiral Karl Dönitz. His aim was to destroy as many British merchant supply ships and American Liberty ships[6] as possible to starve war-torn Britain into submission. He had seen the excellence of the German navy's Enigma code system in the First World War and was certain his U-boat tactics would choke Britain's imports. However, the security of the German naval cipher was a slight concern and he therefore concluded that group attacks were necessary. The first U-boat to locate a convoy would radio its position and stay with the target. U-boat HQ would centralise the information, including locations of enemy (Allied) vessels, then instruct other U-boats to the convoys' expected position for a combined attack.

Dönitz was aware these actions would break the vital rule of their 'invisible arm' radio silence. But in his view, coordination of U-boats outweighed the radio direction-finding skills of the enemy. He further thought his foe unable to solve the coded sightings and, even if they could, there would be no time for countermeasures. The secret of the intercepted messages prevailed, as Dönitz continued to believe in the strength and invincibility of Enigma. But he was wrong.[7]

Chapter 13

Bletchley Park, the Prime Minister and a Letter

From small beginnings in Room 40, codebreaking developed into an administrative industry of massive proportions, but the quantity and quality of professional and capable staff were not always easy to find, until certain influential managers by-passed the general malaise of government red tape. Daisy and Dot were two of the many necessary civilians urgently trained at Bletchley Park to undertake the task.

Developing Bletchley Park 1939-1943

As Germany invaded Poland, Commander Alastair Denniston and his recruiters were prepared for war. Adcock and Birch had interviewed, trained and compiled an emergency list of staff, and on 3 September 1939, the list was implemented. Cambridge intellectual, Gordon Welchman, was one of the first to begin the secret journey to Buckinghamshire. The new recruits had apparently received a coded message saying, 'Aunty Flo is unwell' and to 'keep 10/- in their pocket for a train ticket'. After two days Denniston informed the Foreign Office that all new personnel had reported for duty at the pay rate agreed by the Treasury. Predominantly men, they were paid handsomely at £11.5s.6d per week, equivalent to around £1,750 now, but £600 per year was a large salary then. The extended codebreaking team at Bletchley – the new Room 40 – was ready for action.

* * *

Welchman received the letter that changed his life early in 1939. C.P. Snow, the physicist, novelist and Fellow of Christ's College, Cambridge had recommended him. Adcock and Birch had searched intensely for men with more knowledge and who were less reserved than those found in the military; 'men of the professor type.' They were looking for people who could think out of the box, think more laterally, but still they had to ask, 'In the event of war, would you be prepared to defend King and Country by undertaking secret government work?' Welchman had immediately replied 'yes', and in March attended preliminary indoctrination in Broadway Buildings, London. He was then assigned to the Diplomatic Section who had earlier recruited Dennis Babbage, John Jeffreys and Alan Turing. Over the three-day induction Welchman was impressed and influenced by his group, which included Oliver Strachey for gleaning intelligence from enemy communications, and John Tiltman for the art of 'Bookbuilding'. All would become close colleagues. After initial training he was placed on the emergency staff list and told that in the event of war, he was to report to Bletchley Park, Buckinghamshire, as soon as possible.

It was clear from his early training that Welchman recognised the value of all intercepted messages, and from this his mind engaged seriously on the idea of an intelligence factory. It was imperative to him that once the code was broken and the information extracted through proper analysis, that the intelligence was disseminated to the right people in the right way. It was a challenge, but his attention to minute detail equalled his view of the wider picture. He admired the individual qualities in his colleagues but was frustrated by inconsistencies in operations including slowness of communications, unorganised storage of decrypts and the lack of lateral thought on how intercepted messages could be used. He needed an efficient system to decode all messages, regardless of high or low codes, produce intelligence reports, relay to commanders in the field, and store all information for future use. His aim was to devise a specific system for intelligence to always be useful, not just for a day.[1] Soon he revealed his plans for comprehensive analysis, a method that no one at Bletchley had previously grasped. The potential use for coordinated information – from intercepted traffic between departments, rapid solving of ciphers, decryption of messages, intelligence extraction, re-encryption of messages and access to an organised retrieval system – was huge. At the same time the system had to constantly keep up with advances in cryptology and new technology.

By the end of 1940 his plan for intense compartmentalised work – in huts – expanded quickly. Welchman also started recruiting for his own specialist area where staff were required to work on breaking German Army and Airforce codes. This department was known only as Hut 6 – where Enigma codes were broken using different methods. Some of his best codebreakers were chessmen, who crunched through code puzzles as if they were chess moves. But more help was needed.

***

Commander Denniston, the first director at Bletchley Park, and Barbara Abernethy his feisty assistant, were instrumental in managing the site and thousands of personnel from the beginning. But Denniston generally believed central Foreign Office pessimism that the complex Naval Enigma was impossible to break when he said 'You know, the Germans don't mean you to read their stuff, and I don't expect you ever will.'[2] (Though to be fair, he recognised the importance of hiring people with electrical engineering experience instead of modern languages).[3]

On 4 July 1941 Welchman wrote to the Deputy Commander Edward Travis for more resources. Messages in Hut 6 had increased and were becoming more difficult to handle. A third more office space was requested, along with additional senior and junior administrative women. More chessmen were definitely not needed. The women were divided across Hut sections, with an average of twenty-five in each, headed by a temporary junior assistant principal. In Welchman's Hut 6, out of sixty-seven staff, three were supervisors. All Welchman's requests had the support of Travis, but other senior staff at Bletchley or those further up the line in the Foreign Office, did not respond to his needs. In the meantime, there were other lower codes to be broken to help produce the main intelligence, and suitable professional staff were required for this area too. In early National Archive documents, employee numbers for certain sections were higher than others; sixty in Hut 3, forty in Hut 4, ninety-three in Hut 6. In comparison, Dilly Knox's Research Section had only eight.

A Clandestine visit to Bletchley Park

While Welchman and Travis were frustrated by lack of resources for the many different codebreaking sections, Churchill was intrigued by developments at the secret station deep in Britain's countryside. He made a note to visit when he was next at Chequers in Buckinghamshire, the official country residence of the Prime Minister. However, the sixteenth century mansion, near Aylesbury, was considered by governing ministers to be too much of a prominent landmark and therefore unsafe. The country estate had a long sweeping drive visible from the air and seemed an easy target for the Luftwaffe. With this in mind, Churchill's cabinet strongly recommended an alternative venue to avoid danger. It was then that MP Ronald Tree offered the use of his country home at Ditchley Park, Oxfordshire. The sizeable estate was surrounded by large mature trees which provided necessary camouflage over the drive, perfect for the Prime Minister's safety and onward visit to Bletchley. The house also had an excellent wine cellar.

Churchill's first visit to Ditchley was early November 1940. Special telephone lines were installed, including a scrambling system. Accommodations for his advisory staff were provided along with billets for the full guard of the Oxford and Buckinghamshire Light Infantry. He enjoyed his weekend in the hospitality of his host Ronald Tree and said he would return the following week. However, en route to Ditchley the second time, he opened a top-secret message which made him return to London.

The Enigma decrypt he received indicated another massive attack on London within hours. Churchill said he was not going to spend another peaceful evening in the countryside while London was under heavy attack and immediately returned to his war rooms in the centre of London. That night, 14 November 1940, over 300 German planes bombed Coventry instead, just 30 miles north of Ditchley.[4] Many lives in the city were lost and buildings destroyed. Churchill and his entourage had narrowly missed the disaster; some say deliberately. Over 100 tonnes of high explosives were dropped on sixteen British cities, during The Blitz (September 1940 – May 1941); Coventry was one.

At the time he was unaware of Bletchley's growing needs and his visit was delayed. Not until September the following year was a clandestine visit possible and he met some of those employed in his 'most secret of secrets'. On 6 September 1941, a day of much excitement, Churchill spoke from a pile of rubble in the Bletchley grounds. In his unofficial address to the small group of mostly civilian staff, he thanked them and gave his support to their work of National Importance. 'All so young,' he commented. He also went into Hut 6, according to a young Welsh Typex operator, Maier Thomas, who 'turned to soup' when Churchill asked her if the clunky machine she used, was difficult to operate. Sworn to secrecy she panicked and couldn't say anything, but Gordon Welchman came to her assistance with another comment to divert the Prime Minister. It was a great honour and memory for those on that particular day shift.

Dear Prime Minister

Recognising Churchill's support for their work, Welchman, Turing and other Hut 6 colleagues, Hugh Alexander and Stuart Milner-Barry, were galvanised to compose and deliver a well thought out letter to the Prime Minister. Pipe-smoking Stuart Milner-Barry was friends with Welchman at Cambridge and was now his deputy at Bletchley. He was a calm and avid tactical thinker, demonstrated by his success as a stockbroker and an international chess player. Hugh Alexander, also from Cambridge and a British Chess Champion, was a former teacher and head of research at John Lewis Partnership. Their goal was to be *au fait* with the personalities of the German Enigma, its cipher clerks and radio operators. Milner-Barry's specific work involved analysing decrypts from Zygalski sheets handled by John Jeffreys and other colleagues. Turing had recent success using the Banburismus codebreaking method aligned with the Bombe machine, proving Commander Denniston's earlier thoughts wrong, and which gave the group confidence to go ahead with their positive action. The idea had Commander Travis's agreement but by-passed Denniston who was absent, partly due to ill health. All that was needed was approval from the head of MI6, Stewart Menzies. It was also thought unnecessary to involve others such as Dilly Knox and his team, due to past disagreements and exclusions.

The Letter

October 1941. The highly confidential two-page document explained the lack of human resources and the urgent need to expand personnel for the codebreaking operation: additional staff for the overworked Naval Enigma department in Hut 8; more people at Grade III for training on information analysis and retrieval, and on the mechanised Hollerith section (the night shift was cancelled due to staff exhaustion, creating overall delays); military and Air Force Enigma in Hut 6 needed more trained typists and decoders to handle interceptions, including 'Light Blue' intelligence from the Middle East, and the promised quota of Wrens for Bombe operation needed to be delivered. They praised Deputy Commander Travis and pointed out their previous requests were impeded by other staff and government officials, as their work was secret and others, therefore, were unaware of the importance of their organisation and that their need was now extremely urgent.

Milner-Barry rushed to London by train and taxi to 10 Downing Street, where he delivered the letter to a personal aide of Winston Churchill. With the first part of his task complete, he was told the letter would be passed to the Prime Minster. On reading the contents Churchill, immediately catapulted their requests to high action status and sent a handwritten note to his Chief of Staff, General Ismay, instructing him to give them what they needed and stamped the order ACTION THIS DAY! Without that rubberstamp Bletchley's mission might have failed. A process was implemented at once and staff numbers and facilities at the war station improved, leading to faster, efficient codebreaking.

The subsequent reshuffle in SIGINT (Signals Intelligence) by Colonel Menzies, stemmed from this pivotal communication and Churchill's quick response. Denniston had been in Washington discussing Japanese naval ciphers with American cryptographer, Colonel William Friedman, Army Signals Intelligence, but due to this new area of concentration and a few health issues, he did not return to GC&CS. By February1942, Denniston had moved to the Admiralty offices in London. Travis became director to carry on the serious business of code cracking at Bletchley.

Not all the activities of GC&CS were at Bletchley, and not all SIGINT was conducted by GC&CS. The first link in the chain were the listening stations, often referred to as 'Y stations' where rows of operators at receivers searched the airwaves on various frequencies, for enemy radio signals. The stations were located around the country and overseas. For example, Oliver Strachey, chief of ISOS (Intelligence Service Oliver Strachey), who worked on low-level hand ciphers at Bletchley, went to Ottawa as chief cryptographer of the Examination Unit, the Canadian version of Bletchley Park. Known to President Roosevelt, he took with him code breaking keys for high-level Vichy French and Japanese diplomatic codes. This was another part of the top-secret liaison, to promote transparency and cooperation between the American and British governments. The Japanese encryption was complex as it used versions of kanji, hiragana and romanisation symbols, but Strachey helped break the code even though he could not speak or read Japanese.

* * *

Under Travis, Welchman organised departments, with precise systems and improved machines. His aim was to smooth out wrinkles of disagreement between the message-receiving departments of the Army, Navy and Air Force, and assess and implement efficient solutions. If GC&CS was to play a significant role in assembling, analysing and disseminating intelligence it had to be slick. Different departments each had a strict order of reporting and flow of authority – names, positions, department heads, managers, supervisors, clerks and a multitude of assistants – all with individual tasks and responsibilities. Huts (departments) were part of a well-planned structure that, when typed into a report, created a massive organisational flow chart. Each diagram was accompanied by lists of telephone extensions, stamped in red ink 'Top Secret' or 'Most Secret,' and together they formed one of the largest Top Secret telephone lists in the country.[5]

However, the organisation still seemed confused to some and an attempted explanation was made in a general memo by Nigel de Grey, March 1943:

> *I suppose if you were to put forward a scheme of organisation for any service which laid down as its basis that it would take a lot of men and women from civil life and dress some of them in one kind of clothes and some of them in another, and told all those dressed in black that they came under one set of rules and all those dressed in white under another and so on, and then told them that they had a double allegiance, firstly to the ruler of their black or white or motley party and secondly to another man who would partly rule over all of them, but only partly, any ordinary tribunal would order you to take a rest cure in an asylum. But suppose that the tribunal were somehow foolish enough to adopt your idea and in order that you might begin your work said, 'We will now lend you some tools – they may not be quite*

*what you want but you must make do with them, and tell us
when they get blunt and we'll see if we can sharpen them
for you,' some higher power would presumably lock up the
tribunal as a public menace – or, if it were in Russia or
Germany, shoot them out of hand. Yet that is in fact the
precise organisation of Bletchley Park. Now it happens that
Bletchley Park has been successful – so successful that it
has supplied information on every conceivable subject from
the movement of a single mine sweeper to the strategy of the
campaign, and the Christian name of the wireless operator
to the introduction of a secret weapon.*[6]

* * *

By 1943, Welchman's machine was well oiled and running fast.
Ultimately, there were few situations where GC&CS could not shed light.
After the capture of another Enigma machine and codebooks, a further
surge in codebreaking took place. The theory was simple; they must
solve the daily codes with a prepared formula, to discover the German
plans and where their military divisions assembled. Staying on top of the
intercepted messages and their minute detail and analysis was crucial
and intense work. Bletchley's success came as staff numbers grew and
advances in machine technology seriously embraced the integration of
all forces. However, only heads of department saw the bigger picture. All
employees had signed to abide by the Official Secrets Act which resulted
in all information being tightly guarded within departments; clerks,
administrators and decoders were told their area of expertise and that,
in most instances, was their only task. General staff did not know the
details of 'the product' in the next room, but interception, cryptanalysis,
translation, intelligence analysis and dissemination were all connected
and flowed smoothly between each department when appropriate. The
links were the key; it was everything Welchman wanted; efficient work
on a factory-like basis, a conveyor belt of fast, confidential useable
information with trustworthy teams of highly trained professional
people. The highly secret, organised process of Bletchley Park was fully
informed, for the most part, and turning the tide of the war.

* * *

'My Most Secret Source.' Churchill revived his First World War system of BJ telegrams, to see and 'feel' the intelligence. But there was no way he could see everything. Instead his version of 'headline news', was extended for the Army and Air Force, and a selection was delivered to him via SIS, including diplomatic messages. Blue Jackets can be seen with his initials at The National Archives and Public Records Office, Kew, South West London.

Chapter 14

Living in Digs

The Prime Minister did not return to Bletchley during Daisy's Work of National Importance, but she heard about his visit and realised she was part of the needed staff injection pouring into Bletchley in 1942-1943. New recruits were arriving at 500 per week. Daisy was fortunate, though she didn't think so at the time: 'It was boring and all hush-hush; we didn't ask questions, we just did what we were told.' A phrase she repeated often to her daughters and others when asked, 'What did you do at Bletchley Park?'

* * *

After seven weeks of intense training in Elmer's School Registration Room, Daisy passed and joined the Naval Section. The training taught her the foundations of registering, decoding, analysing and recording Navy, Air Force and Army messages, called 'traffic', into a useable form for other crib and decoding rooms. The tasks for each section were almost identical. The goal was the same, but the codebreaking route could be different. Registration – dates and times, Cribs and Kisses, sorting into different types of message; Decoding – finding other key elements that helped crack the code; Analysis, intelligence reports for military chiefs; Recording and Indexing; Categorising and Storing for future use – were all important functions of each hut or military section.

She settled into Bletchley life and moved to a billet where she shared a room in a house in Leighton Buzzard, whose strange name, she discovered, came from Old English, Leah-tun, meaning 'farm in a clearing in the wood', or from Leestone as mentioned in the Domesday Book. 'Buzzard' likely came from the Dean of Lincoln who had two parishes called Leighton or Leah-tun (or Leestone). At the time Theobald de Busar was prebendary, or honorary canon. The dean added

Busar's name which eventually evolved to Leighton Buzzard. The other parish became Leighton Bromswold.

Leighton Buzzard's brick manufacturing was the cause of the strange smell Daisy experienced when she first arrived. The rancid stench of silica-rich sand, mixed with lime, produced steamed bricks. As well as these, local industries produced tiles and glass for the region and beyond. From dawn to dusk, hot furnaces bellowed smoke and fumes from tall chimneys, peppering the atmosphere with ash and brick dust. Daisy lived with Muriel and Jack Gotzheim, a young couple with a family business connected to the industry. Jack drove trucks to transport sand and Muriel worked in the office. They owned their house at 5 Queen Street, just a short walk from the station. The digs Daisy shared with Mary Goddard, from Chesterfield, were spacious and comfortable. Both agreed their room was far superior to the cramped hostel they had shared with several others in Wilton Avenue. After light conversation they realised they had attended the same message analysis training course at different times, but they never discussed details of their work. Mary and Muriel became two of Daisy's life-long friends.

The commute to Bletchley was usually ten minutes by train. Daisy was able to buy a newspaper or magazine at the station and from these she diligently collected related snippets of war news. Searching for Stan was never far from her mind. Her Bletchley friends and colleagues also saved Far Eastern news reports from their local papers, which elevated her hopes of finding him alive. In her mind's eye she could hear him saying, 'Chin up my love – no news is good news – keep smiling.' Some nights, sleep was difficult and morning fear often lay heavy like a rock in her stomach, but she pressed on with her job while carefully saving the cuttings. She tried to build a picture of his capture and anticipated survival. Surviving was the only positive thing she could imagine.

One cutting read 'Never Gave Up Hope'. She collected many articles hoping they would lead to his whereabouts. A long distressing fifteen months had passed since the capitulation, and since she'd heard from Stan – the delayed letter written before the defeat. Was he still alive? Daisy was determined to find out more; she just couldn't discuss the details. Through intelligence she knew that other camps existed, and reports of others meant he might still be alive, but what were the atrocities? There were so many questions. Newspaper reports said obtaining official notification of PoW's locations was difficult, unless captured loved ones

(Daisy Lawrence Archive)

sent letters. Even then, they might not be received for months. Their Japanese captors were not allowing letters home. Why?

* * *

On 17 May 1943, the BRUSA Agreement (Britain and USA) was signed after a month of discussions regarding intelligence message sharing and TOP SECRET ULTRA reports.[1] The talks took place under orders of Churchill and Roosevelt. This was a formal extension to a previous document in October 1942, known as the Travis-Wenger Arrangement: Memorandum for Op.20 or The Holden Agreement (J.N. Wenger and US Director of Naval Communications, Captain C.F. Holden were the signatories). Soon after the official signing three military officials, Colonel Alfred McCormack of USA Special Branch Intelligence, Colonel Telford Taylor of Military Intelligence and Colonel William Friedman, Army Signals Intelligence, visited Commander Travis to implement the extension and train more American staff at GC&CS. Now more digs were needed for a new breed of personnel as British RAF Wing Commander, 'Jim' Rose, Analyst and Deputy Head, selected a dozen Americans to work at Bletchley Park, mostly women. It was part of the extended intelligence relations. Until then Daisy knew little of Washington's involvement.

* * *

Daisy completed the work given by her supervisor. 'I remember going up steps to an office. Nobody explained the whole picture, though we had a good idea of what we were doing.' Sometimes she worked alone in a vast cold room with code paperwork from another department. 'The machine there made a terrible noise when then messages clanked around the pipes above. Sometimes they got stuck,' she recalled. Her careful transcription of endless blocks of four or five meaningless letters or numbers was one of the first measures in unravelling coded messages received in a daily delivery tube. Her job was officially classified as 'identifying unusual features in enciphered signals'. Most of the information from signals was gibberish and indecipherable. 'We learned to recognise certain things. I had to work out what was different. It was all very boring.'

With the help of her keen memory, Daisy diligently carried out her duties, using specific logbooks and hand-made manuals to identify types of coded letters and numbers on thin slips of paper. Important 'differences' were passed to another hut, via her supervisor, or logged into Hut 7's indexing system. All messages were categorised, cross-referenced, and transferred to a filing system to capture and store information for future analysis. Some were colour-coded. With each notecard and message placed appropriately in Bletchley's extensive index filing system – each with a profile, a certain subject or person – official intelligence was being created. Senior Navy staff went to her section to retrieve information which might have seemed insignificant at first but now had intelligence value. Enemy message enciphering was often sent in several parts on different days, to avoid detection. Here components of each message puzzle were compiled for intelligence reports to the Admiralty.

* * *

At the beginning of May 1943, Daisy discovered she had access to Bletchley's second-hand bicycles; anyone in the park could use them. Sitting all day was making her plump. She favoured the black heavy-framed model with a basket in front for her handbag or picnic and ventured out into the fresh air of the countryside. Hay fever was sometimes a problem, but that didn't matter now. After London's smog, she enjoyed her new rural surroundings, especially cycling with friends to the fields for lunch or a rare relaxing half-day from work. Rationing meant they pooled their coupons to obtain picnic ingredients – hardboiled eggs, bread and butter. Lettuce and tomatoes were abundant in the countryside as people grew their own. Each friend brought their own flask of hot tea. The excursions reminded her of pre-war camping trips. 'Change was as good as a rest…,' from the bustle of Tooting, but still she worried about Stan.

Then on 24 May came the day Daisy would never forget. She had been at Bletchley four months and some of her mail still went to Wilton Avenue. A young messenger girl from the hostel found her in the office and handed her a telegram. Peggy Weston from Barnsley saw the exchange and noticed Daisy was upset. 'What is it?' she asked. Daisy stuttered, 'A telegram from Mitcham, …Stan's mother.'

Peggy was concerned and rose to take Daisy to another place with more privacy. But the other girls in the room begged them to stay. Daisy was frightened and a coldness crept over her body as she started to shiver; she thought she might faint. Her face was pale; tears welled in her eyes. She knew the telegram held news she didn't want to hear. She forced her eyes to the window. It was a warm day, but she was freezing. The message was sent at 12.15pm. She imagined Mrs Moore an hour before, running to the Post Office opposite the Clock Tower in Mitcham's Fair Green. It was now one o'clock. Her heart raced and her hands shook. She stared at the beige envelope and tried to open the top edge with one of her sharper fingernails but it fell to the ground narrowly missing a full cup of tea. She reprimanded her clumsiness and quickly bent to retrieve the telegram, catching her head on the edge of the desk. Carefully unfolding the delicate paper, she focused on the top line. She was frightened to move her eyes further…but she did.

Clutching the telegram, she leaned forward in the chair as if she was about to be sick. Instead she took a deep breath and began to cry with relief. He was alive. The other girls cheered as they gathered around to peer at the message. They hugged her as she wiped her eyes, laughing and crying at the same time. 'That's wonderful, Daisy,' said Peggy, 'Now we can celebrate!' News spread quickly and Dot came as soon as she heard. Soon they all enjoyed extra portions of cake in the cafeteria, courtesy of Mrs Budd, washed down with lashings of tea.

Before long everyone in Tooting and Mitcham knew of Stan's survival. Mr and Mrs Moore, Frank and Doris, could not contain their joy at the wonderful news that he was still alive. They had received brief official notification from the government at last confirming he was a Prisoner of War. Everyone was informed, including the local paper. They still didn't know his exact location, but Daisy treasured the newspaper cutting and kept it safe beside the telegram.

A telegram arrives…. (Daisy Lawrence Archive)

Driver Stanley Moore, whose parents live in Edenvale-road, Mitcham, have just received news that he is a prisoner of war in a camp in Malaya.

Four Co-op Men are Prisoners

All Reported to be in Japanese Hands

Four members of the staff of the Tooting branch of the Co-operative Society, who were all with the R.A.S.C. (18th Division), have been reported prisoners of war in Japanese hands. They are George Appleton, Stan. Fitsh, Charlie Brooks (all of Tooting) and Driver Stanley Moore, whose parents, Mr. and Mrs. F. Moore, Edenvale-road, Mitcham, have just had news that he is in a Malayan camp.

The relatives of the Tooting men received news earlier.

Driver Moore, who is 27, joined the Co-operative Society at the age of 14 and worked there until he joined up in 1940. He was educated at Tooting Graveney School. He served in India before going to Singapore, where he fell into Japanese hands. His family, who had been without news of him for 15 months, have been told that they can now write letters and that the Red Cross are preparing to send parcels to the camp, which they have not yet been able to visit.

Emma Moore's press announcement: "Four Co-op Men Are Prisoners". (Daisy Lawrence Archive)

Chapter 15

The Workings of Bletchley Park

In a confusing mass of different huts and sections, the developed 'workings' of Bletchley Park were actually quite straightforward. Essentially Welchman had devised an efficient hub and spoke system for each cipher. The Foreign Office, SIS and MI6 were centre with the commander and his deputy. Around them were the Army, Navy and Air Force with listening stations for each section. Around these were Wrens and Foreign Office Civil Servants – regular civilians, most of whom were women – with Chief Administration Officer, Alan Bradshaw, a naval officer and one of the first at the mansion and GC&CS, who was said to be the administrative 'glue' that held the departments together.

Structure

All groups worked under the Official Secrets Act for the government, allocated to a specific military section or cipher within the structure. Their specialist job targeted a specific process in handling enemy message intercepts, including diplomatic messages: interception, delivery, decoding, identifying, working with faster codebreaking machines, solving enciphered codes, re-enciphering, reading, analysing, disseminating, indexing, filing, where a resulting 'central file' of information held millions of messages. Analysts often returned to this cache of data to search for past information or message components that held clues to unbroken codes and the enemy's plans.

Leaders from all military sections were informed by their section heads through intelligence reports and acted on or developed strategies based on the best information received. The section leaders did not advise on war strategy. However, more details have recently come to light regarding a special group of officers who met regularly to analyse options for future combat tactics and 'Orders of Battle'. In October 1942 this secret group of approximately six people, mostly from the Air Section, met in Room 149 on the top floor of one of the new Bletchley blocks, possibly Block B. They became known as the Western Front Committee (WFC). With vital information at their fingertips, they planned for the invasion of Europe, catalogued enemy supplies, positions and strengths. This ultimately led to an unprecedented position of intelligence influence for D-Day.[1]

In general day to day running, section heads or managers controlled sub-sections, each with a supervisor for each shift who in turn had a team of people. It was a production line of management, supervision, code-breaking, processing and precise message analysis – using slow manual methods, 'pen and paper', or faster mechanical methods using Bombes and other similar machines. From hut to hut, each section completed its individual task to unravel and usefully disseminate all messages. The section head, and his or her team, acquired a basic grasp of the contents of all wireless traffic (W/T), German, Italian or Japanese, so that all messages from intercepting stations could be used advantageously. To be successful, a net of secrecy, close contact and co-operation between the Intelligence Sections of the Army, Navy, and Royal Air Force was essential, at home and abroad. Some intercept stations were as far away as Australia, Africa and India, as well as the similar system created in Washington.

'Y' Stations listened while Bletchley Park collected and watched for peculiarities in traffic as well as signs of changes of procedure. They were vigilant to enemy operator personality changes, modified ciphers and ready to adjust their deciphering methods. Once results were gathered from day to day 'housekeeping', the urgency and usefulness of messages was analysed and conveyed to the appropriate department head. From there intelligence reports were sent to the Admiralty for further transmission to commanders in the field, where decisions were made on future lines of diplomacy, attack or defence. For most of the time all Allied forces were prepared for enemy manoeuvres, surprise attacks and emergencies through the information coming from the Bletchley operation, but one period in history was tragically missed or ignored.

When the Second World War started, Nigel de Grey was re-assigned to Intelligence at Bletchley, to concentrate on German Enigma traffic. He was a Foreign Office civilian. In September 1941 he provided a report to

Winston Churchill with the first references of mass destruction of human life by German police battalions, who systematically levelled villages and 'removed' populations – likely consisting of Jewish families and their sympathisers. One signalled message boasted over 30,000 executions 'in the central area'. Following a veiled warning from Churchill to Germany in a speech to the British parliament 'to end such atrocities', a German circular cautioned that no further references to 'sensitive operations' should be made on German wireless channels. It was hard for Churchill to be candid without revealing his intelligence source – that Bletchley Park could read all German messages – but the Allies did little to save the Jewish people in 1941. Not until 1945 were the full horrors of the Holocaust known. Did the codebreakers at Bletchley know? Could they have done more? According to the Jewish Virtual Library in 2014 more than 250 people from the Jewish community worked at Bletchley Park during the war.

The Mansion, Huts and Blocks

As Daisy looked back, years later, she agreed the departments at GC&CS were confusing. Many seemed to be duplicated with origins in different sections. Trying to bring them together and explain was not always straightforward. Simplified, each different type of code garnered a new department string, and certain supporting departments worked for all or many strings, such as Hollerith and the faster codebreaking machines.

Huts 1 and 2 housed transport, cafeteria and maintenance staff.

Huts 3 and 6 decrypting German Enigma Army and Air Force intercepts/reports.

Huts 4 and 8 decrypting German Enigma Navy intercepts/reports.

Hut 5 was a Cipher Operators' Training School, a Medical Centre and the Security of Allied Ciphers section.

Hut 7 Navy, Army, Japanese, decrypting Diplomatic messages and reports, central filing, Index Library, early Hollerith.

Hut 9 was Administration, Finance, Personnel and Billeting Office.

Hut 10 Air Section.

Hut 11 Bombe machines and Wren operators.

When the blocks were built some of the departments moved into the new facilities, but often kept the original number of their hut.

Block A was eventually Naval Central Ref/Administration, incorporating part Hut 7 – some Hollerith, Air Force and Jafo (Japanese Forces – Japanese Army and Airforce Intelligence), though the Air Force eventually moved to Block F.

Block B was Naval, incorporating some of Hut 7, and is said to have included the secret Western Front Committee in room 149.

Block C was Hollerith (also in Hut 7), Air Force and Jafo.

Block D was Air Force; Hut 3. Hut 6 moved there too, with their arm of Traffic Analysis SIXTA (formed originally at Beaumanor in Leicestershire). A small tunnel under the road connected Block D to Block E.

Block E Communications held mostly Typex and Teleprinter operators.

Block F was Air Force and the Newmanry.

Block H was Colossus.

As an example of movement, part of the Naval Section known as Hut 4, was responsible for intelligence from German Naval Enigma messages deciphered in Hut 8. It also included Italian and Japanese signals from non-Enigma ciphers. The department was called Hut 4 because the Naval Section started in Hut 4, 1940-1942. When the department moved to the new Block A in 1942, it was still called Hut 4. Fortunately, most staff knew where their department had moved to in the grounds!

People

Daisy was in Hut 7, which had moved to Block B (Naval Intelligence) in 1943, although later this department was to be found in Block A. Daisy worked on Japanese Naval codes, handling intercepts from Japanese merchant shipping under cryptographic expert Hugh Foss, head of department. However, her immediate boss was Captain (later Major) H.E. Martin of the Army Intelligence Corps.

Hugh Foss's immediate superior was Frank Birch, Chief Commander of the Naval Section of Bletchley Park. Here their personnel produced intelligence reports from German Navy Enigma signals decrypted by Hut 8. They also decrypted and produced intelligence reports from non-Enigma naval ciphers, including Italian and Japanese signals. These were diplomatic messages from ambassadors to their High Command. Though somewhat lengthy with many characters, making it harder to decode, the teleprinter intercepts were useful in terms of minute detail. The information may not always have been urgent, but it was a wealth of information, vital to understanding how the enemy worked and their future war strategies.

Foss, at 6ft 5ins and fluent in Japanese, was an imposing figure for Daisy, who was comparatively, diminutive and knew zero Japanese. He had masses of bright red hair, a wild red beard, and frequently wore a kilt and sandals. He was a Scottish dancing fanatic and some called him eccentric as his habits did not quite fit with theirs. On night shifts he was often found studying Japanese as he took a break from cryptography. While this was not unnecessarily unusual, during winter months he also wore a baby-blue knitted pixie hood across his beard to keep his whiskers in place!

Alan Turing, the eminent mathematician – often referred to as Prof, though he wasn't a professor – was known to Daisy. She found him a very polite man; always opening doors for the ladies, but he said little. 'He was just another introverted Oxbridge Boffin, or Dons as they were called.'

Turing, five years older than Daisy, had arrived at Bletchley in 1939 at the age of 27, just as war was declared. He had studied at Princeton University in America, where he obtained a doctorate, but returned to England when his special talents were required for war work. 'There were several men of the professor type', Daisy continued. She also confirmed that he was known for riding around the grounds on his bicycle wearing a gas mask due to allergies. While this was amusing to all, Daisy sympathised since she also suffered from hay fever, though she would never have worn a gas mask for that reason. In 1943 Turing worked mainly at Hanslope House, on Enigma intercepts and Bombe development, but he was a regular visitor to Bletchley Park a few miles further south.

Dons, mostly from Oxford or Cambridge universities, had a history of continued acceptance into the Admiralty or Foreign Office; their dishevelled appearance and eccentricities were often forgiven. In fact, one might say the Foreign Office was completely lax and made of 'interesting people'. New military recruits to Bletchley Park were struck by the informality of the place, especially in dress habits: jumpers and corduroy trousers, everyday frocks and jackets. There was no rigour, uniform or regimental parades for them, many of whom were still extremely young but considered the best minds in the country.

When Turing returned to England, Enigma encryption of the German navy messages was considered unbreakable. Some tried but gave up and decided to move on to other codebreaking activities. But Turing remained keen. Before his involvement in 1939, the Polish codebreaker Marian Rejewski, used a mathematical technique called the permutation theory to solve the connection problem between the typing keyboard and the entry drum inside the machine.[2] Knox and Turing both tried this, but after several attempts with no results, a secretary known as Mrs B. suggested a more logical and simple answer for the wiring to be in alphabetical order following the QWERTY style keyboard. The very idea was considered ridiculous since the connections must be scrambled for security. However, the Poles confirmed this was correct. When the Germans came to solder the machine wiring by hand it was too risky for it to be confused and this method was indeed used. Knox had struggled for months, but understanding this simple step was one of the greatest achievements in cryptographic history. Knox later went on to break Abwehr codes with the help of his assistant Mavis Lever. Meanwhile, Turing's further analysis of the Polish work yielded successful results as he continued to fully grasp the mathematical mechanics of rotors and reasoning behind the complicated functions of Germany's daily Enigma coding system. Using the initial Polish Bomba, he went on to develop to The Bombe mechanical system leading to faster codebreaking. However, he could not reproduce every decryption key. For this he needed to acquire complete up-to-date German decryption tables. Eventually these codebooks were forthcoming, and results escalated, but not before Ian Fleming had become involved.

* * *

Daisy was aware of Lieutenant Commander Ian Fleming but didn't believe he worked at Bletchley since his Foreign Office position often took him abroad; to New Delhi she thought.[3] Nevertheless, he was a regular NID visitor as personal assistant to Rear Admiral John Godfrey, whose office was in London's Citadel.

Eight years her senior, the future James Bond author was a strikingly good-looking man with wealth and good family connections in merchant banking. He was difficult to miss. At 6ft tall, he towered above most when he visited the Park. Author, Joel Greenberg, in his book *The Architect of Bletchley Park,* replays a scene where he attempts to help Turing:

'Following Turing's results to quickly solve the keys, Bletchley recommended that MI6 'capture' one or more German Enigma codebooks; this achievement would hold the key to daily coded messages. The German enciphered code changed at midnight which meant each day's cipher was different. The manual deciphering method took several days, but the team needed fast results to validate their theories. The situation became more and more desperate and a scheme to capture the keys was seriously considered. The scheme belonged to Ian Fleming who, in his bi-monthly reports to his superior, was well aware of Turing's problem. He wrote to Godfrey on 12 September 1940 and mooted the following:

I suggest we obtain the loot by the following means:

Obtain from Air Ministry an air-worthy German bomber. Pick a tough crew of five, including a pilot, W/T (Wire/ Telegraphy) operator and word-perfect German speaker.

Dress them in German Air Force uniform; add blood and bandages to suit.

Crash the plane in Channel after making S.O.S. to rescue service on P/L (plain language).

Once aboard rescue boat, shoot German crew, dump overboard, bring rescue boat back to English port. In order to increase chances of capturing an R. or M. (German mine sweepers) with its richer booty, the crash might be staged in mid-Channel. The Germans would presumably employ one of this type for the longer and more hazardous journey.

As an outside influencer and somewhat of a loose cannon – enough to throw any department off course – Fleming later found fame and fortune through his fictitious spy stories, but in this case common sense prevailed. 'Operation Ruthless' was cancelled, a major disappointment to Turing, and his colleague Peter Twinn. Frank Birch, Head of the Navy Section relayed their response in a letter on 20 October, 1940:

Turing and Twinn came to me two days ago, like undertakers cheated of a nice corpse, all in a stew about the cancellation of Operation Ruthless. The burden of their song was the importance of the pinch.

Undeterred, Rear Admiral John Godfrey remained keen to deceive the enemy. He called this 'fishing'. 'The Trout Fisher,' he wrote in a top-secret memo, 'casts patiently all day. He frequently changes his venue and his lures. If he has frightened a fish, he may give the water a rest for half-an-hour, but his main endeavour, viz: to attract fish by something he sends out from his boat, is incessant.'

For his efforts Godfrey would later become the model for Fleming's 'M' character in the James Bond spy novels.

Known as Godfrey's 'Trout Memo', this was distributed to chiefs of wartime intelligence on 29 September 1939. It was issued under Godfrey's name but showed all the signs of Lieutenant Commander Ian Fleming. Godfrey said Fleming had a 'marked flair' for intelligence planning and was particularly skilled at dreaming up what he called 'plots' to outfox the enemy. They were called 'romantic Red Indian daydreams', but they were deadly serious. The memo laid out numerous ideas for bamboozling the Germans at sea, the many ways fish might be trapped through 'deception, *ruses de guerre*, passing on false information and so on'. The ideas were incredulous and imaginative. The memo continued, saying: 'At first sight, many of these appear somewhat fantastic, but nevertheless they contain germs of some seriously good ideas; and the more you examine them, the less fantastic they seem to appear.'[4]

PROCESSES and CODEBREAKING MACHINES

How much fun some must have had thinking up scurrilous ideas and applying Latin schoolboy nicknames to serious highly classified plans and codebreaking systems of national importance.

Banburismus: This is a type of alphabetical netz method of Bigram and Trigram tables, devised by Alan Turing, where messages overlapped printed paper sheets, ten inches by several feet wide. Corresponding letters were marked or punched with a pencil in the hope that the dark spots matched when several sheets were piled together. Good matches could reveal the Enigma code for the day, but the system was only used if Cribs and Kisses were not available. The method's unusual name simply derived from its being printed in Banbury, Oxfordshire.

Jeffreys' sheets: John Jeffreys was a research Fellow at Downing College, Cambridge, and joined Bletchley with fellow mathematician Gordon Welchman in September 1939. He worked in the Cottage with Knox, Turing and Twinn and was charged with manufacturing Zygalski sheets, a task that took three months to complete. This was another type of mathematically designed perforated sheet, named after Polish mathematician-cryptologist, Henryk Zygalski. The method was also known as the 'Netz', or Net Method. Jeffreys' design was a similar stack of perforated sheets, 'as a catalogue of the effect of any two Enigma rotors'.[5]

Cribs and Kisses: As mentioned, these are the logical analyses of words at the top and bottom of Enigma messages. A Crib, for example, could be a standard message heading such as *Wetterbericht* which translates to 'Weather Report'. Daisy used this method of reading regular headings in her work. The 'clear' or 'plain' text provided a way for codebreakers to find the code for the day. Stuart Milner-Barry observed Enigma operators often used addresses and signatures that were long and typical, and a good source for cribs. A crib could be thirteen characters long but still recognisable to the intended German recipient. Kisses at the end of a message, were a linguistic feature, and provided a 'closed loop' for the Bombe machine. Analysts looked for duplicate kisses, such as 'xx' which could relate to a pair of identical messages sent using different ciphers, one of which had been broken.

Parkerismus: This was devised by Reginald Henry Parker to reveal repeat keys used by German Enigma operators. He worked in Hut 6, which moved to new Block D (6) in 1943 (the department was still called Hut 6). A separate group of staff within the section formed a group to deal with problematic research keys.

The Hankey and Blisters: Information on incoming messages and their discriminants were recorded on a chart called the Hankey (which eventually became known as the Hankey-Panky in true Bletchley style). This directed messages bearing identified discriminants to the correct Bombe list, a 'Blist'. The messages were indexed and registered by FO civilians on a Blist or Foss Form (created by Hugh Foss) and were used to create a Bombe menu for the fast codebreaking machines in another hut. The 'Hankey' was named after its designer John Hancock, TSAO (Temporary Senior Administrative Officer). Naming systems after their Bletchley inventors was a serious but simple business. Who would guess the meaning of these outside Bletchley? Even people inside the Park found the weird monikers bemusing. Women working on Bombe Lists soon found they became 'Blisters!'

The Bonsall Tip: Bill Bonsall, came from Cambridge where he read Russian, French and German at St Catharine's College. He was initially turned down for military service due to a heart murmur, but later interviewed with two men from Bletchley Park. He arrived in 1939, read and signed a form acknowledging the Official Secrets Act. Armed with the task of breaking codes of Luftwaffe pilots, he played a key role in intercepting communications during the Battle of Britain. The Air Ministry later decided his section was also best placed to interpret and analyse enemy plans, before their planes appeared on radar. Bonsall worked closely with representatives of Bomber Command and the American Air Force to provide a bigger picture of what had happened, what was happening and what could happen. This information became known as 'The Bonsall Tip' and effectively aided the fruits of codebreaking. At various times his section handled more than 2,000 intercepted messages daily, via wireless telegraphy (W/T) or radio telephony (R/T). With the 'Bonsall tip' the Air Ministry was provided with simple but immediate warning of crucial tactical information. Bonsall also recommended that major air force bomber raids carry German-speaking radio operators, who would not only record raw material for intelligence, but could also provide instant clarity for their formation commander using immediate translation such as, 'Germans approaching', or 'they're in a different position now'. The Air Section reports were originated by Bonsall and two other colleagues, Millward and Prior. They became known as BMP reports.[6, 7]

Bookbuilding: This process was mentioned during a conversation with Daisy in the mid-1980s: 'We used a system called Bookbuilding.' She was sitting in her usual armchair at home, in the bay window. 'But it was nothing like your kind of book publishing,' she emphasised, a reference to my profession. 'We made collections of important decoded messages for future analysis, and military commanders, mostly navy, came into our office to collect the intelligence.' She placed a finger on her lips and considered her statement. 'As far as I recall they weren't Enigma messages; I didn't know the name 'Enigma' until the 1980s. I worked on Japanese mostly; Lorenz was a codename I remember, with others such as Purple and Tunny. Some were called "fish codes". The names were all quite odd when I think about it.'

When asked, she confirmed that through Japanese diplomatic intercepts, they could read the messages of German High Command. 'After our department heads, and other sections assessed the information we provided, the reports, index cards and files were returned to our department to re-file. It was like a library.'

Crucial information on German activity could be obtained from messages sent by Japanese ambassadors and diplomats in Europe and other parts of the world. The intercepted messages tended to be long, but often revealed intricate basic details, so that by the summer of 1944, BP had access to a wide variety of enemy communications. Small nuances in messages could be game-changing, but unless the intelligence was used in the right way, by the right people, it was of little value.

Daisy remembered it was John Tiltman who had refined the Bookbuilding process that she was connected to in Hut 7. Author, Joel Greenberg wrote: *'He could lay claim to one of the greatest cryptologists of his generation.'* Could it be that Tiltman's Bookbuilding ideas came from the city via his father? The aims and vocabulary of the financial world seem similar, where 'Bookbuilding' is an organised system. Or perhaps it was something more subtle, connected to his time in India.

David Kahn in his 1967 book, *The Codebreakers: The Story of Secret Writing*, tells the story of an Indian group of subversive spies who tried to hoodwink the American government. But their secret messages were exposed by William Friedman, who found their code to be based on a German translation dictionary. Codes from this type of base enciphering were called Book Codes – Tiltman spent several years in Shimla, northern India, and would have been aware of this technique. Dr David Kenyon, Research Historian at Bletchley Park, confirms that Book Codes are a complex form of encryption, especially when a foreign language is involved. The translation dictionary is in two parts, one part reversed. Words or phrases are associated with a group of digits in the first dictionary, and these are used to create a message. The decoder uses the second part of the dictionary to translate the message from numeric codes.

> *From there, you require a second book which has random sequences of digits on each of its pages. You select a page, add the digits from the second page to the numbers in your encoded message to come up with new numbers and send it off. To solve the code, you must have the page number of the second book to subtract the second set of numbers used and use the reverse dictionary to decode the new numbers and therefore, the message. This method was applied to solving Japanese codes with great success. It was a separate world. One team worked only on JN 25 - Japanese Naval Codes. If they identified the meaning of a number, they would write it on large rolling sheets of paper to compile a complete dictionary.*

Thus, you have the 'book'. Bookbuilding is a process where one tries to figure out and fill in the numbers. This process is lengthy and relies on statistical analyses. Further research shows that Daisy's work included these processes under Major H.E. Martin. Over time codebreakers manually filled in the gaps for the missing numerals and words with increasing success. This process was called 'stopping' and some clerical assistants were called 'Stoppers'. The improvement process was also referred to as Emending, with the goal of completing a book. JN was the prefix given to all Japanese Naval codes, in Daisy's case JN11, JN25 and JN 40. The relevant sections worked to find all the relevant groups of numbers to recreate phrases in that particular code book. Their efforts gradually built the key to the majority of Japanese intercepted messages for that code.

Tiltman was also a builder of relationships and a persistent supporter of co-operation between British and USA cryptanalysts. In the mutual quest to break codes and analyse future enemy plans, he helped achieve a smooth exchange of information between Washington and Bletchley. He was promoted to brigadier and became Deputy Director of GC&CS in 1944. After the war he became deputy director at GCHQ and later worked in America.[8]

Codebreaking Machines

The methods and machinery invented for codebreaking are complicated to explain, but briefly their function was to find faster ways to break codes and process intelligence. (Apart from Typex and Sigaba these machines did not decipher or encipher messages themselves.) Many others have already provided details of the complicated mechanics, but here is a summary.

The Bombe

Dilly Knox had been one of the most important codebreakers from the Admiralty's Room 40 since 1914. After the merger of departments to form GC&CS, he tackled the secret ciphers of rising European dictators and achieved the great feat of reading Italian naval Enigma messages in April 1937. By 1939 Knox had moved from London to Bletchley Park with the esteemed Captain Ridley cluster and set himself up in Cottage 3 by the stable yard, next to the mansion. His team included John R.F. Jeffreys, Alan Turing and Peter Twinn. But it was not until 1939, after a second meeting in Poland, that he and his colleagues made progress in deciphering intercepted messages originated by the German Enigma machine. The information received from the young

Polish codebreakers via the French was useful and meant he could start dissecting the Bomba. Both he and Foss worked diligently to replicate and improve the manual and mechanical solutions to Enigma and the Bomba, but it was Turing who fully embraced the task and developed a successful combination search machine. 'Nobody else seemed interested,' Turing is reported to have said, as he persevered with the machine. His version was called the Bombe and it was the first electro-mechanical machine to speedily break Enigma keys regularly.

Knox encouraged Turing's experimentation of the Bombe, along with Jeffreys' Polish Netz method. With these projects underway, he concentrated on breaking into Enigma machines without a 'stecker' plug board. The German Defence Enigma had no plug board, but had frequent changes of code-wheels, and Dilly and his team went on to regularly attack and decrypt Abwehr messages from autumn 1942. This enabled MI5 to gain control of German spies stationed in the UK and aided the development of the secret double-cross system. He built a devoted team, some of whom were excellent codebreakers, including Mavis Lever. Dilly became Chief Cryptographer at Bletchley and received the CMG (Companion of the Order of St Michael and St George) in January 1943. Unfortunately, however, Daisy barely knew him because he died at the end of February 1943 from cancer.

After a slow start, Turing successfully tweaked earlier Bombe designs to achieve reliable results. His machine replicated the action of several Enigma machines wired together. It was considered to be the brainchild of Turing, but to some extent it was also Gordon Welchman's when he introduced the idea of a diagonal line board. Peter Twinn was also involved and at build stage presented the requirements to Harold 'Doc' Keen, Research Director of the British Tabulating Machine company (BTM). During 1940 there were two prototypes built of the electro-mechanical machine – affectionately known as Victory and Agnes, with the most sophisticated model being delivered to Bletchley on 11 March 1941. This was known as the Jumbo bombe.[9] The improvements provided faster codebreaking results daily. As part of the process, analysts in Hut 6 assessed messages from the German Army and Air Force and passed initial message headers, cribs, to the Bombe operators. Hut 8 analysts did the same for Naval messages. The new, faster machine, with the manual decoded header information, was superior in design to previous attempts and quickly eliminated millions of 'negative' code combinations which reduced the amount of time it took to achieve a 'Stop', or a 'positive' cipher, the crucial moment where the code could be broken. However, there were often many false Bombe 'Stops' in a day, before the correct combination was found.

Created to serve and built to perform in secret, Bombe machines – consisting of rotating drums, multiple dials, switches and wires – were constructed by engineers at BTM. More than eighty were made requiring 700 staff to maintain and operate them. Many Bombes were also installed at country houses around Bletchley and at Eastcote, in London, where they were mostly operated by Wrens. Each machine weighed a ton and took several staff members to keep it working twenty-four hours, every day of the week. The size of a large wardrobe, at 7ft long, 2ft wide and 6ft tall, they towered over their operators.

Turing's aim was to break the enemy's code every day, both sides of the Atlantic. Once the solution was found it was shared with other departments, and incoming messages were deciphered immediately by using the same settings and reversing the process through a replica Enigma machine.

Turing conducted a substantial analysis, without electronic aids, to estimate how many Bombe stops would be expected according to the number of letters in the menu and the number of loops. Combining three Enigma rotors from a set of five, the rotor settings with twenty-six positions, and a plug board with ten pairs of letters connected, the military Enigma still had nearly 158,962,555,217,826,360,000 different settings (159 million, million, million – with eighteen zeros). The number is impossibly high and unfathomable for most.

American William Freidman had already broken Japanese codes and with exchanges in information through BRUSA, he expanded the system of intelligence bartering. German Enigma machine intricacies and decryption methods were shared with America's military hierarchy, including Bombe development and operation in exchange for a large amount of information on Japanese codebreaking. The negotiations were signed off by Travis and Captain C.F. Holden, the US Navy Director of Communications. Consequently, a newer version was manufactured by National Cash Registers (NCR). Working with technician, Joseph Desch, Turing provided advice for his updated Bombe machine during a secret visit to NCR in Dayton, Ohio. By the summer of 1942 a version of

Bletchley Park's Bombe machine was ready for the US Navy and twenty American NCR machines were delivered to Washington DC. The NCR Bombe was larger and heavier than the UK version, and the combined design-updates had reduced the time to achieve a successful 'Stop'. In its third life, the once-Polish Bomba was now faster and more efficient than all previous designs, helping all codebreakers to decipher many more enemy messages and hunt down Wolfpacks. Allied troop ships and supply convoys were now safer.

Fish Codes, British Tunny and Heath Robinson

From Tiltman's bookbuilders, to the construction of the Heath Robinson machine and Colossus – Max Newman and his team were crucial to the codebreaking success of the German Lorenz teleprinter cipher and the Fish Codes.

Newman went to Bletchley in 1942. He was a Cambridge graduate whose dissertation considered the use of 'symbolic machines' in physics, which became a precursor to his later thoughts on computerised machines. As a lecturer in 1935, he inspired Turing to start his own pioneering work *Entscheidungsproblem* (Decision Problem) using a hypothetical computing machine. In 1937 he accepted an invitation at Princeton University for six months. After the assignment he returned to Cambridge, but when war was declared and Nazism against Jewish people was on the rise, he sent his young wife and children back to America. He stayed in Cambridge, but began to assess his involvement in war work, or lack of, and his close friend, Patrick Blackett – connected to the Aeronautical (Radar Defence) Research Committee chaired by Sir Henry Tizard – recommended him to Naval Intelligence.

After an interview, Newman agreed to go to Bletchley. At first, he was concerned the work would not be sufficiently interesting or useful, plus his Jewish heritage came into play. The issues were eventually resolved and he was invited to work on Enigma, but instead he chose the Testery to work on the non-Morse cipher Lorenz. The department was named after its leader Ralph Tester and included Jerry Roberts, John Tiltman and Bill Tutte.

Originally from Suffolk, Tutte arrived at Bletchley in 1941, before Newman. He had graduated in natural sciences, specialising in chemistry, from Trinity College, Cambridge. Later, during his post-graduate research, he became involved in preparation of a paper on the mathematical problem 'squaring the square', with three friends. It was published in 1940 and because of this his supervisor, Shaun Wylie, who was already at Bletchley, suggested he join GC&CS. After a short training course Tutte, labelled 'a brilliant mathematician', was soon assigned to the Research Section, where he later met Max Newman.

Captain Jerry Roberts recalled that Hitler's 'secrets writer' was considered unbreakable. Lorenz was a far more complex machine with twelve rotor wheels instead of Enigma's four or five. It was one of the most advanced encryption systems in the twentieth century, manufactured by C. Lorenz AG, in Berlin. From SZ-40 the machine was improved twice to SZ-42a and SZ-42b. Around twenty German stations communicated across occupied territories in Europe and every morning a different key would be used, making daily deciphering impossible for codebreakers. But in an off-guard moment, a German operator referred to a codename *sägefisch* (sawfish). This gave the codebreakers an advantage and from then on, the group called the Lorenz codes Tunny as in tuna fish.

With 'header' starts, repetitive actions and careless mistakes of enemy operators, known as 'slip-ups' or 'cillies', Tutte was able to excel in his mathematical research using just two digits. On this occasion instead of encrypting the word 'nummer' (number), the German operator always abbreviated to 'nr'. From this and following a specific grid pattern learned on his cryptology course, Tutte was able to comprehend and appreciate the whole structure of the complex twelve-wheel Lorenz cipher, which he found to be an additive cipher machine to a data system (SZ stood for *Schlüssel-Zusatz* meaning cipher attachment). While he and Tiltman had access to other electric cipher mechanisms it was astonishing they never had access to a real 'Tunny' encrypting machine – Lorenz. With Tiltman, Newman and their team of linguists, Tutte continued to read the first 4,000-letter intercept. It was a massive breakthrough and the start of deciphering top-level and highly secret 'Fish Code' messages. The German High Command had believed their 'secrets writer' superior to any other cipher system.

With this vital source, Max Newman convinced Edward Travis that Tutte's manual method could be mechanised. Soon after, in December 1942, he was asked to begin this research in a new section called the Newmanry. With Donald Michie, two engineers and sixteen Wrens, a machine with a teleprinter was developed. Known as the 'British Tunny', construction progressed in January 1943, and by June a second prototype was ready. Wrens applied the nickname 'Heath Robinson' to the maze-like machine, after the amusing drawings of complicated inventions and machines by popular cartoonist William Heath Robinson. Wrens made sure the thin paper tape that went through the machine at high speed ran smoothly through every cog and wheel. If it stretched and snapped, they had to re-glue it. If the code wasn't revealed with the first reel of tape, another spool was chosen until a result was found.

The Newmanry operated its faster codebreaking machine in Hut 11, employing over 200 people. Alongside Newman, Tiltman and Michie, was engineer Tommy Flowers. His new remit was to improve Heath Robinson, which over a short time, had become too slow and unreliable. German enciphering machines now had six wheels, instead of five, adding another stream of codes and making intercepts more difficult to decipher.

Colossus

Flowers was the son of a bricklayer from Poplar, East London. As a teenager, he undertook a mechanical engineering apprenticeship at the Royal Arsenal in Woolwich, which led him to evening classes at the University of London. There he earned an electrical engineering degree and in 1926 at the age of 21 he joined the General Post Office (GPO). Between the wars the GPO controlled all communications in Britain, including the telephone company whose cables were installed in many different countries through third parties, including Germany. As a result, employees at wireless stations with the help of GPO engineers, were able to intercept and listen to German messages. From 1935, Flowers explored electronics for telephone exchanges at GPO research in Dollis Hill, north-west London. By 1939, he was convinced an all-electronic system was possible. Recognising his talents and enthusiasm, GPO director, W. Gordon Radley, asked Flowers to join the secret government establishment at Bletchley Park. Already cleared for GPO security, he was asked to help Alan Turing design and build a decoder for the Bombe machine in February 1941. The project was abandoned but Turing, impressed by Flowers' work, introduced him to other cryptanalysts working on German Lorenz. It became obvious to Flowers, in 1942, that electric motor synchronisation of the Heath Robinson could be many times faster by using electronic radio valves.

Flowers, a Londoner, was not 'a man of the professor type' and perhaps that was the reason why his ideas were not respected at the time. The Lorenz cipher, however, was considered 'more important to break than Enigma', but it was a while before he could eventually apply his own form of electronic engineering. Meantime, he joined GPO engineers Gil Hayward, Allen (Doc) Coombs, Bill Chandler and Sid Broadhurst to build the first functional replicas of 'Tunny' machines – British Tunny and Heath Robinsons. By February 1943 Flowers' ideas were permitted. Now he could expand on his electronic plug board expertise to design a better and faster codebreaking machine experimenting with thermionic valves and building on the essential information and manual experience of Testery codebreakers, including Tutte and Newman.

There were some malfunctions, but valve failures were not as common as one might imagine since they performed well through 1943. Shaun Wylie had also transferred to the department and his breakthrough came when he indicated a different way for the machine's motor wheels to quickly 'Break' or reach a 'Stop'. From this Flowers' team produced a reliable and successful digital electronic computer comprising 2,000 radio valves. It was the world's first, and an astonishing and massive achievement using several electro-mechanical relays, all directly coupled. Flowers and his team named their invention Colossus.

It filled a huge room. It was a large sounding name, for a large invention, perfectly apt for the inspired version of an enemy machine. Flowers said decades later that 'Colossus' was the name given simply because it was big, no other reason. From this, deciphering methods of numerous daily codes greatly accelerated and output of Tunny Fish Code decrypts increased by twenty to thirty times.

As war progressed, a further ten of Flowers' computer processors were built, all slightly different, depending on the requirements of codebreaking teams. It was indeed a colossal and necessary invention, especially when you understand the huge role Colossus played in helping to bring the war to a close. A key D-Day message decryption was its most successful achievement.

Daisy knew of 'another machine at the back, not too far from our office'. She'd heard it was bigger and faster, but little else of the Lorenz cipher replica. Colossus was the first and only electronic processing machine not just in the war, but the world. Due to Bletchley's high level of secrecy and Top Secret Ultra classification, nobody could disclose its purpose or

Colossus. (By kind permission Director GCHQ)

existence. The invention remained hidden for more than thirty years, as those involved with this incredible achievement complied with British law and the Official Secrets Act. Churchill had ordered the machines to be completely dismantled in 1945, because he thought they might fall into Russian hands and be used against Britain and her Allies. But two survived at Eastcote and were later moved to GCHQ, Cheltenham.

Despite high security, seeds of this new technology scattered lightly to germinate in other countries and subsequent successes in the computer revolution were claimed elsewhere. Flowers, codebreakers and other engineers could only look on with tight lips. Colossus was finally decommissioned in 1959 and 1960 and America advanced the science (mostly at MIT – Massachusetts Institute of Technology) under high security, where British specialists, including Gordon Welchman, helped develop the computer systems we know today, including data storage, word processing, information processing and search engines – Google[10], for example. But it should never be forgotten the first working electronic computer in the world was Colossus: a fast, British, invention designed and built during the Second World War by general post office engineer, Tommy Flowers and his team.

Hollerith

Another process, the Hollerith punched card system, was introduced to Bletchley in 1940 by Frederic Freeborn and brothers Ronald and Norman Whelan. Freeborn was Head of Hollerith Machine Operations and Ronald Whelan, was deputy head. His brother Norman was supervisor. Freeborn was recruited to Bletchley from BTM. Hollerith's American invention was based on the binary method of collecting information and was the first mechanical version for data processing – a search and retrieval system. In high regard at Bletchley, the department soon became known as the Freebornery. Its base was in Hut 7, but later expanded to Block C.

By 1943 Bletchley's vast storage system of manually filed cards, mechanically classified and sorted punched cards were useful to all codebreaking sections and were designed to track all messages, including those which appeared to be irrelevant. The collection was used by all codebreaking sections. The invaluable database identified past, current and future cribs, deciphered messages and evaluated enemy strategies. As a manual decoder, it was part of Daisy's job with many others, to spot the 'differences' in the original messages. If found, the variations to procedure or code, no matter how miniscule, had to be noted. A slight change in a regular message could mean a change in military operations, something cryptanalysts needed to understand and inform Army, Navy and Air Force commanders throughout the war.

> *The Hollerith machine was like a small piano. You could have what they called a tear-up. One of the punch cards would become slightly damaged. It would block the machine, and all the cards coming up behind it; you had to be very quick to turn it off.*
>
> Doris Phillips, Hut 7, Block C.

The American inventor of the tabulating system was Herman Hollerith, son of a German immigrant. He graduated in 1879 at the age of 19 with a degree specialising in mines. In 1882 he joined the Massachusetts Institute of Technology (MIT) teaching mechanical engineering, where he conducted initial experiments with punched cards. In 1890 he won an important competition to tabulate American Census information. His invention, which quickly summarised the data, is regarded as the start of a semi-automatic mechanical information retrieval process that dominated the data scene for nearly a century via The Tabulating Machine Company, later known as International Business Machines (IBM). Little did he know his invention would later be used as part of a secret weapon in global conflict.

The copyright to build and distribute the tabulation machines in the UK was held by BTM and, before the war, stores including the Tooting Co-op, where Daisy worked, installed the punched card system for stock control. She was not an operator, but aware of its vast capabilities to speed up the manual brain systems of humans. The machines were successfully marketed throughout Europe and well established by 1940. Daisy was not aware the American government used the machines to capture information about race, nor was she aware the German government used this technology to record the location and status of Jewish populations.

With over two million messages each week, the Freebornery grew quickly, as staff converted original intercepts to modern Hollerith punched cards. Bletchley initially had an E6/6 tabulator, a horizontal sorter, a card reproducer, a non-electric key punch and a verifier. Later an IBM 405 Tabulator was installed. The aim was to screen and classify messages in both a manual and mechanical information retrieval system. Through the back-up manual system, the original contents of messages – either hand-written or typed on a paper ticker-tape strip, pasted to a card – were indexed according to the type of message received, coded and cross-referenced to at least eight perceived categories then filed into small cardboard containers, resembling shoe boxes.

The encoded, decoded and categorised messages were then processed through the punched card tabulating system. This early form of faster 'sent' and 'received' data processing was used on a day to day basis, with each punched card securely filed for future reference and fast retrieval by codebreakers and military chiefs. By 1944 more than 500 staff worked in the Block C Hollerith section. They were nearly always referred to as Hut 7 employees or Hut 7 Hollerith employees, because of the department's original location. It was indeed an 'intelligence library' of massive proportions; likely the first of its kind.

Hollerith machines and manual 'googol' filing. (By kind permission Director GCHQ)

Chapter 16

Working and Waiting

After the official news of Stan's survival, Daisy wondered when and what she would hear next. She continued to read and re-read newspaper articles for more information – 'read between the lines' as she had been trained. For light relief she often read the other side of cuttings stored safely in the shoe box under her bed. Each was a brief snapshot of a window in time; life as it was a few months or years before, on the back of a bulletin. One was the Greyhound Race line-up. She and Stan went to the greyhound stadium once. With pennies to wager, she won seven shillings and sixpence. She imagined the noisy and happy scene. Looking at the names again, she considered the dogs she might choose now. Nearly all resonated for one reason or another, but she narrowed her choice to 'Good Prime Minister' and 'Tread Wearily'. Certainly, the latter was how she felt at times. The brief news also revealed waitresses at Debenhams earned 37/6d per week, plus a daily lunch, which was fine as long as the rationed food was edible. The pay amounted to £1.17s.6d (nearly £2) per week and was good then. The equivalent today would be around £87 per week.

Further tips, or 'tip offs', were forthcoming for Daisy to locate Stan. She was given a useful hint from a Bletchley well-wisher to pursue a certain source of information. There was a way to contact army personnel trapped in the Far East. She was to write to the Vatican War Enquiry Department in London, which she did, and received a handwritten reply saying they had little news but would try to pass on a 25-word message. Daisy read between the lines and replied.

The messages were being radioed, Daisy realised that, but the nuns couldn't say, and Daisy couldn't admit she knew. All was conducted in secrecy. It seemed odd to Daisy that nuns were not completely truthful. Her moral guilt was assuaged however, in the knowledge that the whole country was a team and everybody, including nuns, had to do whatever was needed to fight evil. She hoped her twenty-five words would permeate

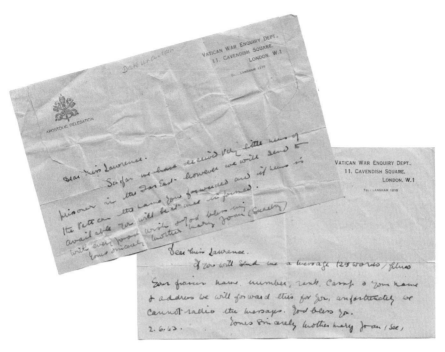

Letters from the Apostolic Vatican War Enquiry Department. (Daisy Lawrence Archive)

official protocol, but sometimes she felt she was getting nowhere. Daisy and Stan's family were desperate for news of his exact location and treatment. Arduous months had passed since the capitulation.

* * *

Daisy's employment at Bletchley came at the time when, as told by author David Kahn:

> *By mid-1943, the U.S. and British cryptanalysts had developed such familiarity with the German naval Signals organisation, they rarely failed to find a crib, and had enough high-speed Bombes to try many cribs. From August of that year, naval Enigma was read regularly and rapidly without significant interruption for the rest of the war. This triumph, the result of hard work by people hidden in the shadows and the daring of men at sea, was the greatest extended intelligence exploit of all time.*[1]

It was the beginning of Daisy's intense work.

Despite the codebreaking triumphs attributed to Bletchley, Pamela Gibson who also worked in Hut 7, thought the work boring and something of a disappointment, especially since she had great ambitions in a completely different direction. Pamela worked on German codes. She was slightly older than Daisy, a debutante from a prominent family that was 'well-known and highly respected as one of provenance'. She was fortunate to have travelled and her privileged schooling ensured she spoke German and French more than adequately, as well as some Italian and Spanish. She was recommended to Bletchley Park by a distant relative because of her language skills, but she also pursued a career on the stage. As an accomplished actress, she worked in serious theatre but when war started, she appeared in troop shows for ENSA, including during the Blitz. 'Performances were never cancelled; we just hoped bombs wouldn't fall on us,' she recalled in a BBC interview for Desert Island Discs.[2]

Before going to Bletchley, she had interviewed for a major West End play, 'Watch on the Rhine', at the same time the 'interesting war work' was suggested. The part in the play was offered, but the war interview came soon after. Cambridge Don, Frank Birch, pursued her because of her interest in the stage, and when he read about her experience with languages, he realised she would be useful for what he had in mind and asked her to work at Bletchley. She had to decide. Her first serious West End theatrical role? Or mysterious undercover work for the government? She reversed the question to Birch: 'What would you do?' His reply was 'Well, the stage can wait, but the war can't.'

At 26 she thought it was exciting and expected to be dropped in France or similar, but her languages were not fluent. Instead she found herself in Hut 4, then Block A, Naval Section, and later in the Indexing Library, Hut 7. There she painstakingly read and sorted 'snippets of information', small slips of German coded paper, ready for classifying, similar to Daisy's tasks.

Pamela recalled:

> 'Initially the codes were broken and sent to something called a Zed room. This happened in the Naval Section, the Air Section and the Army Section, but all separately. When the

codes were broken, the texts were sent to a room where they were put into proper German. After translation, they came to us and we made a note of everything of importance in the signal and indexed it, so the people working in intelligence could come and get all the information. For example, the ship, the *Scharnhorst* was allocated an index card. Every move it made, intercepted by Signals, would be written on the card and cross referenced with the ports it visited, plus any other information we had. It was a very large index.'[3]

Pamela became head of a Naval Section Records department. As a TSAO (Temporary Senior Administrative Officer), she was in charge of younger staff and attended meetings with other heads of sections. In the radio interview, she admitted she always thought the job as head of department was given to her because she couldn't type.

Daisy couldn't type either. Both were mild mannered and used logic in handling intelligence, which they learned to manipulate during training. They classified all Naval, Air and Army section's messages to the appropriate index card file systems, including many Ultra reports. Pamela confirmed: 'In our department we knew everything we were working on. We understood what we were doing.' The various codebreaking methods were important, but equally important was the analysis and information discovered from the communications. It is likely that Bletchley Park's techniques for message analysis are used today and explains why little is written about the central filing and indexing in Hut 7, Block A and Block B, as the systems may still be classified. Daisy echoed Pamela's comments:

> 'We had to write different reference codes, co-ordinates etc. on cards and file in various places, depending on how they were annotated. We had a book of numerical codes to complete and allocate messages to specific files and categories. They were often colour coded.'

She also explained that information when carefully collated, built a picture of an event or process – a huge memory bank – for intelligence officers and military commanders. Accuracy and cross referencing in minute detail was imperative to compile information into a form of reference; a 'search engine'.

> 'It wasn't just filing. Rather it was discovering information of vital importance and piecing the story or puzzle together.' Salient components and puzzle pieces. If one piece was missing, they had to find it. This applied to all the codebooks they replicated; some were just full of numbers.

Snippet by snippet, like a puzzle, the information was compiled in what they called the 'back room'. The data cards filled multiple filing boxes. It was a huge storage facility for Navy, Air Force and Army providing the bigger picture for those who needed more – military commanders and chief codebreakers. Cross-referencing and more cross-referencing, information on the specific military plans of Germany, Italy and Japan grew from a simple manual 'search' file, pre-dating Google and Metadata. The information was then sent to the Hollerith section for faster automated cataloguing. Daisy was familiar with punched card machines from her Co-op days but was just as proud of the more reliable manual system. Either way Bletchley's vast data collection was invaluable.

Further research indicates that after smooth transition from the systems at Bletchley, military commanders at the War Office and the Admiralty made it their policy to relay copies of their ministries appreciative reply summaries – which included ULTRA intelligence – back to Bletchley. This meant the Bletchley sections' watch advisers could follow the thinking of the ministries and see how their work was interpreted and distributed.[4]

* * *

After a busy week, Daisy looked forward to when she could combine two or three days off to visit London. During the train journey home, via Euston and Clapham Junction, she would often see Bletchley people. Joan Clarke was one. She lived in West Norwood and travelled south through London. The slightly younger thick-set woman, about the same height as Daisy, nearly always read a book or a newspaper. If they passed in the mansion grounds, they would give each other a nod of recognition. Perhaps their limited train discussions might have centred around the weather and newspaper articles, or war news in the public domain and boyfriends. Joan might have mentioned her friend, Alan, but never gave his full name.

They might have played Battleships. Daisy learned this portable pastime at Bletchley. 'All we needed were two pencils, and two pieces of graph paper with 10 x 10 squares,' she recalled. Their tasks at Bletchley were serious, but this light activity helped pass the time. The game of attack was popular and long after she left her secret Work of National Importance, Daisy replicated the grid technique on offcuts of white Formica laminate for her children. Each player used a black chinagraph pencil (a kind of porcelain marking wax) to plot an imaginary armada of battleships, cruisers, destroyers and submarines. The fun was to accurately plot your enemy's numbered and lettered squares on the grid to blast each other out of the water![5]

'Joan was one of the 'brainy types,' Daisy remembered, 'one time, I mentioned Stan was a prisoner of war in the Far East; she might have been instrumental in my transfer to Japanese codes.'

Recruited to Bletchley in 1940, Joan Clarke was distinguished in Mathematics Tripos. Decorated with scholarships and prizes for her achievements, she was more than equal in her codebreaking abilities to the 'men of the professor type'. However, she was not awarded a degree and, as a younger woman, was only paid a temporary woman clerk's wage of £3.15s.0d per week; sixty-eight per cent less than Welchman. Clearly, 'women of the professor type' were not considered as important. For her to qualify at a higher level, she had to be registered as a 'linguist', despite languages being one of her lesser skills. However, she didn't expect parity and wasn't offered the same position as a man; employment equality between sexes was non-existent. Most women conformed to a lower status leading up to and during the war. Only after 1945 did the balance begin to shift in a male dominated world.[6]

At Bletchley Joan worked in Hut 8 on German Naval Enigma ciphers, Banburismus and Cribbing. She was also Alan Turing's girlfriend. They were like-minded spirits with whom he could imagine the unimaginable, relating mostly to their codebreaking work at Bletchley Park. After a growing friendship they became engaged, but the relationship ended when Turing had doubts about the union because of his homosexuality. Clarke was upset by this sudden change, but they remained friends until his death in 1954. Joan Elisabeth Lowther Clarke (Murray) died at her home in Headington, Oxfordshire in 1996, after battling cancer. She was 79 and one of the longest serving members of Hut 8.

Chapter 17

Intelligence Triumphs

When Daisy went to Bletchley, she knew nothing about Intelligence work. Her training was purposeful but guarded, and results, if she heard of any, were not discussed. However, certain examples were eventually realised as triumphs. Here are some of her colleagues' stories.

Peter Twinn

Twinn was hired by Dilly Knox at GC&CS in February 1939. He had an exceptional mathematical brain and innovative ideas. Within hours of studying the internal plans of the Enigma machine received from the Poles, he had unravelled its code-wheel wiring. A few days later he solved earlier 1938 intercepts and was possibly the first British cryptographer to fully solve an Enigma message. With German keys changing regularly little progress was made until the summer of 1941. The capture of German codebreaking materials from weather ships and U-boats meant Hut 8 was able to read the Home Waters key, Dolphin, used by German Navy surface vessels and U-boats in the North Sea, until the end of the war. Twinn later assisted Alan Turing in development and building of the Bombe and, when Knox was absent, continued to lead successful analyses of German Abwehr Enigma messages while running ISK (Illicit Signals Knox).

The Herivel Tip

John Herivel was the son of a civil servant from Belfast. He won a scholarship in Maths to study at Sidney Sussex College, Cambridge, where Professor Gordon Welchman recognised his talent for unravelling mysteries and later recruited him to GC&CS. During one of Herivel's more relaxed evenings in front of the fire, a thought occurred to him about Enigma machine operators – a stroke of genius in fact – where he considered that if one was so wound up in instructions, it might be a good idea to think laterally and do something different, even the opposite. He applied this thought to the German Enigma operator and asked: 'What if he was lazy? Would he decide to take a short cut?'

This alternative lateral thinking came to be known as the Herivel Tip. Herivel asserted that one should not assume all rules for enciphering were followed; some enemy operators may well take the easy route. Codebreakers were advised to apply this to all messages and sure enough, many codes were broken faster; some German operators had, indeed, become lazy and daily codes were often revealed by making a different assumption. When successfully employed by Hut 6, the method had significance in breaking the difficult encryption of Code Red used by German air and land forces. It was a pivotal moment and Herivel was heartily celebrated. Turing's mechanical Bombe became more successful a few months later, but the method of 'Herivelismus', as it became known, was an important tactic in codebreaking. By 1940 John Herivel had already gained experience and admiration; he was young, confident and still only 21.

The Battle of Cape Matapan

Mavis Batey (née Lever) was one of the first of Dilly Knox's 'girls' installed in The Cottage during 1940 at the age of 19. Born to a seamstress and postal worker from Dulwich, South West London, Mavis spent her formative years not far from Daisy's, in Norbury. She attended Coloma Convent Girls' School and progressed to University College London, to study German and the romance languages. Her main interests then were arts and culture, and the philosophy of German-speaking countries. At the outbreak of war, her education led her directly to London's Foreign Office where she was asked to check personal columns of *The Times* for coded spy messages.

Before long she was transferred to Bletchley and recruited as assistant to Knox. Now, closely involved in the interception and decryption of messages, her powerful translation skills led her to become familiar with the distinctive styles of individual enemy operators, two of whom she determined had a girlfriend called Rosa. This insight allowed her to develop a valuable codebreaking technique and in late March 1941, she made a successful breakthrough to decode Italian Enigma – an outstanding feat since the Italian navy sent few Enigma messages.

Her first successful decoded message was: 'Today's the day, minus three.' This was followed three days later by one that reported the sailing of an Italian battle fleet. The fleet comprised one battleship, six heavy and two light cruisers, plus destroyers. They were preparing to attack an Australian and British convoy. To maintain the secrecy of Bletchley's discovery and planned counterattack, a plausible event was staged a day or two before, when a low-flying reconnaissance plane indicated to the enemy that the Allies had 'discovered' their location and plans. It was usual for such false reconnaissance to take place so that the enemy would not be suspicious. The message interceptions resulted in an Allied victory on the south-west peninsula of Greece, at the Battle of Cape Matapan, 27-29 March 1941. They sank numerous enemy ships and lost only three people (2,300 enemy troops perished and 1,500 Italians were taken as PoWs). As codebreakers were rarely told of the outcomes of their deciphered messages, it was a surprise when the commander of the British Fleet visited Bletchley Park. 'Our sense of elation knew no bounds when Admiral Andrew Cunningham came in person to congratulate us.' Mavis recalled this friendly rhyme by Nobby Clarke, Hut7.

> *When Cunningham won at Matapan*
> *By the grace of God and Dilly*
> *He was the brains behind them all,*
> *And should ne'er be forgotten. Will he?*

In December 1941, Mavis went on to solve the code for messages between Belgrade and Berlin which enabled Dilly's team to unravel the wiring intricacies of the Abwehr Enigma, previously thought unbreakable.

U-110 Capture

Alan Turing's quest to obtain an enemy code book had been realised with the capture of U-110 on 9 May 1941. Its captain, Fritz-Julius Lemp, under Dönitz, had claimed a quarry of victims in March, including several merchant ships in the Atlantic. As Lemp's submarine shadowed the westward-heading OB 318 convoy, he transmitted a sighting report which was intercepted by British Intelligence. Efficient direction-finding located the submarine's transmitter and OB 318 altered its course. Dönitz, however, ordered the 252½ft U-boat to maintain contact and attack if possible, which it did the next day – the hunt was then on to capture U-110.

An escort ship in the convoy, the Royal Navy corvette HMS *Aubretia*, traced U-110 using sonar (ASDICS)[1] and, with destroyer HMS *Broadway*, depth charges were dropped to blast the U-boat out of the water. But the new Atlantic Type IXB survived and surfaced. HMS *Broadway* prepared to ram, but instead fired two depth charges beneath to stop the craft from scuttling. Rather than destroying the submarine, orders were to capture the crew and their codebooks. The Royal Navy's HMS *Bulldog*, a British B-class destroyer, conveniently positioned in the Atlantic for what turned out to be their most important task, closed in for the pinch. Battle raged and under gunfire from *Broadway* and *Bulldog*, Kapitänleutnant Lemp eventually gave orders to abandon ship and set the craft to self-destruct.

But, as U-110's crew surrendered and boarded the navy tender alongside, 28-year old Lemp saw the submarine was not sinking and attempted to swim back to destroy the German records and systems. A gun battle ensued, and fifteen men were killed through drowning or gun fire, including Lemp. Thirty-two German Navy personnel were captured, along with German Enigma Codebooks, daily schedules, lists of daily rotor-arm settings, and an Enigma Machine. The next day, under Churchill's orders, the submarine was quietly sunk while being towed to Iceland. The Enigma machine and codebooks were taken to GC&CS at Bletchley. Turing now had the bounty he needed for more efficient codebreaking. Some of the water-stained lead-lined books were used for Daisy's training.

Soon further 'captures' or 'pinches' were made. Turing's Hut 8, and Bletchley's message processing centre was able to decrypt and analyse German Navy Enigma messages at a faster pace. The capture of U-110 by HMS *Bulldog*, and its codebreaking prize remained highly classified for many months. Later named 'Operation Primrose', this treasure and the event was one of the war's best-kept secrets. Churchill gradually provided information of this operation to President Roosevelt, calling his secret source 'Boniface', a cover name for a non-existent spy, and the covert Bletchley operation of Top Secret Ultra.

The Sinking of the *Bismarck*

The British had hunted the German battleship since the sinking of HMS *Hood* on 24 May 1941. Of the 1,418 men on board only 3 survived. The *Bismarck* had sailed in early May, and *Hood* with the newly-commissioned *Prince of Wales* and other British capital ships, was determined to stop the German ship from reaching the Atlantic. The *Bismarck* was first spotted by two British heavy cruisers, the *Norfolk* and the *Suffolk*, and by 24 May the ship and its cruisers were in the Denmark Strait between Greenland and Iceland. HMS *Hood* and *The Prince of Wales* intercepted, and a battle ensued. The *Hood* was struck by several German shells and sank. This was a profound loss for the British as the ship was perceived to be invincible. *The Prince of Wales* also tried to stop the *Bismarck*, but it too was hit and limped to safety in Iceland. Meanwhile, the damaged *Bismarck* moved on undetected toward occupied France for repair, though most reports said the ship was still in the North Sea.

Meanwhile, an intercepted message transcribed by 27-year old Jane Hughes (Fawcett), in Hut 6, was initially considered one of 'general housekeeping'. But she noticed a reference to the port city of Brest in northern France. The German Enigma operator had communicated to the Luftwaffe general that his son was aboard the *Bismarck* heading to Brest for repairs.

The British fleet thought the *Bismarck* was controlled by German Naval Headquarters at Wilhelmshaven, but in fact it was from Paris. Since it was 'just a vessel heading to a French port', it was missed by Admiralty intelligence. But Jane thought the information and location she had in her hands was important and relayed it to her supervisors. Through Jane's transcription of the ship's exact position, the US Navy located the *Bismarck* 700 miles off the coast of Brittany in the Atlantic Ocean. British warplanes and naval vessels attacked and the most formidable of German battleships was sunk on 27 May 1941. This was the first time a codebreaker's decryption led to direct victory in battle.

'It was very hard work, and incredibly demanding,' said Jane when she was finally able to talk about her work. 'A lifetime of prohibition on not revealing codebreaking systems and activities, then being asked to talk about this in the late nineties was overwhelming. I never told anyone, not even my husband.'

Reflecting on the men who died on the *Bismarck* – more than 2,000 German crew members were killed – she said, 'I thought it was a great tragedy, but then everything in war is a tragedy.'[2]

The Battle of Kursk

Another major decryption success from Hitler's 'Secrets Writer' messages was achieved by Captain Jerry Roberts and his group, during the battle of Kursk, south of Moscow. After Stalingrad – a long but pivotal battle in the frigid winter of 1942/43 when the German Sixth Army and elements of the Panzer Division were defeated in the city's streets – the pendulum started to swing the other way. Known as the 'Turning of the Tides,' Russia was fully prepared for future attacks. As Hitler moved troops from his Western Front, in preparation for another battle, the Testery deciphered a stream of messages indicating another German attack. This time, as a 'reliable source', the Allies were able to warn Russia of vast numbers of men and weapons approaching the city of Kursk. The decrypts from Bletchley indicated map references and exact details of the strength of the enemy's fighting power and planned pincer movement.

The massive attack, in the flat cornfields of Kursk, was one of the largest tank battles in the war and Russia was able to fight them off. The Allies had the upper hand because German plans were known in advance, but it was important another faux mission was put in place to protect Bletchley's secret work. Messages were never sent to Allied forces directly from Bletchley but through a special route. Another false reconnaissance air mission was ordered, positioned openly and just 'happened to come across' certain key targets, indicating to the enemy that a plausible Allied spy plane had been in the region. Only Churchill and the codebreakers at Bletchley knew the mission was staged. 'Everything,' frustratingly for Roberts, 'was wrapped and re-wrapped in a fictitious ring of spies. But Hitler fell for all of it, even if his generals didn't.'

Many codebreakers suffered mental health problems due to the extreme pressure to decode the messages and then keep them secret, but, nevertheless, a large percentage of intercepted messages were solved. Kursk, the Sinking of the *Bismarck*, The Battle of the Atlantic U-boats, The Battles of Alamein, Matapan, and Colossus had hastened the Testery's codebreaking and reigned supreme during the D-Day landings, all with decrypts from Bletchley.

Cryptogam?

When codebooks were retrieved from the bottom of the ocean, by chance, it was discovered that a specific type of technician should restore the large tomes to a usable state. In this arena an unlikely recruit to Bletchley was Geoffrey Tandy. As a graduate of Oxford University reading Botany, his pre-war expertise was in algae at Britain's Natural History Museum. In 1939 he registered for service, but his papers were misconstrued by the War Office, who thought his work on cryptogams to be the same as cryptography. But cryptogam means 'hidden reproduction' or 'hidden marriage' – a reference to the duplicate reproductive habits of ferns, moss, lichens, fungi and algae – an area where Tandy excelled. The misunderstanding led him to Foreign Office employment at Bletchley, Hut 4 and later Block A, for Work of National Importance. However, his odd science was not in vain, and his wartime breakthrough came when sodden German codebooks were recovered from sunken U-boats or from the ocean floor. He knew exactly how to act with the soggy pages and used his expertise to carefully dry and restore the heavily leaden tomes without damage. His actions and knowledge ultimately saved crucial keys to provide an important contribution to decryption. Known as 'seaweed man', he rose to be Naval Section VI's Head of Technical Intelligence. Tandy only published two scientific papers at Oxford. A lack of productivity, it seems, from a 'hidden marriage' of his own, for Tandy, the cryptogamist shouldered the burden of running two families in tandem for most of his life.[3]

Meanwhile, linguist Agnes Jean Tocher, moved to Commander Tandy's section after VE Day to head the typing pool which also produced Gestetner lists of German captured documents. She said, 'Commander Tandy was a great character.' Of the young typists (probably Typex operators) she confirmed they were brilliant with their specially adapted machines, but they didn't know any German, and didn't understand what they were typing. Agnes, therefore, checked everything.[4] Prior to the move she was head of watch in the 'British Plot' team, where she helped maintain a visual mural of allied and enemy shipping.

Vivienne Jabez-Smith linked her boss, Commander Geoffrey Tandy, and her work to a type of indexing, similar to Daisy's tasks.

'My work in Naval Section VI involved keeping indexes of strange references to unidentified pieces of equipment. I gradually built evidence of, usually, a new weapon, or kept tags on U-boat commanders and any other significant names which might crop up in traffic. We were backed by a library composed of captured documents, their English counterpart and technical manuals. I was in charge of the captured documents section. Paper of all kinds from captured surrendered boats, naval depots and bases, arrived in our vast hut to be sorted recorded, examined and translated, if required.'

One batch she remembered, 'consisted of the entire set of construction drawings of the *Tirpitz*,' a German battleship, 'which, when folded, covered six wobbly adjacent trestle tables.[5] Gradually we acquired the drawings and manuals of most of the secret weapons we had puzzled over; and in a letter from some research institute, I remember a reference to heavy water, the first time I'd heard of this.'[6]

Typically, small and large triumphs at Bletchley Park were known only to a few, and all were kept secret to the end of the war, and for decades beyond.

Chapter 18

Rationing and Writing

War was crippling Britain and rationing had a serious effect on the population, especially in London. Daisy's family pooled coupons and other resources. Brothers, Harry and Bill and Ciss's husband, Ernie, sometimes came home with 'something' from 'someone they knew' and a good, perhaps illicit, feast was had by all. But when they left for war treats, such as extra meat, fruit and sugar, were few.

* * *

The system of meting out food was not new to Britain. Growing up just after the First World War, Daisy learned how to be frugal and not waste a thread of cotton or scrap of meat. The carefully collected threads were used for darning socks and meal leftovers were made into soup. The country had faced starvation during the 1914-18 war, when the British government was reluctant at first to control food markets. Their stiff upper lip meant 'business as usual'. The German plan in 1916 was also to starve Britain into submission by sinking the country's food supplies. Voluntary rationing was introduced then, in a scheme endorsed by the king and queen. Compulsory staged rationing was introduced for bread the following year. The situation became critical when wheat provisions decreased to just six weeks' supply and local governments took matters into their own hands.

In July 1918 ration books were introduced for the first time for butter, margarine, lard, meat and sugar. Average energy intake decreased only three per cent, but protein decreased by six. It was illegal to consume more than two courses for lunch or three courses for dinner in a restaurant. Fines for such dalliances were imposed, as well as for those who fed pigeons or stray animals in a public place. Rationing then, however, was said to have benefitted the health of the country through the 'levelling consumption of essential foodstuffs'.

Studying nutrition at Cambridge University at the beginning of the war, Elsie Widdowson from Wallington, Surrey and Robert McCance, from Ireland, personally undertook specific tests to see if the population of the United Kingdom could survive with only domestic food production. There was a real fear that German U-boats would achieve their goal this time and supplies would be stopped from entering the country.

They used 1938 food-production data and fed themselves and other volunteers, one egg, one pound of meat and four ounces of fish each week; a quarter pint of milk per day, four ounces of margarine, unlimited potatoes, vegetables and wholemeal bread. They also participated in two weeks of intensive outdoor exercise to simulate the physical and strenuous wartime work Britons might have to perform. In total they cycled 80 miles and walked 30 miles in a week and climbed 5,000 to 7,000 feet. At each rest point their diet was supplemented with adequate amounts of rations, bread, potato, cabbage and carrot, etc. After three months the scientists' health and performance remained excellent.

The only negative results showed an increase in time required to consume the necessary calories, due to the additional bread, potatoes and vegetables and what they described as 'a remarkable increase in flatulence', presumably due to the high amount of starch in the diet.

Elsie Widdowson's Nutrition and Strenuous Exercise List – a 1940 recipe for wartime health. (Wellcome Collection)

The British government now felt prepared. Petrol rationing was immediate in September 1939, followed by bacon, butter and sugar in January 1940. Successive ration schemes for meat and other provisions, such as tea, jam and biscuits continued throughout the year. Cereals, cheese, eggs, lard, milk, canned and dried fruit were also rationed. In 1942 the Combined Food Board was set up to co-ordinate worldwide food supplies for the Allies with special deliveries from Canada and the USA to Britain. Almost all foods, apart from vegetables and bread, were rationed by August 1942. Strict rationing inevitably created illegal buying and selling at high prices. People taking advantage of this 'black market' crime were called 'spivs' by Londoners.

Many controlled items were rationed by weight, but meat was rationed by price. Game such as rabbit and pigeon was not part of the rationing programme, but limited in availability. Young children were so accustomed to wartime restrictions they hardly believed certain fruits existed. Imports such as lemons and bananas were unobtainable for most of the war, but oranges continued to be sold. However, greengrocers reserved this vital source of vitamin C for children and pregnant women, if they could present their ration book. Other un-rationed fresh fruits were also in short supply, such as apples. These, too, were restricted as sellers introduced their own controls.

Grasslands were ploughed to grow crops and many families grew vegetables in their own gardens, flowerpots or window boxes. Communities were encouraged to 'Dig for Victory', in a highly successful campaign involving a network of garden allotments. Daisy's father shared one with neighbours next to the railway line. If they hadn't worked hard to grow a variety of vegetables it would have been difficult to feed their families and bridge nutritional deficiencies. Long queues were seen at fishmongers and fish and chip shops, but fish was not rationed, even when the price increased as war progressed. Some considered the quality of wartime chips 'below standard' due mainly to the low-quality of frying fat available.

Clothing was also affected. A points system was introduced in June 1941, but clothing coupons were not issued. Instead unused margarine coupons were valid for garment purchases; the allowance was one new outfit per year. As war dragged on, points were reduced until buying a new coat meant using almost a year's supply of coupons. By July 1942 the basic civilian petrol ration was removed. Vehicle fuel was then only available to 'official' users, such as emergency services, bus companies and farmers. Priority was always given of course to the armed forces. Fuel supplied to 'approved users' was dyed red; its use for other, non-essential, purposes was an offence and culprits were fined or sent to prison.

Food supplies consumed by the poor and working class were subsidised: bread, flour, oatmeal, meat, potatoes, milk and eggs. The same First World War rules for restaurants were applied, with an added restriction of a maximum of five shillings, per restaurant meal, per person.

Bananas were rare in Britain, especially during times of war. In the First World War, their shortage led to the popularity of the music hall song 'Yes, We Have No Bananas', co-written by Leon Trotsky's nephew, Frank Silver. Similarly, during the Second World War bananas disappeared from the grocery stores. After the war the Labour government decreed a National Banana Day, when every child was to be given a banana, but some had more than their share.[1] Fresh bananas were not a necessity for Daisy since she liked hers ripened to the point where some might consider them inedible. Her favourites were always heavily bruised or black.

The result of the Widdowson and McCance study was secret until after the war, but it gave confidence to the government that rationed food could be distributed equally, including to high-value war workers, without causing widespread health problems. Britons' actual wartime diet was never as severe as the Cambridge study, since many imports from America had avoided U-boat attacks, but again, rationing improved the health of British people. Infant mortality declined and, discounting deaths caused by hostilities, life expectancy rose. Everyone had access to a varied diet with enough vitamins. Bread, surprisingly, was not rationed until after the war ended, in a controversial move by the government, when supplies had to be shared further around the crumbling British Empire as their economies began to fail.

George Orwell's column 'As I Please', in *The Tribune*, mentioned that from 100,000 tons of paper, allotted to the Her Majesty's Stationery Office (HMSO), the War Office used twenty-five per cent. This was more than all the book trade put together. Paper was so desperately short that even the most popular of 'Classics' was liable to be out of print. Many schools lacked textbooks and new writers had no chance of being

Standard Rationing - World War II

Standard ration quantities were limited to only 25% of the population's pre-war consumption, and staged each week, from larger amounts to smaller amounts by the end of the war.

FOOD

<u>Milk</u> was supplied at 3pt (1.7 l) each week with priority for expectant mothers and children under 5; 3.5pt (2.0 l) for those under 18; children unable to attend school 5pt (2.8 l), certain invalids up to 14pt (8.0 l). Each consumer received one tin of milk powder (equivalent to 8 pints or 4.5 litres) every eight weeks. Cheese 8 oz (227 g) - 2 oz (57 g) Vegetarians were allowed an extra 3 oz (85 g).

<u>Eggs</u> if available, by 1944 the allocation was 1 per week, invalids and children 3, and expectant mothers 2.

<u>Sugar</u> 16 oz (454 g) - 8 oz (227 g)

<u>Loose Tea</u> 4 oz (113 g) - 2 oz (57 g)

<u>Meat</u> 1s/2d. bought about 1 lb 3 oz (540 g) of meat. Offal and sausages were rationed 1942-1944. When sausages were not rationed, the meat to make them was so scarce they often had a high proportion of bread.

<u>Bacon and Ham</u> 8 oz (227 g) - 4 oz (113 g)

<u>Preserves</u> 1 lb (0.45 kg) or 2 lb (0.91 kg) of marmalade *per month*, to 2 lb (0.91 kg) marmalade *or* 1 lb (0.45 kg) preserve *or* 1 lb (0.45 kg) sugar to make your own jam.

<u>Butter</u> 8 oz (227 g) - 2 oz (57 g)

<u>Margarine</u> 12 oz (340 g) - 4 oz (113 g)

<u>Lard</u> 3 oz (85 g) - 2 oz (57 g)

<u>Bread</u> was not rationed until after the war

<u>Sweets</u> 16 oz (454 g) *per month* - 12 oz (340 g) *per month*

NON-FOOD

<u>Clothing</u> 66 coupon points for clothing per year, 1942 cut to 48, 1943 to 36, 1945 to 24. In 1945, an overcoat (wool and fully lined) cost 18 coupons; a man's suit 26–29 (according to the inner lining); men's shoes 9, women's shoes 7; woollen dress 11. Children aged 14–16 received 20 additional coupons. Clothing rationing points could be used for wool, cotton and household textiles. Extra points were given for work clothes, such as overalls for factory work. No points were required for second-hand clothing or fur coats, but their prices were fixed. Before rationing, lace and frills were popular on women's underwear but these frivolities were banned so that cotton could be saved for more important items such as uniforms. From March to May 1942 austerity measures were introduced restricting the number of fashion details on clothes such as buttons, pockets and pleats. Clothes rationing did not end until March 15th, 1949.

<u>Soap</u> Four coupons each month. All types of soap were rationed. By 1945 one coupon would yield 4 oz (113 g) bar hard soap, 3 oz (85 g) bar toilet soap, ½ oz (14 g) No. 1 liquid soap, 6 oz (170 g) soft soap, 3 oz (85 g) soap flakes, 6 oz (170 g) powdered soap. Coupons were allotted by weight or (if liquid) by quantity. Babies, selected workers and invalids were allowed more.

<u>Fuel</u> The Fuel and Lighting (Coal) Order of 1941 came into force in January 1942. Domestic coal was rationed to 15 long hundredweight (1,680 lb; 760 kg) for those in London and south of England, where the climate was milder; 20 long hundredweight (2,200 lb; 1,000 kg) for the rest of the country. A long hundredweight is equal to 112 lbs. Heating was prohibited "in the summer months". Some coal, such as anthracite, was not rationed, and in northern coal-mining areas, this was eagerly gathered to keep families warm in the bitter winters.

<u>Paper</u> Newspapers were limited from September 1939, initially at 60% of their pre-war newsprint consumption. Paper supply came under the No. 48 Paper Control Order on 4 September 1942 and was controlled by the Ministry of Production, an interim department created to fill a gap in the machinery of government between the Ministry of Supply, Ministry of Aircraft Production and Admiralty on the one hand, responsible for supply to the Armed Forces and the Ministry of Labour and National Service on the other, which was responsible for the distribution of labor between civilian occupations, war industry and the Armed Forces. It was a critical part of the British administrative organisation that contributed to victory over the Axis during World War II. By 1945 newspapers were limited to only 25% of their pre-war consumption.

Standard Rationing Quantities World War II. (Public domain)

published. Even established writers had to expect a gap of a year or two between completing a book and seeing it in print. Orwell continued:

> '…incidentally, the export trade had largely been swallowed up by America. The HMSO's contemptuous attitude towards books drew much anger from British publishers. But in fact, the English as a whole, though somewhat better in this respect than Americans, had little reverence for books at all. Before the war small countries such as Finland and Holland had a larger consumption of books per head, and often a remote town like Reykjavik had a better display of British books than any English town of comparable size!'

He based his comments on an earlier pamphlet published by Mr Stanley Unwin, of the publishing company, George Allen & Unwin.[2] Was Bletchley Park and the War Office using all the paper?

* * *

Many other consumer goods were difficult to obtain due to timber rationing and shortages of other components such as razor blades, baby bottles, alarm clocks, pots and pans. Sales of wrapping paper were prohibited, you had to re-use, and Christmas trees were impossible to obtain. Fathers saved wood scraps to build toys for children's Christmas gifts, and party balloons and sugar for birthday cakes were unheard of; war brides, and there were many, had to do with cardboard wedding cakes!

Daisy wondered whether she would have a real wedding and a real cake when Stan returned, because he would return, she was sure. 'It won't be a stylish marriage; I can't afford a… cake?!' Daisy mused, as she sang to herself.

Chapter 19

From SW17 to PO Box 111

When Daisy left her parents in January 1943, she was told to tell them she was a filing clerk 'doing government work'. Her first new home was the draughty assembly hall at 2 Wilton Avenue; adjacent to Bletchley Park. Whether she was supposed to divulge this hostel facility is unclear, but it was the address she gave to Emma Moore, Stan's mother. Daisy's mother and other family members, however, could only send correspondence to PO Box 111, Bletchley, Bucks. Daisy laughed when she saw the secret address and felt it a safe and satisfying omen far from home. Her address in London was also 111, this time 111 Kenlor Road, Tooting, SW17. The Lawrence family thrived on happy coincidences.

Letters frequented PO Box 111 via Bletchley's main post office. For security a coded lettering and number system was used when the Park's administration office annotated and delivered mail to each employee's department. Nobody outside was supposed to know their department name or number. Rumour later said women secretly went to collect their letters from Dorothy Perkins in Bletchley, the popular purveyor of women's lingerie and stockings, but this is a myth as PO Box 111 was most likely Dorothy Perkins in Oxford Street, London, not Bletchley.

* * *

Daisy's collection of newspaper cuttings grew – anything to do with the Far East. Mail from abroad was still not getting through and newspaper journalists speculated around the country with alternative reports. She had written several letters to Stan but didn't know if he received them. Newspaper cuttings were all she had. One explanation was forthcoming on 13 August 1943, headlined 'Captives' Mail Lost'. A flying-boat belonging to BOAC (British Overseas Airways Corporation) had crashed in Eire on 28 July. Out of some 30,000 letters and postcards from Japanese Prisoners of War only 2,570 items were salvaged. The Postmaster General expressed his sympathy by trying to appease relatives with a written statement saying: 'The protecting Power will be asked to take steps to expedite further consignments of mail from the Far East.'[1]

This was no consolation to Daisy, as she turned over the article to read 'Grunts of Satisfaction'. According to the Food Ministry, since 1938 the number of hogs marketed in Canada per year increased from 3,500,000 to nearly 8,000,000 in 1943. Most of these would be slaughtered for Great Britain.[2] Daisy sometimes read the news to Mary when their shift ended at four. They would take a cup of tea to their room and read or sleep until dinner time. They didn't think they would be tasting much of the Canadian pork. She tried to take her mind off food and find another method to contact Stan. Her evening routine was often the same; tea, newspaper cuttings, dinner. Flipping through each, she reread one that shouted:

> *WE WANT NEWS OF 60,000 BRITONS!* Sixty to seventy-five thousand Britons – including many women and children – are caught in the Japanese invasion and still unaccounted for.'[3]

Daisy knew the number was high and that she was one of the waiting sweethearts the article mentioned. Even the tiniest scrap of information would be something to hold her sanity. The family understood he was alive, but where? How was his health? Was he badly treated? What had become of the 18th Division? Still so many questions. The Japanese government was to blame. They promised reports with names, but nothing was forthcoming. Government officials, the General Post Office and British Red Cross were doing their 'utmost', they said.

* * *

Sometimes Daisy worked back to back shifts because her department was excessively busy and extra staff was needed to deal with an increased volume in messages, especially in emergencies. On those occasions she rested overnight in female sleeping quarters. The make-shift huts were cold, especially during winter months. The room was often stark with a small bed, a bare lightbulb and a gas stove for heat. It was hard to sleep there, but sleep did eventually come, only to be woken by the next shift and another exhausted woman getting into the same bed, almost before Daisy got up. 'The bed was still warm! Nobody seemed to care about clean sheets back then. There was a line inside the sleeping area, over the stove, for drying stockings and underwear and there always seemed to be a smell of gas,' said Daisy. 'You just turned the taps off as tightly as you could, after trying to dry clothes or make tea.'

Daisy admitted the cold was frightful, caused by the in-built ventilation system – numerous cracks and holes in the walls. 'To stop the draughts, we rolled up pieces of newspaper, or any kind of paper we thought rubbish and stuffed it into the cracks.' Numerous pipe holes created by poor plumbing were blocked this way to prevent draughts. Several were disused work sheets with coded messages, which they weren't supposed to use, but they didn't want to freeze. Decades later some were discovered during hut renovations.

* * *

Daisy continued reading the papers. A headline read:

> 'More than 500,000 people await news of their relatives caught in Shanghai, Singapore, Malaya and Java. Arrangements were made over a year ago with the Japanese to give names of British prisoners and to let mail through. Japs Don't Care!'

She'd heard about the Japanese attitude toward prisoners and now vented her anger by throwing the newspaper on the bed. A Japanese soldier, when taken prisoner, is considered a failure and his family is not notified. He is as good as dead because they believe he should have died fighting for his country – nobody is interested, not unless he died a hero. That families would want to know about prisoners of war was inconceivable; Japanese leaders could not understand why anyone would want information on military failures.

But Daisy realised she was in the right place to investigate further. As well as the Red Cross and the nuns, she had become aware of a secret listening service in India that intercepted Japanese broadcasts and picked up prisoners' names. However, she was in a quandary because she knew how PoW names were obtained but could not tell anyone as this was part of her top-secret work. She could not reveal anything about this to family or outside sources, such as Stan's family, but she decided there might be a few people at Bletchley who could help.

* * *

Daisy understood little about Dot's section at Bletchley. They both adhered to the strict rules and did not discuss their work. However, she knew Dot was a proficient typist and was probably a Typex operator. Dot later divulged she was first assigned to Hut 5 before Block E, where Naval Section staff processed messages from several sources, including the Balkans and Japan. Hut 5 also had a Cipher Operators Training School, Medical Centre from June 1943 to late 1945 – and the Security of Allied Ciphers Section.

Dot recalled her Typex schedule: 'Our shifts were 8am to 4pm, 4pm to midnight, and midnight to 8am. While daytime shifts were fully staffed, only four or five women worked together at night, which at times could be very busy, especially if a major event was happening or about to happen in the war. It was gruelling. We had a day off every sixth day and met up socially, whenever we could.'

Daisy's schedule was similar. However, on days off, she enjoyed her free time with new Bletchley friends when they ventured into the countryside, usually Stony Stratford. The panoramic views were refreshing after a long shift. Rolling green fields, trees flowers, birds and animals provided a peaceful interlude to the stress of intense war work which, at times, glimpsed death and destruction. Bletchley Transport also took them to Woburn, a pretty village with quaint Shakespearian thatched cottages and white Georgian architecture, adjacent to the Abbey. Here they enjoyed gentrified surroundings and browsed small country merchants, though some shops were quite sparse due to rationing. Occasionally rain prevented an excursion, but a film or play presented in a church hall in Bletchley or Leighton Buzzard was a pleasant alternative.

She wondered if it was a coincidence that some of her Bletchley friends were employed by the Co-operative society before joining the Foreign Office. Mary was with Co-op Insurance in Chesterfield, Dot and Daisy worked in Tooting, and much later it was discovered that their Co-op friend, Peggy Johnson, was also involved in similar work at Beaumanor, the listening unit connected to Bletchley. Apart from the volume of personnel needed, the Co-op had a good reputation for hiring reliable staff, and these professional young women could be recruited without drawing attention to themselves. Perhaps it was also because some larger Co-op stores operated Hollerith punch card systems.

Speculation escalates when you also notice the austere looking GPO telephone exchange adjacent to the store in Tooting. The large structure with multi-paned opaque windows is a block from the Co-op's 1920s grand façade. Was this part of the DTN (Defence Teleprinter Network) and one of the switching centres discreetly positioned around Britain? Were they connected? Imagination suggests that a tunnel runs beneath the High Street to connect the buildings, perhaps with a link to Tooting underground stations too? Was this a secret unit for intelligence gathering, or even a secret get-away route? Balham station was badly bombed, but was the target Tooting's telephone exchange? All are just a short distance from central London and the Admiralty. It's also perhaps worth mentioning here that urban legend claims that Du Cane Court in Balham High Road escaped destruction as it was thought the lavish Art Deco building was to be used by Hitler's military officers after he invaded England![4]

Chapter 20

Block E, Typex Communications

While Daisy worked alone with small slips of gibberish, indexing and 'stopping', Dot Edney worked as a typist in Block E, converting re-constructed messages into reverse code using a Typex machine. Block E, Communications, was last in the codebreaking process before re-coded messages were passed to commanders in the field and the Admiralty. The department's machines were not the usual typists' typewriters, but specially developed British enciphering machines replicating the German Enigma Model C.

In 1926, Foss had studied a smaller version of the machine, which led the British government to form a Cipher Committee. Their aim was to investigate replacing inter-department message book systems with cipher machines for the Foreign Office, armed forces, India and Colonial offices. By 1942, Foss's standard Typex design was a key piece of imitation apparatus for Block E. In a large noisy room, in smoky conditions, many young women including Dot, trained to operate the secret machines. When a plain text message was typed in, Typex would produce the same information encrypted. The encoded message would then either be taken or telegraphed to the Admiralty or commanders in the field. A reverse process could also be achieved to read coded messages, and to strip the first layer of messages that often were superenciphered. (This is a cipher on top of another code or cipher – in other words double enciphered.) Unlike the German military machine, Typex had a minimum of 120 different wheels or inserts from which to choose. Five-wheel inserts could be selected from a set of twenty-eight. Operators arranged the wheels inside, as instructed. This could be any of 7,687,680 different ways compared to Enigma's 60 or 336. German counterintelligence would have needed to find electrical wire parings for 120-150 wheels, considered insurmountable at the time.[1]

* * *

Dot was assigned to Block E, from February 1943-1945. She had a wonderful outgoing personality and was often the life and soul of the Communications Department. Even when she and the other girls were under strict instructions from their supervisor to be quiet, there was always a mischievous twinkle in her eye. She laughed and joked, but always carried out her duties seriously – though at times, she wished she was back at her normal typewriting machine.

Each of the black Typex machines resembled a large typewriter with additional wires and keys. Once the cipher for the day was broken, the Typex machines could be set using the cipher key and intercepted messages were typed into the machine for decryption, or re-encrypted if the message was to be sent to military chiefs in code. The section operated much like a typing pool with women typing thousands of 250-character messages into the machines. The original messages had been encrypted in Germany by Enigma, where a different code was used every day. When re-set to the new position, the Typex letters revealed coded German words. 'I couldn't make head nor tail of any of it!' Dot exclaimed.

As part of a team of women, she worked on four-digit codes. The work was laborious and had to be accurate, but the touch-to-key response was slow – like typing with the weight of a slow elephant on each key. Gone were the fast skills of these experienced typists – seventy to eighty words per minute – now they could only manage twenty. The slow pace was frustrating. Dot typed coded messages exactly into the Typex machine and each produced German text. Some, on thin strips of paper tape, were stuck to the back of an original message and passed to another hut for translation and analysis. Typex operators said they didn't understand what they decode or recode, or why, but when the work increased substantially, they knew something of major strategic importance was afoot. Often, they stayed late to complete the work.

Despite its importance Block E was reputed to be one of the unhappiest parts of Bletchley Park. Not only was work tedious but noisy machines, lack of natural light and ventilation led to a high rate of sickness and resignation. Weariness, general debility, gastritis, nervous anxiety, breakdown and psychoneurosis were some of the causes, while others simply blamed too many night shifts. Management said it was lack of morale and suggested robust ways to combat the problem with firm instruction on the significance of their work or, perhaps, playing music over a loudspeaker; a short-lived remedy as it disturbed the deciphering and decoding work of other departments.

The secret wing of Block E was the heart of Communications. After rapid expansion the section had 710 personnel, peaking to 1,425 in 1944, and represented about fifteen per cent of GC&CS staff. Most were either WAAF or Foreign Office civilians working on Typex or teleprinters. Alfred 'Sidney' White, arrived at Bletchley near the end of 1942, around the same time as Dot. Previously he was clerk-in-charge, awaiting call-up instructions at Bletchley's branch of Barclays Bank. It was certain all men would be called up to fight, and it wasn't long before he received papers to join the RAF as accountant officer. White happened to mention this to one of his bank customers and gleefully joked: 'You'll need to visit a different branch in future!' The man appeared surprised and followed his astonishment with a puzzled expression. The customer was Commander Edward Travis who, having left White with a hint of his plan, within days, offered him an alternative way to 'join up'. White signed the form complying with the Official Secrets Act and received an official letter to confirm his new employment. This clearly stated his position was 'instead of active service'.

In 1943 Sidney White became head of the department's Cipher Office and deputy head of Communications. His assistant was Erin Papworth, and his secretary was Doris Davy, known as 'Davy'. He returned to the bank after the war, but died in the 1960s. Erin continued working for the Foreign Office until her retirement. White's family stayed in contact until she died in the 1990s. However, like Sidney, she divulged little information about their time at Bletchley.[2]

Chapter 21

Culture or Intellect?

Daisy switched an early December shift to make time for wrapping Christmas presents in Tooting. Her old suitcase on top of her wardrobe at home held festive green and red pre-war paper for re-use. She studied each of the pieces and if still flat and not too creased, trimmed the ragged edges to neatly wrap each present. Fastened with re-purposed brown twine, her gifts were modest, but those for special people were tied with red ribbon. It seemed an age since she'd bought the silky spool from the Co-op before the war using her staff privileges. In the corner of the empty case, she noticed faux silver rings and the small card from a well-wishing friend when she and Stan became engaged. Christmas Eve 1940 seemed long ago.

* * *

Daisy wondered what she had fallen into when she first arrived at Bletchley Park. Civilians and military personnel came from many places and social backgrounds – from urban masses, small town country girls and London debutantes with little commercial experience – to knowledgeable and experienced people from various forms of business or government and smart university professors. Most made her feel welcome, but initially, she felt uncomfortable around the superior Wrens, professors and debs with lofty attitudes. However, she soon adapted and made friends with other women in similar bewildering positions. She wasn't involved with Y Stations, intricate workings of Bombe machines or Typex. Her job, she always maintained, was clerical. Sometimes she extended her description to 'figure work'. Over 10,000 people helped to break codes at GC&CS and most were women. It was, however, typical and symptomatic of the time and pre-war hierarchy, that mostly 'men of the professor type' were employed as department heads. Mathematicians, linguists, chess champions and crossword puzzlers, 'experts in charge', they gave themselves the name 'The Golf, Chess and Cheese Society'. After a few weeks of hard work Daisy found everyone's 'Work of National Importance' equally valuable as they fulfilled the tasks for which they trained.

Londoners also had a special bond and this expanding group was where Daisy gravitated. The group reminded her of the Co-op friends she missed, and of course her fiancé. She still didn't know where he was exactly, and had received only one letter from him, written on 6 February 1942, a week before the Japanese invasion of Singapore. But at least she had the May 1943 telegram from his mother saying he was safe.

A few weeks before receiving the telegram, Daisy met Stan Sedgwick in 1943. Originally from Yorkshire, he was raised in the small Surrey district of Woodside, now known as Norwood, a short distance from Daisy's home in South London. He reminded her of her fiancé. Glad to find kindred spirits, Sedgwick felt comfortable in the London group's company. He was 29, she was 26. It was a worrying time for Daisy, but his silly cheeky rhymes and poems made her laugh and allayed any insecurity she might have had. He was also good at crossword puzzles and Daisy enjoyed considering his plausible solutions to clues, across and down. She discovered they also had dancing in common as he was secretary of Bletchley's Ballroom Dancing club.

Before the war, Daisy and her fiancé Stan often danced together at Co-op social evenings. Everyone admired how they waltzed as one to the melodious notes of a live band or a tinny gramophone record. They glided with ease. Now Daisy had the same magical feeling of that care-free time when she danced with a new partner.

Stan Sedgwick had arrived at Bletchley in an interesting way after he entered a crossword competition. Months before, in a ruse to find top-performing people for intelligence work, Lord Camrose, a friend of Churchill and owner of *The Daily Telegraph*, agreed to run a crossword-puzzle event, in January 1942, where contestants would have twelve-minutes to answer clues. Several people took part and five contestants submitted correct answers, prompting Camrose and his editor, Arthur Watson, to publish the same cryptic crossword in the newspaper the next day. Unknown to many, including the editor, the compilation was to secretly test others for work at GC&CS. Over a period of weeks promising crossword-solvers were assessed for skills in logic, ability to quickly decipher cryptic clues and trustworthiness. Stan Sedgwick was one of the 'lucky' competitors and, after hearing from

Colonel Nichols of General Staff regarding a 'confidential matter of National Importance,' he was duly employed at Bletchley Park.

Not long after he arrived, Sedgwick suggested ballroom dancing as a fine distraction from worries and tedious work. Dance evenings became popular in the ornate mansion ballroom, which eventually became known as 'The Hop', a moniker influenced by the few American male officers at Bletchley. The Jitter Bug was popular at the time, but Sedgwick's dance choreography leaned more toward the Big Band jazz sounds of Glenn Miller and Duke Ellington. Harmonies of crooners and spooners were replicated on an HMV gramophone playing black, slightly warped and scratchy, records.

The Bletchley socials often produced clusters of female wallflowers – Wrens and civilians around the periphery of the ballroom, sitting like turrets on a fortress surrounding a jousting ground, while a mixed collection of couples danced. Others stood close to an open window smoking cigarettes. The dark-oak panelled room with its opulent ceiling of gold-feathered crests and emblems was a heavy sight for some women, as they longed for a proffered hand, an invitation to take to the floor. There were few accomplished ballroom dancing men, but whether a waltz, foxtrot or quick step, eventually everyone would dance. Some men felt sorry for the lonely ladies and considered their invitation an act of kindness and duty. Women frequently danced together, and if Stan Sedgwick was not present, Daisy danced with Dot or Mary. 'We had to, there was no-one else,' they lamented years later. But it wasn't always dull. In a rare treat of raucous fun and exercise, everyone collapsed smiling with exhaustion when Hugh Foss played his lively Scottish dance records and one of their favourite tunes – the Gay Gordons!

* * *

Stan Sedgwick also had a penchant for cars and aspired to own a Bentley before any other automobile. Consequently, he spent many years borrowing cars from friends and family before he finally acquired a 3-litre model sometime during the war. Whether he drove or acquired any of the 'transport' cars at Bletchley is uncertain, but Daisy recalled at least one occasion where she was able to ride with her friends in a Bentley. A 'chauffeur-driven' trip to the Buckinghamshire countryside for a summer picnic was perfect.

CULTURE OR INTELLECT?

It seems Sedgwick's position was not at all boring or junior, as he worked on non-Enigma signals from German and Italian air forces to produce intelligence reports. His area of expertise was meteorological codebreaking, an important function in strategic planning. Later he worked on Jafo (Japanese Forces – Japanese Army and Airforce Intelligence) on signals decryption, a section formed in 1944. After VE Day, May 1945, many personnel previously engaged on German codes also transferred to Jafo.[1]

* * *

While it is not at all certain Daisy and Stan Sedgwick danced together, it is certain he was at Bletchley at the same time and worked on Japanese intelligence. He may also have been the person who arranged for her to receive the Air Section's invitation to the Second Anniversary Ball on 9 September 1944: 'Dancing at 12.00 hours – from The Commanding Officer and the Officers and Men of Station 111.'

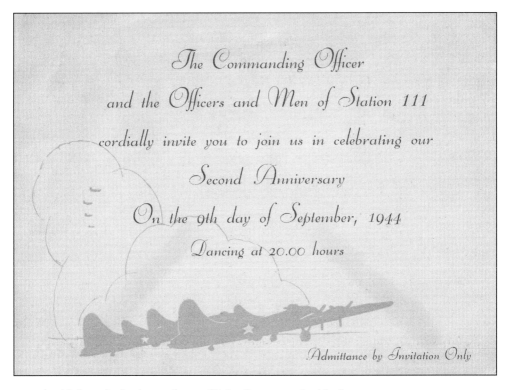

The Commanding Officer

and the Officers and Men of Station 111

cordially invite you to join us in celebrating our

Second Anniversary

On the 9th day of September, 1944

Dancing at 20.00 hours

Admittance by Invitation Only

An Airforce invitation to dance. (Daisy Lawrence Archive)

Daisy saved one of his rhymes – an irreverent A-Z of prominent Bletchley people, a twenty-six person 'Who's Who of Bletchley Park connections'. Verses start: A is for Anthony…., B is for Budd etc., each humorously highlighting an individual flare or nuance of a notable Bletchley or wartime character. This version of his rhyme was written at the end of the Japanese War in August 1945 and can be found in Chapter 33. Check out 'S is for Sedgewick'. (The rhyme includes his name with an additional 'e.')

Chapter 22

Wrens

There was great admiration for the women in uniform. They always looked magnificent. Daisy sometimes wondered why she hadn't joined the Women's Royal Navy Service (WRNS); perhaps she wasn't offered the chance. Affectionately known as the Wrens, this vast and impressive group of females was formed during the First World War in 1917. It was disbanded 1919 but revived at the beginning of the Second World War in 1939.

Wrens were needed for wartime work and complemented the positions of men called up to the Navy and other armed forces overseas. A slogan 'join the Wrens – free a man for the fleet', encouraged many women to sign up. They were cooks, clerks, wireless telegraph operators, Bombe operators, radar plotters, weapons analysts, range assessors, electricians and air mechanics. Some also trained as pilots and flew transport planes. Women in the military were not sent into battle, nor stationed on boats, but on land across the country, often far from home. Training units – some called 'Wrenneries' – were at various places such as Mill Hill in London, Wesley College, Headingly, Leeds, or Tullichewan Castle, Scotland. Ordinary Wren to Director, ratings' titles were suffixed with their trade such as 'Leading Wren, Operator' and 'Chief Wren, Telegraphist'. Some qualified for 'Writers Special Duties X' along with other various ranks stationed at Bletchley. A few were sent to work in intelligence overseas. By 1944 the force consisted of 75,000 women. They had a good education, were reliable and trustworthy and they'd learned how to 'keep mum'.

* * *

The Wrens in Intelligence were mainly tasked to operate highly classified and fast codebreaking machines, such as the Bombe and Colossus. Daisy didn't know the names of the special machines in Hut 11 and Block H then, but knew the header information she sometimes provided, helped find the solution to the enemy's daily code. Later in life, when she admitted she was reading diplomatic messages, she confirmed that she didn't know anything about how the codebreaking machines worked. 'Absolutely nobody could enter those huts or buildings without additional security clearance. Only Wrens were there, along with high grade civilian supervisors or department heads. No one was permitted without a special pass.'

After their shifts, weary Wrens rode Bletchley Transport to their billet at Woburn Abbey. Sometimes this was the same bus as Daisy's which meant an additional forty minutes. She could take the train, but on cold foggy nights the door-to-door route felt more comfortable. When Wrens were aboard, she often heard snippets of conversations and complaints. Murmurs of aching backs and legs, stuffy working conditions, and badly lit rooms without windows – the oily stench, hot machines and endless clattering were uncomfortable for the secret machine operators.

The Wren's huts had several Bombe machines in one room. They stood for long periods operating, setting and re-setting drums and plugs. The equipment was noisy and smelled awful. Chemical fumes from black lubricating oil were obnoxious, and potentially dangerous, especially if used liberally to maintain the machine's efficiency. Their working conditions were unhealthy, a situation that would not be tolerated today. Daisy was glad she worked in an office.

Wren operators waited for their machine to reach a successful 'Break' or 'Stop'. Once the machine was set it could take five to twenty minutes to wait for the call and 'job up'. Some stops didn't work, so the Bombe was constantly loaded and reloaded. Jean Valentine (Rooke) was a Bombe operator at Adstock, a satellite station 11 miles south west of Bletchley near Winslow, Buckinghamshire. She was short in stature, but still accepted for the Wrens in 1943. She had trained at Tullichewan Castle, where her living conditions were not designed for personal comfort. The eighteenth-century ancestral home of Scottish aristocracy had less than pleasing facilities, and extremely primitive plumbing. When Jean's group of Wrens moved to London, she was interviewed for a mysterious position, said to be Top Secret. She passed the evaluation test easily, she was after all a hard worker, but at the final decision the committee seemed concerned about her height because she couldn't quite reach the top of a Bombe machine. Having already divulged secret information to her, they eventually said, 'she would do', and a small wooden platform was specially made for her to work her Bombe machine accurately.

WRENS

The Wrens were well trained in setting up and running the complicated machines, which aimed to produce results faster than human brains. Combinations of billions of numerical options ran through the machines to find a logical match. Every 'Stop' was critical to read the enemy messages of the day and to defeat Hitler's aggressive plan. They understood what they were doing. Codebreaking was important war work.

* * *

Ruth Henry (Bourne) from southern England, decided to join the Wrens in 1944. Her training, also in Scotland, consisted of dull routines – drills, square bashing and cleaning floors. Sometimes she took part in socials and plays; the light-hearted times were fun and uplifting. After two or three weeks, Ruth learned she was to be posted to 'special category: HMS *Pembroke* 5.' She thought this meant fulfilling Her Majesty's Service on a ship. The only information she received was that she would be SDX. This translated to 'Special Duty X'. Ruth and the other young trainees asked what X stood for, but experienced fellow Wrens just laughed and said: 'We have no idea what it means, but it isn't 'Y'!

It wasn't until years later she discovered 'Y' stood for wireless stations and 'X' stood for Station X, the rogue pseudonym for Bletchley Park. Ruth was a Bombe operator at Eastcote and later Stanmore, both were satellites to Bletchley, closer to London. There, large banks of Bombe machines were installed and changing drums and settings was Ruth's main job, day in, day out. It was boring, but at the age of 18 she was doing her bit for the war.

In 1944, Shirley Cottrell (Wheeldon) became a Wren at 19 after she left Kodak, a large employer close to her home in Harrow, Middlesex. One of the questions she was asked was: 'Would you be prepared to work in water?' She didn't much like the idea, but because it was the war and she did not want to be released, she said yes. Her Wren number was 93020. Shirley's training was in Mill Hill where, after several tests, she learned she was down for 'Special Duties'. Shirley didn't know what that meant either but followed instructions and went with a group to Woburn Abbey. It felt marvellous to be quartered in such a magnificent place. The next day they went to Bletchley Park to sign a form agreeing to abide by the Official Secrets Act. She didn't know what she was in for but was quite fascinated.

Wrens – Smooth operators – Shirley Cottrell (left) was part of the Newmanry team working on Colossus, while Ruth Henry worked on Bombe machines. (Shirley Cottrell Wheeldon and Ruth Henry Bourne. Photos provided by Bletchley Park Trust)

At Kodak Shirley had operated an early microfiche machine and she also knew the functions of Hollerith the punched card accounting machine, though she had never used one. With this new industry knowledge, she was assigned to The Newmanry. There she worked with high-level codes and fast codebreaking machines with strange names: Fish Codes, Tunny, Heath Robinson and Colossus. Her first day at work after training was D-Day, 6 June 1944.

* * *

Civilian female codebreakers were respectful to the Wrens and other Women's forces, but Daisy felt there was always an air of 'them' and 'us' – uniformed versus civilians – that feeling of slight inadequacy lingered within her for many years.

Chapter 23

The Listeners

While Peggy Johnson was stationed at Beaumanor in Leicestershire, she often corresponded with her best friend, Daisy. 'I loved her and always found her a sincere and really true friend. But I never knew about the important work she did at Bletchley during the war.'[1] Daisy didn't know about Peggy's listening work either.

Peggy left the Co-op before Daisy, in late summer 1942, to join the women's branch of the British Army, ATS (Auxiliary Territorial Service). All that Daisy had gleaned was that Peggy and her smart uniform had travelled north after training. Not until fifty years later did Daisy discover her friend was a 'Listener' and that their roles in the war were connected. Peggy had the opportunity to mention this to Daisy and Dot in 1976, but she chose not to say anything. The main interest then at Bletchley focused only on famous codebreakers and inventors of speedy codebreaking machines and methods. Why would anyone be interested in lower grade employees? Peggy's secret was safe because people knew little about the Listeners, but the tasks of codebreakers largely depended on their diligence. They were the first link in the chain. It wasn't until 1996, at a family celebration, that the codebreaking friends felt safe to discuss more about their wartime work and how they were recruited. This time Peggy confirmed, 'Yes, I was with the Y, ATS Royal Signals, Beaumanor.[2]

Close to her home in Raynes Park, Peggy thought she had signed up for Wren training at Southmead, Wimbledon, SW19, but somehow she was diverted to ATS training elsewhere. Only Navy Wrens trained at Southmead, under Commander Freddie Marshall. Special Duties training there would have been similar for the ATS Y Operators as well as the Women's Auxiliary Air Force (WAAF). In Gwendoline Page's book, *They Listened in Secret*, Wren Joy Banham

(Hale), recalled her experience, after her Wren New Entry course at Greenwich Naval College:

> 'Twelve of us made our way to Southmead, a training and drafting depot for Special Duties. It was a huge neglected Edwardian mansion – complete with ballroom – situated between Wimbledon and Southfields. Against all the rules of the Official Secrets Act, a course member's sister told me I would learn how to listen to German radio operators on German ships as they relayed messages in the British Channel. I would have to write down what I heard. The sister spoke with great confidence having already completed the three-week training. I was only 18, a former County Grammar schoolgirl, and found I had to compete with superstars from sophisticated upper-class families. But I applied myself, and with my German and new nautical terms, I easily passed the end of course test.'[3]

Foreign Office civilians learned their listening skills alongside military personnel. They were mostly women from upper middle-class families; the men were often educated Jewish refugees from Germany and its occupied territories. Rows of wireless operators sat at receivers searching the airwaves for enemy traffic. However, different stations engaged in different types of signals, such as enemy high-frequency Morse and other signals such as radar or navigational guidance beams for bombers, also referred to as 'noise'.

Peggy revealed little about her war days, but her station at Beaumanor Hall was one of the largest and grandest of the war offices in the country. The acquisitioned former home, near Loughborough, was converted to an intercept station with disguised cellars, bomb-proofed outbuildings, stables, 196 radio sets and around 1,300 War Office Y Group operators, known as WOYG Staff. They called themselves 'Woygites' or 'Beaumaniacs'. Men with dashing credentials were known as 'Manor Beaus'. The Royal Corps of Signals, Royal Navy and Royal Air Force Y operators all trained at Beaumanor, but mostly this was home to Royal Signals.[4] The first wave of newly trained ATS ladies arrived February 1942. Many were billeted in surrounding villages and Garats Hay Hall, but in March 1943, in an organisational conflict to transfer operators overseas, Gordon Welchman wrote angrily to GC&CS Commander Edward Travis:

> 'The whole object of training operators in 'E' interception (code for Enigma German messages) is to produce intelligence by breaking 'E-boat' traffic. This is a highly technical matter of which GC&CS alone can speak with authority. The decision to transfer thirty-eight of our best ATS operators from Beaumanor was taken without consultation with GC&CS, and a request for information was not even answered.'

His missive continued for several paragraphs, the essence being:

> 'Two important facts are that the mere number is not nearly so important for the production of intelligence as the quality of the operators and that high quality can only be achieved by experience. ...recruits from an ordinary training school are of little use until they have had special training. Entrusting a frequency to an operator who is not up to the necessary standard entails missed traffic and corrupt texts. This means a loss of intelligence if the traffic is broken, and it may mean failure to break codes. Only too often a message is passed which would have given a good chance of breaking a key, but the vital portion has either been missed or is corrupt.'[5]

Welchman kept his experienced Y Operators. They used the same Bletchley twenty-four hour, three-shift system which was crucial to consistency. All were highly valued. 'Y' men and women were called 'Listeners'. When Enigma messages eventually came through to Bletchley, via plain language radio traffic (R/T) or Morse code, wireless traffic (W/T), they had first been intercepted by secret 'Y' stations around the British Isles and overseas territories. One operator wrote:

> 'We spent our four hours on watch, listening; twiddling the knobs on our receivers up and down frequencies the German ships and bases used and, apart from any plain

language we might pick up, we were mostly listening to coded messages. They used three, four or five letter codes. We had message pads that were blocked out in squares; we wrote down the letters as we heard them. Very often they were interrupted, faded or distorted so you really had to listen very, very closely. When a German ship came up on one of the frequencies, usually a carrier wave came up first. You would latch onto this and see if it turned into speech. Then the speech would normally start with the call signs of the sender and of one or two other ships, or places, or whomever he was sending to. The German signal man would then start reading out the alphabet letters; with names like Anton, Berta, Caesar, Dora, Emil, Fritz, and so on.'[6]

On duty Listeners called themselves 'twiddlers' while they listened to find a German signal. The wireless frequency units intercepted, were part of various radio networks. The 'twiddled' reception knob searched for the best setting to pick up an enemy transmission. When the click or squeak of a signal was heard the operator immediately switched to the setting, turning the R/T signal to speech or Morse code. If R/T they had to write and think fast to identify the source – German aircraft or German naval vessels? Men from the Civilian Shore Wireless Service initially covered Morse W/T interceptions, but later, accomplished female listeners trained in Morse. Those selected often attended Brownies, Guides or Scouts as teenagers and had prior knowledge of Morse and semaphore. However, wartime trainees found it strange to be coached to high-level speeds of twenty-five words per minute, only to receive Morse messages and never send any.

After student operators completed training, they discovered why. In special intercept stations such as HMS *Flowerdown* – a large land-locked Royal Navy building near Winchester – seventy-five trained Listeners sat at monitor stations in a huge room facing a supervisor called 'the controller'. There Morse monitors only listened, noting all the beeps and peeps on a single frequency, to produce 'a schedule' in intercept operator jargon. Messages were never sent. They only listened. Their eavesdropping work was sporadic; some enemy stations transmitted often, others hardly at all. On those occasions, it is said, many operators spent their time knitting.

But, as soon as a message began, a flurry of activity started as the Listener grabbed a pencil. He or she noted the time, the frequency and signal strength, the addressee and the sender. Next, the Morse message was replicated into the small grid rectangles on the same intercept form. Operators only wrote clear and certain letters; guesses were not permitted. It was better to indicate an omission rather than speculate. However, the German operator's transmissions were usually precise and uniform, resembling a 'goose-step' march. When the message was complete the Listener ripped the intercept form from the pad and held it high, ready for the controller to collect; at times they could be holding one message for collection while trying to write details of another. The controllers relayed the message to the codebreakers.

Signals and intercepts from Y stations were constantly relayed to Bletchley by telephone, teleprinter or dispatch riders. These were men and women who rode delivery motorcycles – some were certainly armed. Important events such as Dunkirk or D-Day, generated far more messages; fast delivery was key to Bletchley's operation.

'We were taught to use a service revolver, due to a real threat of invasion. It was thought that if we were in a vehicle and a paratrooper dropped, they would try to obtain transport, so we should be able to defend ourselves.'[7]

As well as Beaumanor, the army operated stations at Forest Moor in Yorkshire, Harpenden and Bishop's Waltham. The main naval stations were at Scarborough and Flowerdown. RAF stations were at Chicksands, near Bletchley, and Wick in Scotland. Listening stations were also run by the Foreign Office, staffed by the GPO and Metropolitan Police, at Denmark Hill and Whitchurch. Other transmissions such as non-Morse (known as 'No-Mo') were also later picked up via teleprinter, at Knockholt (Kent), Sandridge, and Smallford (St Albans). The SOE (Special Operations Executive) listening room was staffed by operators in Baker Street. Betty Law and Jean Algers were two young women working as FANY wireless operators.[8] Most likely they were trained at Bletchley Park or a connected outstation.

In addition to these units, a raft of volunteers listened in their bedrooms or attics. Ray Fautley was one. Born in 1922 in Camberwell, he later moved with his parents to Cheam, in Surrey. He trained as a chartered engineer at Wimbledon Technical College, after leaving senior school, but in 1941 he was approached at home by a man in a bowler hat and dark suit. His parents were alarmed he wanted to speak to their young son alone but, probably under college recommendation, the man asked if he would become a radio listener. It all seemed very secret and exciting and Ray said yes. As a cover he was recruited into the Royal Observer Corps and became a Voluntary Interceptor. During this time, he worked at Marconi in Mitcham and listened in secret between 8-10pm at home in Cheam for a few nights each week (which played havoc with his girlfriend, and he was once nearly caught). His radio frequency was 7-7.5 megahertz. Each morning he would secretly send sheets of the four, or five-digit, Morse signals he heard to PO Box 25 in Barnet, Herts. The first envelope was marked secret and placed inside a second envelope. He was bound by the Official Secrets Act, unable to talk about his work after the war, and not until 1979, in a BBC2 documentary presented by the late René Cutforth, did he discover what he was really doing for the Radio Security Service. Recently he learned this department was part of MI8 – the signals intelligence department of the War Office, that ran the Y Stations – originally set up by MI5. By 1944 the Section (or Service) employed 3,500, including 1,200 Voluntary Interceptors. Arkley View in Barnet is now known to be the PO Box, where Ray's intercepts were collected and forwarded to Bletchley Park.

Many intercept stations were also positioned overseas including Colombo and FECB dedicated to Japanese traffic.

Message Dissemination

Codebreakers did not decide how to act on the message information received. That was the domain of military chiefs and advisors after information was turned into special intelligence reports and passed to authorised personnel. Special intelligence reports of messages from complex ciphers such as Enigma and Lorenz, usually fell into the covert Bletchley operation of Top Secret Ultra. Some messages were 'adjusted' by paraphrasing, and re-enciphered using Typex, to confuse any enemy interception, but Allied communications security was very effective as the enemy never did crack Typex.

From 1939 Oliver Strachey headed a section at Bletchley Park called ISOS (Illicit or Intelligence Services Oliver Strachey). He was one of the men of the professor type from Balliol College, Oxford, and in between queuing for 3d cups of tea in the canteen (his bill was often £5.2s.0d per month, equalling thirteen cups of tea per day!), he decrypted messages of the German Secret Police on the Abwehr network, and was involved with 'turned' German agents as part of the Double Cross System. This was a covert counter-espionage civilian operation during the Second World War, that only a few knew of. Its operations were overseen by John Masterman, chairman of the Twenty Committee, which in roman numerals reads as 'XX' – double cross. Their HQ was not at Bletchley, but once Enigma codes were broken the intelligence gathered at ISOS was crucial to discovering spy-espionage networks of Germany, picking up their agents in Britain and later turning them for counter-espionage activity and battle-winning deception techniques. With spy names like 'Careless' and 'Lipstick' (even 'Teapot'), one imagines the validity of Ian Fleming's fictional stories, especially when the idea of such an operation emerged in *Casino Royale* (published 1952). Masterman, himself an author, also fuelled the fire and the sensational stories began to lead people to think this true. Of course, it was all fiction – but was it?[9]

Other ISOS deception tactics, as well as the RAF reconnaissance aircraft that kept Bletchley's secret, included false War Office messages to hoodwink and deflect enemy listeners. Tales were transmitted from credible sources to non-existent spies, so-called double agents, whose fake leader, 'Boniface', ran a fake spy network, who provided plausible reasons as to why Britain was aware of enemy's plans. The fake spy was also the code name protecting Churchill's Top Secret Ultra. Different deflection techniques were used, some already mentioned, others were Operation Bodyguard and Operation Fortitude which led Hitler to believe the spurious location of the D-Day invasion.

Secrecy was maintained in a game of bluff and double bluff, while the Allied listeners, decoders and codebreaking machines of Bletchley Park became increasingly more efficient. Their detailed examination and analysis of all intercepts meant Allied Intelligence knew nearly everything about Germany's plans during the war.

Special Liaison and Special Communications Units

The range of intelligence sources available to Allied commanders in the field varied from basic patrols and reconnaissance on the frontline, to valuable human intelligence (today called HUMINT), Secret Service agents in local areas, resistance organisations and interrogation of prisoners of war. In his book *The Ultra Secret* Frederick Winterbotham[10] wrote about the Special Liaison Unit (SLU) that he said he created to provide a secure system for relaying reports to commanders and the government.

In his early twenties, during the First World War, Winterbotham was captured in Germany while serving in the Royal Flying Corps and became a prisoner of war for over a year. After this ordeal he was asked to join the Secret Intelligence Service in a newly formed Air Section. This civilian role handled a team of intelligence officers operating in Germany, which lead to information on threats and hostilities. Under Hugh Sinclair, Head of MI6, Winterbotham was then hired for his knowledge of German, military systems and experience in Europe, and was well positioned to employ further intelligence personnel to British High Command Field Headquarters. Until this team of messenger analysts was formed, the British military knew little of how to securely manage such vast quantities of secret intelligence information (Ultra) coming from several fronts – Western, Atlantic, European, Mediterranean, Middle East and Far East.

One of the SLU recruits was RAF Sergeant Stanley Clegg, who was at Bletchley Park prior to being assigned to SLU Unit 8. Clegg had studied textiles in a cotton mill at the age of 14 before joining the RAF at 18. Posted to a radio station in the furthest point north of Scotland, he trained as a listener on radio frequencies where messages were intercepted about German bombers about to attack convoys in the Clyde estuary. He later trained as a radio mechanic at RAF technical college in Rotherham. He didn't like the work but because he could type, was able to transfer to a course in codes and ciphers, a subject of which he knew little at the time. Clegg went on to attend a course at St John's College, Oxford and passed the exams after a week of training. Further training in secretive communications led him to report to a place in Baker Street, London. There he met Lieutenant Colonel Gore-Brown who told him that most others on the Oxford course were considered a security risk, but he was fine. 'You can stay to find out more or leave and rejoin an RAF unit,' he was told.

Gore-Brown could not tell him about the job, but Clegg immediately agreed to stay. With three from the Oxford course and others, he was billeted in Hallam Street, Marylebone, London. Most were multilingual but there wasn't much chatter since everything was so secret. He later discovered some were SOE. He never knew where they went exactly, but they were frequently dropped behind enemy lines and picked up a day or two later. Each day Clegg went from Regent's Park tube to St James's Park and walked across Broadway to a building that said: Passport Office. Downstairs he learned more about Typex machines and codes. After a month he was moved to Bletchley. There he remembers working in a cold wooden hut with a linoleum-floor, Enigma intercepts and a hydraulic pipe system for message exchange between huts. After a few months he was transferred to a large radio station in Great Whitcombe, Gloucestershire, at the bottom of Birdlip Hill, where he mainly typed messages.

By 1944 he was on the move again. His work in each place – decoding messages from Bletchley Park – was long and hard; eight to twelve-hour shifts without a break. Algiers, Tunis, Caserta, then Bastia in Corsica and finally, via a landing ship, to Fréjus on the French Mediterranean. In Caserta the night before the Normandy landings he remembered a very important 5Z message coming through from the wireless operator:

> 'No later than 2.15am on the night of 5-6 June, I set my Typex machine up as the first bit of coding came through. I typed the message in and read plain text coming out. It had been sent by the Germans at about 1.25am. Within an hour it had been intercepted, sent to Bletchley, deciphered and sent to us. I then had the pleasure, if you can call it that, of asking for the American and British generals to be woken up so that I could give them the message. I was probably the first person in Italy to know that Normandy was starting.'[11]

The German message intercepted and relayed to the generals revealed: 'Allied paratroops, dropping on the point of Barfleur.' Barfleur is a fishing village on the coast of Normandy.

The Ultra messages of 'Special Intelligence', were crucial communications and also known as Top Secret Ultra Reports. This classification was higher than the next level down – Most Secret. Some German cipher messages were intercepted from Enigma machines, others from Lorenz and Hagelin.[12] All communications came through GC&CS, re-enciphered via secure Typex, or a one-time pad cipher.[13]

Special Communication Units (SCU) were responsible for moving and operating equipment and receiving messages from Bletchley Park, while the SLU was responsible for decryption of messages received and dissemination of this intelligence to commanders. The units were not involved in command decisions. Their job was only to receive and deliver Ultra Reports to the commander and retrieve the message once it was read and understood. The briefing message was then destroyed. Perhaps it might only have been a few words, but commanders had to act on that information as they saw fit. There were no leaks of Ultra – SLU and SCU officers were recruited for their trustworthiness and unerring ability in military command posts. With this tried and tested means of transmission the direct service extended to US commanders. The degree of responsibility varied, but all officers were confident and able to present Ultra reports as valued intelligence to senior commanders, many of whom held many years' service and were often sceptical of younger officers, intelligence sources and the messages they delivered.

This included army commander Field Marshal Montgomery who, in Winterbotham's words 'treated the Air Force boys in blue like mud'.[14] However, Winterbotham felt he had excelled in setting up the system and hired the right people. With a wide grasp of operations in Signals Intelligence (SIGINT) including radar, imaginary aerial intelligence (IMINT) and interception of enemy communications (COMINT), he made it his job to ensure the Ultra Reports of meticulous intelligence analysis, arrived at the appropriate senior field commands and government officials' offices.[15]

* * *

As the seeds of Bletchley Park stories germinated in the eighties, Daisy searched for Winterbotham's 1970s book in the Mitcham library. Some of his claims had been disputed, especially by the CIA Government Library who chimed: 'The Ultra Secret was a prolific source of misinformation.' Daisy tended to agree. She hinted specific indexing was true, but other parts of his account were untrue. 'That's not how I remember things,' she said, 'at least not in our section!' However, it is unlikely Daisy had penetrating inside knowledge of other departments. She would have known little about the detailed operations of the SLU or SCU, just as she knew little about Typex communications where Dot worked. She would have believed the Japanese messages she handled went directly to commanders at the Admiralty. In a way she was right, but SLU and SCU were so secure few knew of their existence as an intermediary.

Chapter 24

Speaking of Japanese

It transpires that working on Japanese codes was Daisy's main function, though she never spoke of her dealings or knowledge of the language to anyone after the war, not even close family members. Leonard Pickles was part of the Japanese Naval section, from mid-1943. He had been a Foreign Office Japanese Linguist stationed in Singapore's British Consulate, just before the invasion and General Percival's capitulation in February 1942. He was lucky to escape, and on his return to England was assigned to Bletchley Park, Naval Section, Hut 7. It is likely Pickles knew of Daisy's situation and her captured fiancé (probably in Singapore) and perhaps explains why she worked on this section too.

She guardedly implied that 'maybe somebody knew' and 'perhaps that was the reason she was moved'. But how much did Pickles know? How much did she know? Could Stan have survived certain horrors because of her work? Was it all a plan right from the start when she enlisted? A conversation at her initial London interview would have revealed she was engaged, and her fiancé was lost overseas in Malaya. He was 'MIA' – missing in action.

The British and American Japanese Codebreakers

Bletchley's NSIJ (Naval Section Intelligence Japanese) were experts at the Japanese Kana and Romaji Morse code systems. Pre-war the section was headed by William F. 'Nobby' Clarke in Room 40, which included Frank Birch, John Tiltman, Hugh Foss and Eric Nave from the Royal Australian Navy who went to Bletchley in 1939. Hugh Foss later became head of the department after 1941, when Clarke moved to Italian intercepts.

During and after the First World War, governments had decrypted as many of each other's diplomatic messages as they could, but in peacetime traffic reduced. However, one source was highly productive in the intelligence world and intercepted on a regular basis leading up to and during the Second World War. This source – of several – revealed diplomatic messages sent from the Japanese Ambassador in Berlin to Tokyo. The resulting decrypts and intelligence gathered were especially significant to D-Day. This might seem surprising as one imagines that only German decrypts would be helpful, but these lengthy teleprinted messages, usefully outlined the full strategies of the Axis powers, 'in a rich seam of intelligence for the Allies'.[1] The Higher Command codes were harder to break, but when their teleprinted messages were successfully intercepted and deciphered, they gave full texts. This was in stark contrast to Enigma's snippets of information gathered over long periods of time.

America's William F. Friedman was one of the first, well-respected Japanese codebreakers in the 1920s and 30s, along with Hugh Foss. Just before the Second World War the Japanese RED cipher, an A-type diplomatic cryptographic machine (different from the naval codebook also called RED) had been broken. But in 1938 Friedman's work discovered that a new Japanese cipher machine was under construction. Friedman's team, led by Frank Rowlett, called this PURPLE, when its first messages began to appear on 20 March 1939. As the Japanese phased out the RED cipher over three months, PURPLE was much tougher to crack and the team spent many months studying its patterns. The breakthrough came when the Friedman/Rowlett team built an exact analogue replica of the cipher apparatus without ever seeing an original machine. PURPLE's code was cracked on 20 September 1940. As Japan, Germany and Italy signed the Tripartite Pact and Japanese troops were stationed in North Indochina, America watched and listened.

By 1941, the shared diplomatic messages between Germany and Japan were efficiently read by America. But Friedman had a temporary nervous breakdown possibly from the mental strain of his efforts on PURPLE, and while he was in hospital, the important US Navy OP-20-G quartet of Sinkov, Rosen, Currier and Weeks, visited Bletchley Park on 9 February 1941. After their perilous journey to Britain, and welcoming sherries, they started to exchange mutual intelligence information. Part of their bullet-spattered luggage included a crated PURPLE machine – a gift for Britain in return for details of the design of Enigma and how the British and Polish had broken that cipher. Their visit was the first of many and the beginning of a renewed trust between Britain and America.

Britain would come to rely on America for expansion into Japanese diplomatic ciphers, and Japan's Ambassador to Tokyo in Berlin, General Hiroshi Oshima, continued to be key. From 1941 it was clear that he was fully accepted into the confidence of the Nazi Powers while maintaining his direct line to Tokyo. That year, over seventy-five of his lengthy messages appeared as PURPLE decrypts in Washington, as America listened closely to protect their interests in the Pacific. Messages – Japanese Traffic – were regularly intercepted between Tokyo and its embassies in, predominantly, Berlin, Rome, Lisbon, Madrid, Stockholm, Istanbul, Ankara and Berne. 'Special Intelligence' reports from Bletchley came to be known as ULTRA, or TOP SECRET ULTRA, while intelligence reports in America carried the name MAGIC.

The term stuck when US Army Chief of Signals, Major General Joseph Mauborgne, called the successful codebreaking team 'magicians'.

* * *

When Pearl Harbor was bombed on 7 December 1941, the attack left America in no doubt they were in the war, but Washington's intelligence analysis had peaked. They said there was no warning of an attack (a matter of much debate). A call for more Japanese linguists at Bletchley was made and an accelerated training programme was created to bolster Japanese Signals Intelligence and, by February 1942 – notably at the same time as the Fall of Singapore – candidates took an intensive course to cram two years of instruction into six months.

The Inter-Service Special Intelligence School (ISSIS) provided this training under Captain Oswald Tuck, a retiree from the Royal Navy. Variations of the course were taught in locations around Bedford and Bletchley producing linguists for the Navy, Army, Air Force and Foreign Office. Some were sent to Bletchley, others went to the School of Oriental and African Studies (SOAS) or government offices in London to work with Captain Malcolm Kennedy, an expert on Japanese economic, political and military matters. Kennedy was associated with Bletchley from 1939-1942. Language teaching methods and decryption improved; the shorter course was deemed a success. By August 1942 the unit consisted of forty people. Partial training was at Elmer's School, but detailed training was in Hut 7. This fits with Daisy's recollection of

176

having trained on Japanese codes from the summer of 1943 at Elmer's School.

As well as electrical cipher machines, codebooks and the manual ciphers of Kana and Romaji Morse codes, there was JADE and CORAL, known as JN 20 by the Allies. This used the same machine technology as PURPLE, but there was another Japanese code system introduced by the Japanese Military Attachés (JMA) in 1941. This was broken by John Tiltman in 1942.

The code was not mechanical, but a book-based system using diagraphs – pairs of letters to represent a single sound or code. The pairs were written in a specific pattern into a special grid called a 'conversion square', then copied out in a different order. For 'superencipherment' a separate table of letters would be added for transmission. With his knowledge of the code's structure and large quantities of messages to practise on, which he called 'depths', he was able to unravel the puzzle. In June 1942 Tiltman created a Japanese section within his military section at Bletchley to work specifically on JMA. This was in liaison with the larger Japanese Naval Section, which integrated fully with Washington and the US Bombes, for a seamless flow of information between America and Britain. While some was not valuable – embassy tittle-tattle and matters concerning attachés' personal situations – General Oshima's included a report on his visit to Normandy in late 1943. It was like striking oil,[2] and in the lead up to D-Day message intercepts increased to over 400,[3] providing important information to the Western Front Committee.

*****

Carmen Blacker, a university graduate and Foreign Office Civilian working on technical intelligence, built a scrap-book catalogue of words and phrases, from Japanese magazines for central records. As few could read or speak the language, Carmen, who was proficient in Japanese, felt her system provided a visual element to their task. She worked diligently in Block B(N) to create the extensive library index that proved useful for codebreakers in their repetitive work, but unfortunately her reference work was not respected by Bletchley's higher powers. As a result, she decided to move her work to SOAS and prepared to leave, but this decision resulted in her being called a traitor. Fortunately, she was not executed under the Official Secrets Act, but 'sent to Coventry' instead. Excommunicated in fact, nobody could converse with her in or outside of the Park. An official notice was circulated to all staff giving the order. No one could speak her name. If they did – Bletchley had its built-in personnel spies – that person's job could also be eliminated. It was awkward and hard for Carmen's friends; no one knew what she had done or why she left; she was ostracised for the rest of the war.

Rising from the dreadful experience, however, Carmen successfully completed her Japanese studies at Oxford, Harvard and Keio and became a Fellow of Clare Hall, Cambridge, where she worked until she died in 2009. Her long-time friend and husband Dr Michael Loewe also worked on Japanese codes.

> 'We would work out the Japanese behind the messages, provide a translation and send it into the next office. They would then consider the value of the messages sent in from us and decide what to do with it. For example, the arrival of three aircraft at 10 o'clock at a specific Pacific airfield may not be interesting on its own, but a number of similar messages, received day in and day out, would be. Such information would be passed on, including to the Admiralty in London.'
>
> Michael Loewe, Foreign Office Civilian cryptanalyst, Naval Section, Bletchley Park.[4]

***

Before the war a few Foreign Office personnel had been posted to outstations such as FECB (Far East Combined Bureau). This unit was initially in Hong Kong, then Singapore. But after Singapore also fell to the Japanese, it re-located to Anderson Station, Colombo, Ceylon (Sri Lanka), then Allidina School in Kilindini, Kenya, before later returning to Colombo. Part of FECB, however, escaped to Melbourne to form the Fleet Radio Unit, Melbourne (FRUMEL).

FRUMEL was a United States, Australian and British Intelligence unit, one of two major Allied signals units in the Pacific theatres of war. The other was FRUPAC Fleet Radio Unit Pacific, also known as Station HYPO, in Hawaii. Their brief was to monitor movement in Japanese shipping, Navy, Air Force and Army, reporting directly to Admiral Nimitz in Hawaii and Chief of Naval Operations OP-20-G, Admiral King, Washington. The Australian unit was fraught with problems between Lt. Rudolph J. Fabian's 75-man code breaker unit, evacuated from the Philippines by submarine and Australia's Royal Navy cryptography support unit, run by Commander Eric Nave who, despite orders, went to FRUMEL.[5] The British Foreign Office civilian linguists, Henry Archer, Arthur Cooper and Hubert Graves of the Far East Combined Bureau (FECB), also arrived there after being evacuated from Singapore in February 1942, just before the Japanese invasion. Fabian, backed by the US Navy's Rear Admiral Joseph Redman, was not interested in any exchange of intelligence material with anyone else, and eventually ousted Nave and the 'British Diplomatic Corps types', including Archer, Cooper, Graves and other British Servicemen and their wives.[6]

Daisy worked with Cooper's brother at Bletchley and learned of the Australian unit during her work on Japanese shipping codes and her search for Stan. Little did she realise a link would creep into her war-time story years later, with a personal connection, perhaps, for Daisy and her family.

The fact is that the process of 'cryptography' would perhaps better be described as interpretation.
Josh Cooper, Head of Air Section of Bletchley Park, 24 June 1941, brother of Arthur R.V. Cooper, FRUMEL.[7]

Chapter 25

Hut 7 and Top Secret Ultra

In the final months of 1942 and into 1943, three units of US Army personnel were sent to assist at Bletchley Park and Ruislip, a satellite station. They called their area of high security the United States, naming each machine for an American city, and quickly learned how to operate Bombe machines manufactured by the British Tabulating Company. Other elements available to them under the Ultra umbrella were Bletchley's deciphering methods. America's role in helping break Germany's naval Enigma was beginning to equal Britain's, but in return they sent information on Japanese codes from PURPLE.

Both units used furtive radio and cable communications through the British Security Co-ordination office in Rockefeller Center, New York, where further secrecy was maintained via a Combined Cipher Machine (CCM) – a combination of the British Typex machine with a receiving adapter in Bletchley to decipher through the American Electric Cipher Machine (ECM). On the American side an adapter was fixed to the machine to receive messages from Typex. The American intercepts were turned into Top Secret Ultra intelligence reports and, using 5x8-inch index cards in open topped file boxes – the same cross-referencing system Daisy used – classifying information into at least two categories, possibly eight. The master file was chronological; index card extensions held individual information such as U-boat and ship positions, map co-ordinates, assignments, new equipment, weather, personal nuances of cipher clerks, status reports, etc. The secure Central Information system mirrored Bletchley's to serve translators, watch officers and high-ranking officials looking to fill gaps in past intelligence.

While American codebreakers kept the intelligence secret safe, only a few people knew that high ranking British codebreakers visited Washington's Navy department. Updated telephone lists of Bletchley departments noted when heads of staff were 'absent' in a semi-official roll call. These lists contained key personnel together with less important staff such as '34 Typex operators' or '12 indexers' and, if absent, a typed note at the bottom that perhaps read: 'Welchman – gone to Washington.' They are held in London's National Archives. One on 1 June 1944 shows, 'Mr. H.R. Foss (OC) is at present in Washington on liaison duties with OP-20-G, "TOP SECRET ULTRA".'

Foss, head of Hut 7, worked full-time on Japanese ciphers, with US Navy Cryptography, OP-20-G. Still an ardent sandal-wearer, he was known by his Washington colleagues as 'Lend Lease Jesus', a nod toward the Lend Lease Act passed in March 1941, and his footwear.

* * *

It is recorded on the Roll of Honour that Daisy worked in the Naval Section, Hut 7, Block B(N), but this is now found to be incomplete. The ramshackle Hut 7 no longer stands. Its structure is documented, but its function and the people who worked there are not. Only a small dot on Bletchley Park's map recognises its former presence, next to a grassy patch behind Block B, where a small 1960s prefabricated structure now serves a local scout troop. All that remains of the original building is the white 'battery room', a small sturdy brick-built electrical sub-station.[1]

Before the estate was occupied by GC&CS, this small single-story farm building was surrounded by undulating fields on the edge of the main estate. But as codebreaking and storage of intercepted messages increased, the shoddy Hut 7 building devoured additional land as the department became essential to the operation. It was 19ft wide by 60ft long. With its maze of extended offices, only a small grassy area, a large tree and a few shrubs were left for codebreakers to enjoy fresh air during a well-earned tea break. The noisy Hollerith punched card operation was also beneath the double-pitched roof and the swell continued as rooms for more machines were added. In September 1941 Ronald Whelan wrote:

> 'By the time of Churchill's visit, Hut 7 had become a commodious erection compared with the modest hut in which we had started our activities. Being a wooden structure, it has been comparatively easy for workmen to tear down walls and partitions and to tack on extensions not once but several times until eventually for a time we had ample accommodation for machines and operators.'

After two years of muddled expansion most of the Hollerith section moved to a new purpose-built Block C, in November 1942. The insulated, bomb-proof building was safer, designed to cosset the deafening machines and protect the secret store of information punched cards. Even though the section had moved, the name 'Hut 7' stuck and followed the Hollerith department. However, the Hollerith Training School, run by Freddie Freeborn, and other training activities remained in Hut 7. By the time Daisy arrived she heard only stories of the recent dispute, including which end of Hut 7 the Naval Cryptography Section would occupy. The argument was based primarily on one important issue – toilets! If Freeborn had his way to occupy the half they coveted, the Navy Section would be without this necessary facility. They argued that Freeborn and the Hollerith section already had access to toilets in their newly built Block C. But Freeborn argued that Block C was now further from Communications (Typex) in Block E where they also needed direct access. But the Naval superiority of Frank Birch won and the rooms at the end of Hut 7, closest to Block B, were converted to individual offices for NSIJ personnel.

With its multiple extensions and labyrinth of corridors, Hut 7 was an inner hive of secrecy. It was also now surrounded by purpose-built concrete office blocks A, B, C, D and E.

The east wing of Block E was one of the closest buildings to the west wall of Hut 7 which made day to day operations with Communications more efficient for the Naval Section. Now the different departmental functions of Hut 7 were widespread including parts of Blocks A, B and C. The urgency to expand intelligence in the Far East after capitulation to the Japanese in Singapore in February 1942, had seemed non-existent at first, despite the event ultimately breaking the back of the British Empire. But with the robust training for Japanese linguists and cryptanalysts, Frank Birch exerted Naval pressure to take full possession of Hut 7. This staff would also process Japanese intercepted PURPLE messages from Washington DC. Now 'Hut 7' became the section moniker for all Foss's areas of responsibility in Japanese naval codes, including JN4, JN11, JN40 and JN25.

Daisy's personal connection to the Far East was no secret at Bletchley. She often spoke of Stan being a prisoner of war but didn't know his location. Although she initially trained on German intercepts, by March 1943 she found herself working on Japanese codes under Major

H.E. Martin. In 2005, we asked if the shift was deliberate; her answer again was somewhat vague: 'Perhaps someone knew he was a PoW and that I was trying to find him.' At first she worked on JN 40, JN 25 and JN 11 with civilian cryptanalysts Mr G.A. Peters and Mr C.A. Ladd, whose 'cryptographic works and translations were always excellent and reliable', as recorded by Major Martin, but when the section split Daisy stayed with Martin on JN 11. The split was contentious with in-fighting between sectional leaders; Martin had formed the original division JN 40 during the last quarter of 1942. According to him there was no hierarchy in the JN numbers as they were chosen completely at random for different codes. Daisy thought it odd that, while they all worked in the Naval Section, Major Martin's title was Army, Intelligence Corps. Confusingly, he worked for the navy but why was her superior from the army? Perhaps this was part of 'sharing information between the forces'. Stan was also Army. Could this help lead to Stan's whereabouts?

Records show Army Major H.E. Martin was a kind and respectful, avuncular person who seriously cared for the staff in his department, most of whom were women. However, when it came to translations, he considered the men more efficient. 'They (women) always showed a disinclination for "ferreting" when the work was wrong or the intelligence incomplete.'

This new information located in a National Archive research during 2018, confirms diligent JN 11 as the Bookbuilding and Translation Party,[2] and at last Daisy's name is listed – several times! The little-seen 85-page official government record of Major H.E. Martin, September 1945, clearly outlines the work of the Japanese Section of Hut 7. It could be described as 'Sour Grapes and Teamwork'. It also indicates the department originated in Block B then moved to Hut 7 in January 1943 for just nine months. In October 1943 they moved again to Block A, Room 141 for ten months, before returning to Block B, room 145 and later Room 45. The report indicates how transient departments could be and shows the potential disruption by the influx of new staff and fickle management decisions. Between VE Day and VJ Day they spent their time back in Block A, occupying rooms 113, 114, 115 and 119.

Daisy worked on Japanese merchant shipping codes, where she collected and categorised Maru[3] ship information on Japanese Merchant Navy cargos, their routes in the South China Seas, and their arrival or eventual demise. Early, in the infancy of the sub-sections it was necessary to maintain certain intelligence records within the Party, and Martin recorded that the first of such work produced a weekly plot chart on the positions of all sightings of, and attacks by, American submarines on Japanese vessels from positions given in submarine intelligence messages. From this information two intelligence factors could be seen: one: the main routes traversed by Japanese vessels, and two: the scope of attack and successes achieved by American submarines. Martin also indicated in his report that 'Admiral Somerville personally commended this particular work'.

But it was obvious to Major Martin that JN11 rarely received the cream of the crop in intercepts. There was a pecking order that was considered controversial and astonishing, since instead of all messages being processed collectively, it was sorted by lower ranks for both urgency and value. This judging of material was disputed, especially by the Air sections, but GC& CS central continued to sort and categorise messages. Martin's feelings were probably emulated from Hut to Hut. The sorting system was: Pile 1 – urgent for translation, analysis, redrafting/paraphrasing for transmission to the War Office, Admiralty or commanders. Pile 2 – could be delayed four to eight hours, before being treated the same way. Pile 3 – would be processed similarly and sent by bag within twenty-four hours. Pile 4 – was Quatsch (German for 'nonsense'), which would receive attention when all other piles were depleted.[4] Some messages deemed worthless might not have been passed on at all. In Martin's opinion, other sections with good translators had the first (and easiest) pick of the bunch, leaving his section to deal with difficult Japanese ciphers which took longer to solve. Latterly, these included the revealing and lengthy Japanese diplomatic messages pertinent to all aspects of the war.

The Bookbuilding and Translation Party JN 11 was formed in March 1943 out of the JN 40 Party, formed by Martin, where personnel handled existing merchant shipping codes. The new objective was to translate every possible message and bookbuild all messages in JN11, 'an arbitrary designation given to this code by the Americans', Martin maintained.

Four stations besides GC&CS worked on JN 11 – Washington DC, Pearl Harbor, Melbourne and Colombo. GC&CS was the headquarters of the British effort and Washington the headquarters of the American. Whereas in the German codebreaking effort Britain took the lead, for

Japanese codebreaking, Washington was the controlling centre. Two processes had to happen before a full translation was made: 1) the encipherment had to be removed from the transmitted cipher text, to provide plain code groups and 2) the decoders then had to look up the Japanese meanings of the code groups in a decode book, but, as JN 11 did not possess a 'decoder' they had to reconstruct one using 'all means available'. The resulting translation led to Bookbuilding. The sources of JN 11's interceptions were mainly HMS *Flowerdown* – via teleprinter, Washington – mostly by air across the Atlantic, but sometimes via cable, and Colombo 'who from time to time signalled us their intercepts'. All stations shared their results to avoid duplication.

The percentage quotas and quality of JN 11 recoveries was favourably commented on by Washington, despite the Party only working on a third of the total traffic. The remaining two-thirds had already been processed by other stations before they received the interceptions. This was put down to slow air transfers or cable. However, they not only maintained a percentage quota of book group recoveries equal to the average of other stations, but their quality was more than once congratulated by Washington compared to those produced elsewhere.

The factor of other stations receiving two thirds of the traffic earlier inevitably meant those people had the pick of the best and the easiest, leaving JN 11 with the hard-going residue. That was the downside, but tackling such hard-core interceptions provided an excellent upside in training material for the team and Bletchley Park. As a result, part of their work fulfilled one of GC&CS objectives which was to train linguists in the complexities of Japanese codebreaking, especially for overseas assignments and other clerical positions. At the outbreak of war with Japan, only eight interpreters were available, but after an intensive training scheme, the deficiency was adjusted and eighteen of the thirty-one trained translators went overseas or became leading hands or heads of other parties.

The Japanese codebook usually changed every three months, except the first which ran for a year. When the change was discovered a letter was added to the code number by the Party to denote the difference, hence JN 11A, JN 11B and so on. The Bookbuilding Party built books for A, B, C, D and E, before Book F was captured. Book G was unbroken as at 22 September 1945. Martin also added that, 'A few book groups were recovered in Book H which came into force on 10 August but had a short existence as the war ended on 15 August.' The rapid change of book codes followed Japanese policy to confine the 'odd' numbered books (I=9) to use within the Japanese Navy, and even numbered books (H=0 or 10) for use by Japanese authorities outside the Navy.

In 1944 Olive Humble worked alongside Daisy, Miss Stott, Miss Martin and Wren Pope. Humble was called up in 1943 and wanted to be a Wren, but to her consternation was shipped off to Bletchley Park. After school she worked in insurance in the City and like many young women had never left home before. At Bletchley she was escorted to the billeting office by an armed soldier and later (in her words) grilled by a senior commander, who stated she could not leave the park for any reason other than death or disablement! She was told to sign the form consenting to the Official Secrets Act, to which she dutifully complied and agreed never to speak of the work at Bletchley – even to her nearest and dearest – or she would receive thirty years imprisonment. Terrified, Olive was allocated to the Japanese section dealing with merchant ships under Hugh Foss.

She described the department as divided in two, one half civilians, the other Wrens and Royal Navy Officers. She was very happy to initially find herself with Wrens and bright young navy boys as this was where she wanted to be from the beginning. Major H.E. Martin, her immediate boss, sat at a table in the middle of the room. He was older than everyone else – 'he looked after us like a benevolent father', she recalled fondly. In Martin's report he considered civil servant clerical staff more apt to have a mind of their own, opposed to the Wrens who always followed orders. Either way, each of the clerical staff, Wren or Foreign Office Civilian, was to be expert in at least one specific process and able to cover for other processes in case of staff absenteeism. Martin's report was keen to outline the method of training used for newcomers.

> 'They all arrived blissfully ignorant of anything to do with Cryptography, so I set about a practical explanation of the composition of a Japanese codebook, the principles of a subtractor,[5] together with the indicating system[6] employed. This was followed by an explanation of the cryptographic processes involved, how the index of code groups was made, the nature of call-signs,[7] and the general methods of processing.'

Seeing and doing, is believing. 'Practice makes, perfect,' I hear Daisy say. Martin continued:

> 'They then spent two or three weeks, studying messages that had already been translated together with all available reference material. They thus gained practice in seeing what sort of fist they could make of these messages, having reference to the English translation if necessary. Strictly enjoined to tackle the least corrupt of the messages, they were gradually initiated into the mysteries of "de-garbling"[8] and also into the peculiarities of the particular code book.'

His training was always supplemented by oral explanations as well as written, and visits to other sections to demonstrate to newcomers the vast jigsaw puzzle of codebreaking. The final stage was reached sometime much later when trainees were competent to make tentative book group recoveries themselves.

In addition to the submarine intelligence charts previously mentioned, a Ship/Cargo/Data/Port list was compiled in four different ways, from data available during the translation period March 1943 to January 1944. Daisy worked on this which proved to be 'of considerable value both to translators and bookbuilders. It formed a ready reference to types of cargo loaded at a specific port, and amounts constituting a "full load" for a particular ship etc. Copies of this were sent both to Washington and Colombo. It also proved of considerable value to the Military Section (army) at GC&CS,' who were producing their own version of shipping codes.

The department's work intercepting Marus, transport and troop ships in the Indian and Pacific Oceans, was so successful they were able to recreate the entire Japanese codebook. To facilitate this Martin 'evolved a special JN 40 Instruction Booklet which contained numerous examples of correctly decoded messages, and others that contained errors and corruptions likely to be found in the ordinary course of work.' This took seven to ten days to work through and proved 'a valuable aid as the trainees thus acquired actual experience, from the start, to cope with the various difficulties they might encounter.'

Two further aids to translation and bookbuilding were also produced. One was a language Trigraph. Normally, this would have been made by Hollerith machinery, but Martin's team created this by hand. Here, every Japanese language group occurring in a message was listed alphabetically, together with the words immediately before and after. The second was a complete analysis of Japanese texts according to the originator – the ship or authority sending the message. This provided 225 different types of messages from 53 originators. Copies were sent to both Washington and Colombo.

Daisy and colleagues used these aids to help decipher intercepts. An offshoot of their department in Kilindini, had trained with them and broke the Japanese merchant shipping code of five figures, where each block represented a Japanese term or syllable. Olive typed these five-figure blocks on to strips of flimsy paper, and in clear English constructed understandable messages, such as: *Otaru Maru leaving Manila at 0200 hrs. for Singapore, arrives at … time.* The messages were then passed to Major Martin, but she didn't know what happened to them afterwards.

Originally known as the Merchant Shipping Code, JN 11 covered subjects such as ship's programs, escort duties, routing, ports of discharge, communication zones, enemy submarine intelligence, weather reports, fuel and ammunition expenditure, personnel and cryptographic changes etc. but eventually lines became blurred as the Japanese government requisitioned merchant ships to fall under the command of Japanese naval authorities, either as naval or military vessels, or as merchant ships under navy or military control. The distinction between 'merchant' and 'naval', was distorted and therefore all shipping communications fell under the Navy Department and, in 1944, though JN 11 was an Auxiliary Naval General-purpose System, it carried major naval codes.

As a result, new types of operational signals appeared with an increase in the variety of routine reports. There was also an increase in the number of messages containing action summaries, movements of German and Japanese submarines, code administration, communications and communications regulations. This showed that convoys relied heavily on airborne cover, and that shipping in the south west came under military control. Mostly part of amphibious operations, Japanese shipping moved westward through the islands, creating a considerable increase in Air and Army message interception.

On 22 April 1944 a note was received from Commander McIntyre:

'I am very pleased with the translations from JN 11. The quality is as high as ever, and the quantity this week has reached what I believe is an all-time high. I am telling DD (NS) about it. Please convey my appreciation to your staff.'

Commander J.P. McIntyre was also in Hong Kong and Singapore, probably as part of FECB. He escaped Singapore in 1942 making it back to Bletchley Park by October 1942 where he worked in Block B. He was Deputy head of the Japanese Naval Section by mid-1943 and became Head in late 1944.

Finally, long miscellaneous signals of tactical and strategic importance appeared and during the last few months of the war, when the Japanese were busy inaugurating the independence of the Netherlands East Indies, JN 11 was used for transmitting lengthy messages of civil and political importance. The extent of ground covered therefore, was comprehensive.

* * *

During Bletchley's Veterans Day interviews in 2014 and again in 2016, Mollie Muetzel (née Brewster) said she was told by Bletchley she had worked in Hut 7, but she didn't recall the descriptions of others, nor did she recall Daisy, or 'Lawrie' as she was sometimes called, or the names of others connected to Hut 7. Mollie, who was 18 in 1944, knew her sister worked at Bletchley Park and when it was time for her war-work she went there too; they never knew what each other did until decades later. Elizabeth Davies (née Ross), at the same interview, confirmed she worked in Hut 7, Block B.

'I was one of the younger-set too,' said Elizabeth, who was born in 1924. 'We arrived relatively late in the war.' As a student at Oxford University, she was approached in the library by a man who asked if she would be prepared to work for the government 'on work of a secret nature'. Elizabeth thought it all rather sinister, but exciting and said yes. But as with Daisy, neither Mollie's nor Elizabeth's paths crossed even though they might have worked in the same building. Shift allocations and specific areas of concentration may well have accounted for that. Elizabeth recalls she went to Bletchley in October 1944 and lived in the hostel outside the main gate in Wilton Avenue, where 'the refectory had thousands to feed and bathe in many shifts'. She was assigned to Hut 7 with Hugh Foss, 'an Anglo Saxon Don', she remarked gleefully, to work on Japanese codes, JN 40 and JN 25 – a five letter code. She also remembered others such as Septimus Wall, Rachel MacOwen, a WAAF and Peggy Jackson NCO (non-commissioned officer).

'We worked on code 70 SERO. The room was large with a long table in the middle and a top table at the end. The T-shaped configuration was divided into five sections.' Her supervisors were Mrs Dawson and Miss Wainwright. 'You stayed at your own section and carried out the clerical tasks you were asked to do,' said Elizabeth. 'Nobody discussed their assignments; only the supervisor saw your work.'

While Elizabeth didn't know Daisy, she thought her work might be more subtle than just a filing clerk or header checker. 'Maybe she was in her solitary office sending us the JN40, via our supervisor, because it was terribly important to know when the enemy messages contained mistakes.'

After the war Elizabeth went to Trincomalee, Ceylon. She returned to another government facility in England, Burghfield, near Reading, Berkshire, and later became an actress working with Claire Bloom.

* * *

The Hollerith training school eventually moved to Drayton Parslow after main punched-card activity transferred to Block C. Hut 7 continued to serve the Naval Section until the end of the war, though many of its departments moved to Block A as well as Block B. After the war part was used for overseas teachers' training before they were dispatched to places in Germany, such as Wilhelmshaven, to teach Allied forces children,[9] but gradually the ramshackle building fell into disrepair. The hut was demolished in 1954. All that remains is the disused 'battery room', a sad ending to this rabbit-warren of history.

Chapter 26

Lonely Girl

Daisy often wore her favourite green woollen dress to work. She handwashed the garment once a week in the cracked porcelain bathroom sink at her billet. It was just large enough for the task. Somehow, the dress and warm liquid suds fitted into the basin, but the resulting dirty water was alarming; pollution from brick-dust or Bletchley's cigarette smoke. After several rinses, she plunged the dress into clean water and continued kneading until the fibres were free of Lux soap flakes. The damp mass was then transferred to a metal pail and carried downstairs, being careful not to trip on the threadbare carpet.

The Gotzheims kept a mangle in the outhouse, a poorly built shed-like structure of glass and wood leaning against the outside kitchen wall. Here she fed the dress between the mangle's wooden rollers, trying not to pinch her fingers. Excess water drained into a large blue enamel bowl below, but care was needed to avoid breaking the ivory buttons or ripping the lace collar. After two or three mangles the flat mass of green fell into the clothes basket on the other side. With most of the water squeezed out, she returned upstairs to hang the dress on the line above the bath to drip-dry. Cold spells took longer for it to dry completely, sometimes twenty-four hours. In winter months, Daisy often dangerously perched an electric fire nearby to aid the process. If necessary, she resorted to her 'second best', a delicate frock of red silk printed with tiny white flowers. Perfect for summer, but thin for winter's chill. On those days she wore her thick grey cardigan which Ciss had knitted for her after she learned of Bletchley's freezing temperatures and conditions. Daisy was also glad of her long grey overcoat and fur-lined boots.

The lofty cavernous room where she sometimes worked was sparse, cold and lonely. 'Awful,' said Daisy. The yellowing-white gloss-painted walls and square pillars were nicotine-stained from the stagnant cigarette

"I worked alone in a vast room with a machine that clanked around the ceiling," Daisy Lawrence (Author)

smoke of previous shifts. Daisy didn't smoke, though she had tried once or twice. The only disturbance to her solitary condition was the sound of the overhead message system and her supervisor arriving with more messages. 'There was a table with an uncomfortable wooden chair and the noisy machine that cranked around the pipes.' Here she worked quietly, apart from the noise of the machine. When asked about the message contents, she always said she didn't know and that it was 'all gibberish'.

But was it? Her pale, slim and well-manicured fingers carefully unfolded the delicate strips to reveal typed four or five-digit codes. She said part of her job was to lay each in front of her and with a keen eye, assess the strange jumble. The codes were both letters and numbers and didn't make much sense at first, but when several were laid on the table, she identified different or unusual features. The messages were generally indecipherable until the code was broken, but headings from messages often followed the same pattern for weather reports and general shipping signals. These were the cribs; standard phrases of letters or numbers following a pattern. She calculated the numbers and looked for similarities; usually double letters were an obvious clue.

She noted and separated the 'different' messages which were handed to her supervisor for further analysis. Daisy always said she didn't know what happened to the messages but thought her work painfully monotonous. Intercepts were marked with a reference code, ready for senior Navy, Army or Air Force personnel who needed further access to the classified information. From that room they were sent to another place via the overhead conveyor system for additional processing and filing.

* * *

Similarities to Daisy's navy work are found in the Air Intelligence section, where WAAF Anne Hamilton-Grace was an indexer from August 1941 to March 1943, producing air-related intelligence reports from Enigma decrypts. She worked on a three-shift system with about seventy-five other people. Their main purpose was to translate, interpret and act upon intelligence received and decrypted in another hut. She recalled the hub and spoke system was complex:

'There was a central operations room called the Central Watch, the "hub", where intelligence was first handled. Here, the spokes, representatives from naval, military and air sections, worked together passing information back and forth through the chains of command. One of the most important tasks was to maintain a minutely detailed indexing system, so that whenever a new piece of information came in, it would be broken down into components and each part recorded in a separate file or card. The idea was to create a database, so that if you needed to find information on a particular ship, office or place, all previous intelligence for this could be accessed.'[1]

Anne's indexing job seemed menial, but it was essential to the smooth running of the hut (and the war), due to the volume of information received and the puzzling coded names within the messages. There were service abbreviations, service jargon, acronyms and slang within the signals, often different from unit to unit. Much is made of the electro-mechanical devices (such as the Bombes and Colossus), but the ability to absorb, annotate, store, retrieve and process the huge quantity of data via these indexers and indexes was just as important.

Their work was all done by hand, with cards and pencils – some coloured – and a great deal of patience and expertise, often in terrible working conditions.

Though one of Daisy's workrooms was at times vast, other people were deprived of space in small huts as Anne revealed in her diary about the late afternoon shift:

> 'At four o'clock, one must leave the car at the end of a long row in the car park (she had learned to drive), and walk to the huts, passing WAAFS who never think to salute an officer. Then enter the hut and into a narrow passage with coat hangers on one side and rows of civilian tin hats of a queer high topee[2] shape, on a shelf above. The passage is so narrow everyone knocks into you as you try to hang up your coat. The cloakroom is literally two by two feet; you can scarcely get the door open, let alone enter to comb your hair in front of the glass. The whole proceedings are the essence of discomfort and sordidity.... I then have to take over from the NDO on watch, where I sit under brilliant light and have so much to do, that I think I am going mad. The job necessitates continuous running between the watch room and our room to check up on maps and cards, and the usual inevitable conversations with Hut 4 over the direct line.'[3]

Turn Around

Hut 7, Block B Navy. Where exactly did Daisy work? A late discovery of a reference number on the envelope of a letter her mother sent in 1944, prompted further questions. Separated from the main address, the mail code was unnoticed before, but reveals she worked in Block A too.

A discussion about PO Box 111 at a meeting with Bletchley's Oral Historian Jonathan Byrne, confirmed most staff mail was received through PO Box 111 directly to Bletchley Park. Correspondence was annotated in the administration office with a specific reference number – usually blocks and room numbers for the employee's location within the Park – disguising their actual department to outsiders. In this case Daisy gave her mother the reference number – the handwriting is the same –

but gave nothing as to her department and the work she undertook. The number was A/141 and is now confirmed in Major H.E. Martin's report. When I asked Jonathan where Block A was, he immediately replied, 'We're sitting in it!'

Was this where she worked? The tall ceilings, the Crittal Windows, the yellowing pillars…now painted a brighter white? The steps she mentioned…? There are steps into Block A, about six, and at the side a fire escape to the top floor. Both smiling and feeling a ghostly presence, Jonathan explained that modern day Bletchley central administration, Block A, was restricted to the public. But why was she listed as Block B on a 1999 list compiled by David Cook, GCHQ Consultant? Daisy had also written Block B, Naval, Decoder, on a form in 2003 – a BP document also unavailable to me until 2018.

As already seen, the department 'Hut 7' was also sometimes in Block A, along with many other sections. A different entry for Daisy's room number, A/141, shows this as Air Section. Here is a sample of the many task descriptions from BP's 553 Roll of Honour entries for Block A alone:

> U-boat signals Indexers and statistical research, NSI Liaison with costal Y organisation, research into enemy coastal defences, Emender – identifying missing or garbled parts of decrypted signals, Communications and Crypto-intelligence, NS1 Liaison with coastal Y organisation, indexing, filing, translating. Linguist. Naval Section German and Japanese. Captured German and Japanese documents. Japanese naval call-signs, Decoding Japanese signals and recording ships' movements. Japanese meteorology specialist. Japanese vessels index, merchant shipping codes JN11, naval auxiliary codes, Japanese cryptography, Japanese Naval Attaché codes. NSIV plotting German and Japanese ships and minefields from information in signals. Japanese decoding including JN25. Submarines and Hydrography disseminated naval intelligence, NSV Clerical support. Mapping, British plot of allied convoys. Specialist in Italian submarines and Mediterranean hydrography. Plotted convoys and submarines. Pacific islands place names. NSII Z Reporting Watch. Teleprinter Operators. NSV Monitored neutral shipping in the Atlantic,

some of which were suspected of refueling U-boats. Air Force meteorological 'Dip sheets'. RAF Air Section Tactical Codes, Decrypt signals re. PoW reports, Room 111 Air Section. NSII Neutral Traffic. Cmdr. JP McIntyre: head of Japanese Bookbuilding E5884 and translation. NSVIII – Records. Naval Section VI Technical Intelligence producing dictionary of technical terms, NS IV and VII Naval Section Library.

Bletchley and its specialist Block A of many central 'administrative' functions was complex!

Chapter 27

Fun and Games

Time to Relax

Daisy reported for duty six days a week, but her schedule did not always follow the usual weekly pattern. Sometimes her eight-hour shifts, or in Naval Section jargon 'watches', would fall on a weekend. Often she could tag twenty-four hours leave to a rest day and rush to London to see her family and Stan's mother. They both needed news. It was hard not knowing where he was, what he was doing or if he was in good health.

When there was no time to return home, she would sit by the lake in front of the mansion to contemplate her situation. Even the croaking sound of frogs was hypnotic. The grounds of the country estate offered tranquillity as she strolled in the sunshine with her thoughts, sat and read a book or just watched the clouds. The mansion was usually the centre for social gatherings and plays, as well as the commanders' main offices. Tony Sale, an early Bletchley historian, noted the study of Commanders Denniston and Travis overlooked the picturesque surroundings 'where summer drinks and social repartee, encouraged codebreakers to mingle in the evening sunshine'. Presumably this distracted them from wartime-worry and tedious codebreaking.

After John Tiltman and his team moved to Hut 5, wartime camaraderie in the mansion dining room was popular when it became the officers' mess. Thespians created a theatre group. Service men and women with stage experience, choir, musicianship, or from ENSA, felt the group of keen talent would help pass the time. Productions of plays, operettas and, occasionally risqué pantomimes were planned every three months and held in the ballroom. Bletchley staff were happy to pay a small entrance fee to cover the cost of scenery, costumes and props. Plays and dances were held regularly, but when the drama group put on a pantomime, a different kind of enthusiasm was evident. Everyone wanted part of the

197

humorous production, which perhaps led some to believe that Bletchley, with its quirky personalities, resembled a mad house.

Frank Birch, according to Daisy and Dot, was the life and soul of the party. He was often seen wearing a bright pea green shirt and a Breton beret around the Park. He was an accomplished actor and comic, and played central roles, one of which was Aladdin's Widow Twanky – a strange combination and good cover for the director of Naval GC&CS. Despite the madness, Birch helped dispel snobbish attitudes at Bletchley with his humour and inclusiveness. Another thespian was RAF Wing Commander Brinley Newton-John. He spoke perfect German and worked on captured documents from German U-boats and, it is said, interrogated prisoners of war. He was deputy head in Hut 3 and Block F, and later head of Japanese codebreaking for the Air Section. Bryn was at Bletchley at the same time as Daisy from 1943-1945. Their paths would have crossed. His roles in the amateur dramatic and operatic societies reached 'star billing' when he played Mr Darcy in *Pride and Prejudice*, The Count in *The Marriage of Figaro* and sang *Lieder* in German – a dashing fellow no doubt. In 2013 his famous daughter Olivia Newton-John confirmed he had a beautiful voice and was pleased he'd passed some of his better Welsh genes to her.[1]

Daisy became involved with Bletchley plays to help pass the time. 'Usherette mainly,' she said. The quarterly performances were usually at weekends. Occasionally, she agreed to be an extra, but she was far too shy to be under the spotlight. Programme selling was preferable and she retained several copies of playbills such as *They Came to a City, Gaslight* and *Dangerous Corner*. Activities were important to the well-being of Bletchley employees and great efforts were made to keep billeted personnel occupied. Some productions were held in local village halls.

The long and irregular hours affected workers' health, but social gatherings helped their sanity. It was exciting to join a fun group, but at times these seemed flippant and maybe resembled a summer holiday camp. But who can blame the need for light relief to lessen the stress of serious codebreaking which often reflected sad and terrible events of war?

During work and play, some men and women became entangled, literally. There were illicit affairs with married men and swapping partners; some secret relationships were long, others short; one can only imagine if their secret work was still secret after pillow talk. If anyone spoke about their work, they were dismissed immediately; the rule of

The Secret Seven: Bletchley girls enjoying evening refreshments at the Eight Belles. Daisy Lawrence (front row, centre left). Mary Goddard (back row, far right). Also pictured Olive Humble, Kath West and Winnie Bull. (Daisy Lawrence Archive)

secrecy was very strict. One time, contrary to 'loose lips, sink ships', a cafeteria incident found two temporary assistants (TAs) fighting over their boss. One was his soon to be ex-wife, the other an assistant whom he'd taken a shine to. Secrets and slander were shouted publicly over cafeteria teacups until a senior supervisor stepped in to halt their personal and intelligence information exposés. Both were immediately sacked. It was a serious offence and their colleagues were mortified.

* * *

The perception that aristocratic debutantes used their family connections to secure a place at Bletchley is partially true. Sarah Norton was a leading light on the London scene before the war; a social X-ray with a waistline of 18½ inches, a fashion trend. Her time at Bletchley was memorable for many, including Daisy. Later in life she was known as Lady Sarah Baring. Sally, as she was called, was one of the many women who decoded, translated and assessed intelligence. But the routine repetitive work which we know was exceedingly boring, meant her experience was no different.

Three years younger than Daisy, Sally also worked in a 'Hut 7' department with Jean Campbell-Harris, the future Baroness Trumpington of Cambridge. Before the war Sally's parents sent her to learn German in Bavaria. As a teenager, she had a wonderful time learning the language and socialising, leading a privileged life very different from many others at Bletchley, including Daisy.

She also enjoyed the benefits of royal connections since her godfather was Louis Mountbatten, the cousin of King George VI. In Munich she became fluent in German which had a huge effect on her future, but not immediately. After war was declared, she wrote articles for *The Baltimore Sun*, an American newspaper, and captions for stylish photographs in *Vogue*. When it was her time for war work, she was employed as a telephone operator at the ARP (Air Raid Precautions organisation)[2], followed by a spell at Hawker Siddeley in Slough, where she helped to build Hurricane planes.

However, as she spoke perfect German someone thought it better for her to try intelligence work. She was duly recommended and interviewed by the London Labour Exchange at Devonshire House, the same office where Daisy was interviewed two years later. Sarah had also never heard of Bletchley Park and received the same travel instructions. In February 1941 she boarded a 10.40am train from Euston to Bletchley and became an early cog in the secret machine. As a linguist, her translation work for Hut 4's Naval Section Index, was actually located in Hut 7. There she helped translate and index German U-boat intelligence.

Her work then passed to Hut 8 where Alan Turing worked. The women in Hut 7 saw Turing often, but he rarely spoke. Sarah once offered him a cup of tea, but his shyness made him back off as if she had a serious disease. He never had the tea or spoke to her. Daisy saw him from time to time in the grounds; silent with his eyes averted to the floor, attire somewhat dishevelled, but everyone thought he was wonderful. 'We were all very proud of his achievements even though he seemed rather odd at times. Of course, we knew only a few details of his work.'

Monotonous as the work was, their important individual contributions cannot be underestimated. Still they savoured small pleasures, like a rare piece of chocolate or interesting gossip, and when the opportunity arose even frowned-upon-fun broke the repetitiveness of downtime and paperwork. Sometimes, however, their larks lead them into deep trouble; especially Sarah, since she was caught on a night shift running down the corridor with a laundry basket containing Jean Campbell-Harris. Sarah and her companion-in-fun were duly reprimanded.

Pamela Rose (née Gibson), supervisor, remembered Sarah as one of her younger girls. 'I had to stop them from going on leave whenever they wanted to see their boyfriends.' And of the incident with Campbell-Harris: 'She was put in a laundry basket then Sarah gave her a push and she careered off down the passage. She ended up in a naval commander's office. He wasn't terribly pleased, I must say,' laughed Pamela.[3] 'She (Campbell-Harris) was just as naughty then as she is now!'

The rules for night shifts changed to avert further frolic and mayhem, and the 'fun group' dissipated. Daisy's associates were now more of 'the sober type'. Sarah kept her job in 1944, despite her high-jinx and distractions, and was later transferred to OIC, the Admiralty Citadel in London. Her title was Special Liaison for Bletchley Park. Years later, reading news of the Rt. Hon. Baroness Trumpington, Dot prompted Daisy to remember the incident, but she struggled to see how the young woman had become the older infamous Parliamentary character in the House of Lords. But gradually she remembered and with a smile was incredulous to learn this was the same person. However, keeping her oath Daisy refrained from divulging anything further about their secret work.

Jean Barker (née Campbell-Harris), or her preferred title, Baroness Trumpington, was outspoken, hysterically funny and often in the news. After marriage, the birth of her son and several years in politics, one of her more infamous moments was a two-finger insult in the House of Lords, November 2011. Then age 89, she was deliberately abusive toward her colleague Lord Tom King of Bridgewater, who disparagingly referred to her advancing years. Opposite of the victorious V sign, 'to go forth and fornicate', she said was, 'a friendly gesture'. The incident was captured on Parliamentary TV cameras, much to everyone's delight!

'Life only really began when I went to Bletchley,' said the Baroness. 'That's when I made my real friends, and it was exciting being a part of something important. We used to meet in Claridge's, throw bread at each other, sing and behave so badly. Five shillings was the most you could spend during the war, so it was as affordable as anywhere.'[4] She retired from the House of Lords in 2017 and died November 2018.

Sarah Norton's notoriety continued when she met William Waldorf Astor, son of the 2nd Viscount and MP Nancy Astor, during a VE Day cocktail party; their marriage was announced within five days. She was 25 and he 37. They had a son, the 4th Viscount Astor, but eventually age difference and personalities proved problematical. They divorced amicably in 1953. Sarah later married Lieutenant Colonel Thomas Baring and adopted a son. After they divorced in 1965, she never re-married. She died on 4 February 2013.

* * *

The grounds around the mansion were always peaceful, especially by the lake. Sometimes Daisy played tennis on the grass courts nearby with friends, but this was not her favourite sport. She preferred hockey in the winter and rounders on the lawn in the summer. She learned to play both at school and was part of the Co-op hockey team before the war; she kept the small trophy. Gordon Welchman played hockey too; his team was the Cambridge Wanderers. Though male and female teams were separate, they would have mutual contact in Mr Forward, secretary of Bletchley Park Hockey Club. Another Foreign Office civilian, he worked in various departments from February 1941 to October 1945. He was also with Jafo.

Team games were played in the late afternoon on the mansion's shaded and sunken lawn. Daisy didn't have a hockey stick, but she owned a rounders bat which she carried to Bletchley after a weekend trip home. As they previously used an old broom handle with a hole at the top for a leather strap, she was quite the star on that occasion. If the sun shone, the teams would congregate by a tree around 1pm. Daisy loved the camaraderie the old English game and mixed sides offered. A tennis ball was easy to find, and two teams of nine were formed. They used jackets or bags for bases. Daisy could certainly hit a blinder! Matches were politely competitive against different huts, though one could expect arguments over the rules. The congenial fun resembled, perhaps, a traditional English summer's Sunday afternoon of cricket, with an aroma of freshly mown grass and the sound of a ball hitting willow.

A long path ran across the grass in front of the mansion, from east to west. Staff called this 'The High Street'. Foot traffic during the week was heavy from the side security gate, labelled the chauffeurs' entrance, to the increasing cluster of huts and industrial office blocks. The setting was mostly idyllic, if one could forget the barbed wire fences and blast proof walls of the ugly purpose-built structures. Their relaxation distractions were welcome, but for Daisy, most of the time, the worry and fate of her fiancé swirled deep inside.

Stan's parents still had no official notification. It was just assumed he was in Formosa. But if he wasn't there, where was he? The War Office held names for only sixty-five per cent of the 100,000 troops captured, and only twenty per cent of 18,000 civilians registered in Singapore. When a name was known to the War Office, relatives were informed. Mrs Moore received hers in May, but without confirmation of his location. More news appeared when an International Red Cross delegate reported on the fate of 50,000 Britons held by the Japanese in Formosa, Tokyo and Hong Kong. Fifteen months after the Fall of Singapore, and fifteen months of uncertainty, he reported that prisoners' lives in captivity were getting easier. Daisy couldn't help but wonder if Bletchley Park knew of this report.

The inspection mid-1943 gave information on food, medical services, hobbies, work and mail and indicated the prisoners' greatest hardship was lack of news from home. Many had not received letters since 1941. He reported that lighting, ventilation, drainage and sewage in Formosa camps were good, all prisoners had a hot bath twice a week and cold showers when they liked. Kitchens were staffed by prisoners. Rations varied – stated by the Japanese to be the same as civilians – workers received extra rice and barley. Small amounts of meat and fish were issued, with fair amounts of vegetables. Captives were trying to raise cattle and poultry to provide additional protein. They didn't receive butter, margarine or cheese, but all camps had ice boxes to preserve food in searing heat. Prisoners receive 150 free cigarettes per month.

PoWs on Formosa were inoculated against infectious diseases – dysentery, typhoid, cholera and smallpox, and cases of beriberi were treated with yeast preparations and something called 'rice polish'.[5] Malaria was treated with quinine. The Red Cross provided other drugs and books. Canteens were run by British prisoners of war and they could write one postcard per month. The delegate reported that fifty-two British officers and 512 Canadians, of varying ranks, lived in a new seven-story wooden barracks of fifty-six rooms. They had a vegetable garden, eighty ducks and sixteen pigs. Prisoners wore clogs and winter working clothes distributed by the Japanese. They were paid for work. Officers could volunteer, but work was compulsory for all other healthy ranks. They had blankets and sheets. In the new camps prisoners played chess, cards and football. A gramophone 'recital' was given for two hours after supper and there were services on Sundays. A dentist attends the camps and regular medical inspections take place; health is steadily improving. Prisoners receive only the *Nippon Times*, but no British newspapers.

Overall the report was positive but reading between the lines the conditions of their grouped incarceration would surely be worse. Daisy could only imagine the horrors Stan was living through.

* * *

On Christmas Eve at 1.45pm she received a telegram. It was addressed to Miss D.E. Lawrence, Box 111 Bly, Bks. *'Mrs Moore received card from Japan. Stan fit & well. Letter following. Love Ciss.'* Daisy wanted to leave then but had to stay until Boxing Day. As a relatively new employee she was scheduled to work Christmas Day. Overjoyed with the news, she found she was able to enjoy herself and happily devoured the food, mince pies and sherry that someone supplied. She thought of Stan again, wondering how his Christmas was, the second in captivity. When she returned to Tooting three days later, there was more news from Harry, still in the Middle East, and a card from Stan.

The austere looking postcard had red oriental markings that stood out ominously on buff-coloured cardboard: Daisy Lawrence, 111 Kenlor Road. An official stamp 'PASSED P.W. 3815' had released the communication. There were no censors or alterations; just reassuring words. Daisy's hands shook. The card he had touched and signed suddenly became very personal. After holding the message close to savour his words, she shared the private message with her family, kissed the card and placed it back on the mantle next to Harry's card and

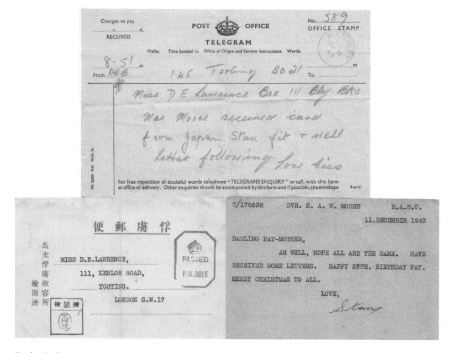

Daisy's hands shook. The card he had touched and signed suddenly became very personal. (Daisy Lawrence Archive)

(Daisy Lawrence Archive)

Stan's handsome pre-war photograph, but they still did not know where he was twenty-one months after capture.

As the Allies planned a strategic attack on German military in Northern France, Daisy read more unsatisfactory reports. The newspaper article of Monday, 5 June 1944, did nothing to increase her hopes that Stan was still safe and alive. However, the British government had at last issued a handbook via the War Office.

Chapter 28

Lead up to D-Day

From the Quebec conference at the latter end of 1943, known as 'Quadrant', America and Britain set a date for major escalation in Europe, including re-organisation of the Far East and South East Asia Command. However, any sharing of secret nuclear energy information was limited. Conferences in Moscow and Cairo followed where declarations of support and plans for post war USSR and Asia were made. Operation OVERLORD was settled by Churchill, Roosevelt and President Inonu, who agreed to complete Allied air bases in Turkey. However, Operation ANAKIM, to recapture Burma from the Japanese, was postponed. In May 1944 prominent prime ministers of the British Commonwealth came together to support the Moscow Declaration and agree their respective roles.

In the lead up to OVERLORD – D-Day – messages stormed into Bletchley. All leave was cancelled to handle the expected surge of secret messages. Listeners collected over 18,000 intercepts, while secure teleprinters and dispatch riders delivered daily batches from every part of Britain and abroad. More than forty motorcycles passed through Bletchley Park's security gates every hour for twenty-four hours, every day of the week. It was a busy time for the message processors – human and mechanical. Not only were incoming messages intercepted, but false information was also dispatched to divert the enemy... who also listened. Agnes Jean Tocher (Smith), a Wren in the Naval Section working on the 'British Plot' recalled:

> 'One of the most important events was the build-up to D-Day. We had a flat-bed plot of the Channel...renewed every day and we plotted like mad, not just the real invasion but the false invasion as well. We were trying to persuade the Germans we were going to invade at Calais, but we were

206

going to invade in Normandy.... We plotted the German
E Boats, particularly dangerous to us in the Channel, the
French fishing boats, and all. It got so busy at that time we
stayed on for a second Watch; it was terribly important to
keep the Plot up to date.'

Agnes Jean Tocher (Smith), WRNS,
Naval Section 'British Plot'.

Preparations for OVERLORD took place around England's southern
beaches, including Mulberry Harbours, known as Phoenix Caissons.
British engineers had built temporary jetties of floating reinforced
concrete to rapidly transfer cargo, troops and trucks to Northern France.
For months they lay submerged, ready to be lifted and towed into place
to create a harbour – another incredible feat of engineering the result of
an ambitious project first mooted in 1917 by Winston Churchill.

Aligned with the weather, Bletchley's Colossus provided crucial
intelligence for the planned operation. In the few days before, while
the Western Front Committee provided crucial strategic information,
the Newmanry and Colossus had broken the Lorenz cipher to reveal a
message from Hitler indicating he had fallen for the faux orders of the
Allies. When the message from Bletchley Park reached Commander-in-
Chief General Eisenhower at HQ Southwick House, Southampton, he was
with other Allied commanders. The trained SLU Typex officer handed
him the message, asked him to read it and keep the contents to himself.

Allied Listeners had intercepted a crucial diplomatic message with
secret orders of battle for Field Marshal Rommel. Through his spies
Hitler had information that the Allied invasion was planned in Normandy
but, as he informed Rommel, he considered this to be false and a trick
to draw German divisions from Calais and the main Channel ports. The
Führer instructed Rommel not to move his troops.

With no room for error and careful to understand and devour the
contents correctly, Eisenhower knew he had five clear days for the
planned Allied Normandy invasion. He could not tell his staff or other
commanders what was in the message, nor could he keep the document.
Under orders and 'with the best information available', he handed the
paper back to the officer and made the decision to go ahead immediately.
He could see Hitler thought the Allied plan a trick and that Allied
convoys would move east along the Channel shores of northern France

to begin the invasion at Calais, where the German Panzer divisions awaited combat. The opposite strategy for the Allied invasion on the western coast of northern France was safe. But due to the weather, the Normandy landings, D-Day, was delayed one day until 6 June 1944, under cloudy skies.[1]

> 'The invasion was put off for twenty-four hours, and that was how our watch was 'on' for D-Day minus one. Everyone knew down the Tunnel (previous watches had come off very upset at missing 'the party'), but even if you'd been dropped from Mars that day you would have known something very big was about to happen. The sight of the whole of Portsmouth Harbour, Spithead, in fact all the water usually seen from the Portisdown Hills, was utterly invisible, covered so thickly with ships it was impossible to see any space between them. It is my most vivid memory of that time.'
>
> Shirley Cannicott (née Gadsby), Special Duty Wren[2]

Daisy read and listened to reports as the Allied invasion played out successfully, but at times she heard harrowing news of retaliatory death and destruction. Her workplace was overloaded, but all knew that Eisenhower's 'best information available' probably came from Bletchley Park's intelligence.

Chapter 29

Letters from Home

After the invasion the SCU and SLU had direct access in France, presenting a different picture for Bletchley. On the battlefield the gathered intelligence now took a more immediate and different form where the goal was to liberate France completely. Codebreakers prepared for another massive increase in traffic. All were highly motivated and, with additional intercepts, daily keys were successfully broken within twenty-four hours. Meanwhile, Germany was still unaware the Allies knew all their movements and strategies.

* * *

It was during this busy period in the summer of 1944, that Daisy received an unexpected letter. She had returned to Bletchley after two days of unplanned leave and no time at all passed before she received an envelope with her mother's handwriting, dated Sunday, 9 July 1944.

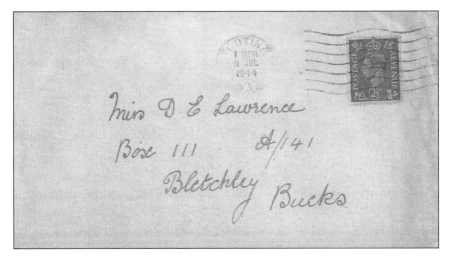

Letter sent to Daisy at Bletchley Park, Block A, Room 141. (Daisy Lawrence Archive)

It read:

Wartime letter from Daisy's mother, Annie Lawrence, 9 July 1944. (Daisy Lawrence Archive)

She was devastated to hear the news of a bomb so close to home, but glad her family was safe. The sooner the children left the better. Daisy's nephew Ron remembered being an evacuee.[1] Pam and Tricia, his sisters, were first to leave to live with their host, Mrs Gaysford, in either East or West Dean, Sussex (he couldn't remember which). At age four he had stayed behind with his mother (Ciss). They returned later in 1944, but then all three children were evacuated as more air raids were expected over London. Ron recalled:

'We walked from Kenlor Road to Smallwood Road School with a small case and a gas mask each. When everyone was there, we walked another mile to Earlsfield station to catch a train to Central London and then another to Lancaster. When we arrived, coaches took us around the streets to see if anyone would take kids from London. Nan (Annie Lawrence) said we must stay together, but who in their right mind wanted three little brats? As Pam was older, she decided to go alone. Those remaining were taken to a large hall where we slept on the floor. I can't remember eating or washing, but we must have done at some point.'

The next day a lady from Scotforth wanted a boy Ron's age. Tricia was somehow billeted with Pam. But later Tricia and Ron went to stay with the sister-in-law of Maurice Webb, who later became Minister of Food.[2] Ron didn't like Mrs Webb. He called her 'the Witch', and compared her to Mrs Voray in the film *No room at the Inn*. Whatever they did – good or bad – they were scolded and he began to wet the bed. When Mrs Webb's husband was on leave, she sent them to her sister's in Barrow-in-Furness. There was a submarine dockyard nearby, so in theory they were just as unsafe as in London. But for that short time, Ron did not wet the bed. It all started again when he returned to 'the Witch'.

Ron and Tricia had fun outdoors and sometimes on the way to school, a US army convoy would drive by. As they did, the children would call out, 'got any gum chum?' Most times they received something. They sent letters asking to go home, but never had a reply. They were later told their mail was opened. One day, Tricia wrote a letter to their mother, but didn't write on the envelope, instead they stopped a man in the street to tell him what they thought and asked if he would write the address. He said yes and agreed to pay the postage. Two weeks later their mother arrived to take them home.

* * *

On 15 August 1944 another somewhat battered telegram arrived at PO Box 111, Bletchley, Bucks for D.E. Lawrence, A/141. The flimsy label on the beige envelope had replaced the original address of 111 Kenlor Road, Tooting, London. Once again Daisy nervously opened the envelope and two folded sheets of paper fell to the ground. The smaller piece was from the Postmaster General, which she dismissed, eager to read the other. It was from Stan. But as she re-read the header from 165 SINGAPORE, she noticed the date: 2 FEB 1942 – pre-captivity.

She couldn't believe that mail more than two years old had finally arrived! The other note attempted to appease recipients: 'This was an

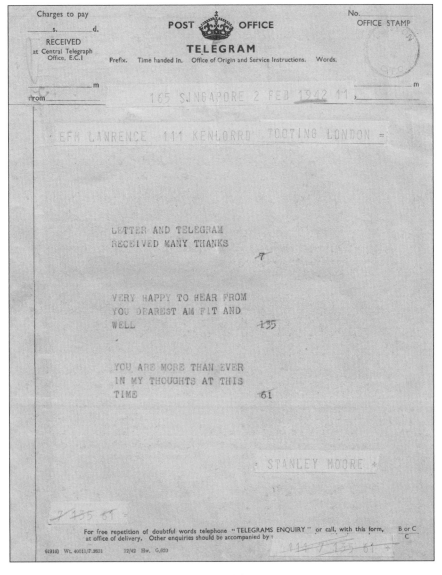

POST OFFICE

TELEGRAM

Charges to pay

s.   d.

RECEIVED
at Central Telegraph
Office, E.C.1

from

No.
OFFICE STAMP

Prefix.   Time handed in.   Office of Origin and Service Instructions.   Words.

165 SINGAPORE 2 FEB 1942 11

EFM LAWRENCE 111 KENLORRD TOOTING LONDON =

LETTER AND TELEGRAM
RECEIVED MANY THANKS

VERY HAPPY TO HEAR FROM
YOU DEAREST AM FIT AND
WELL   135

YOU ARE MORE THAN EVER
IN MY THOUGHTS AT THIS
TIME   61

STANLEY MOORE

For free repetition of doubtful words telephone " TELEGRAMS ENQUIRY " or call, with this form,
at office of delivery. Other enquiries should be accompanied by

'Lost' 1942 telegram. (Daisy Lawrence Archive)

example of 'captives' mail lost.' The letter had been written in Singapore, but was he still there? Confused and disappointed that the only official news anyone was able to provide about Stan's capture, had arrived in May 1943, fifteen months before, she continued her search for clues and ways to make contact via Bletchley; radio messages, newspaper cuttings and leads she could justifiably admit.

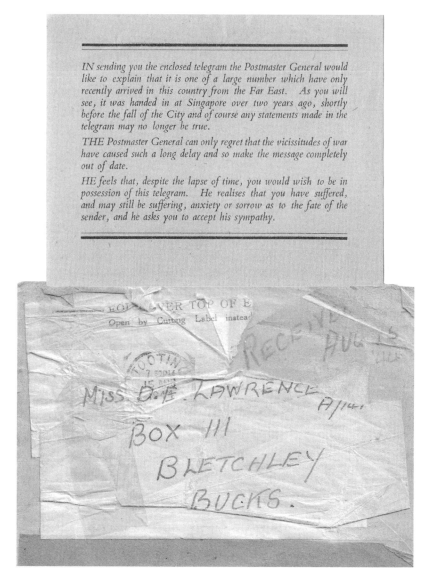

IN sending you the enclosed telegram the Postmaster General would like to explain that it is one of a large number which have only recently arrived in this country from the Far East. As you will see, it was handed in at Singapore over two years ago, shortly before the fall of the City and of course any statements made in the telegram may no longer be true.

THE Postmaster General can only regret that the vicissitudes of war have caused such a long delay and so make the message completely out of date.

HE feels that, despite the lapse of time, you would wish to be in possession of this telegram. He realises that you have suffered, and may still be suffering, anxiety or sorrow as to the fate of the sender, and he asks you to accept his sympathy.

Letter message from the Postmaster General received in 1944. (Daisy Lawrence Archive)

On 11 October 1944 a newspaper report indicated that Japanese-held prisoners would be permitted to cable relatives. The Red Cross would pay. A ten-word cablegram to next of kin, routed from Japan via Geneva, was possible, provided the Japanese were willing to implement this undertaking. Also, next-of-kin could send messages to prisoners of war

CODEBREAKER GIRLS

Aerogram No.158159 via S_I_M_L_A. All India Message Service (SIMLA). "Message cannot be broadcast more often than once every three months." (Daisy Lawrence Archive)

and interned civilians. On 27 October 1944 Daisy received encouraging news from the officer-in-charge of the Radio Message Service. Her messages were being sent, but were they being heard?

214

* * *

Friends continued to comfort Daisy with their newspaper cuttings about the Far East. They gave her hope – just in case one provided a clue. As winter approached, they also helped her occupy her time with trips to Stony Stratford via a Bletchley Transport bus. The small picturesque market town with Roman origins was a welcome distraction. The village's quaint Queen Anne-style houses were surrounded by the luscious green fields of Buckinghamshire countryside. Central to the community were narrow terraced houses, with doors opening to the street, tapering pathways and passages; part of England's rich history and the ancient Roman road of Watling Street. Gordon Welchman also lived there. On market days the place heaved with activity from local tradesmen and travellers. Some frequented the adjacent inns famous in folklore. The Cock or The Bull. For years coachmen competed on the tallest tales and gossip, hoping to be the most believable. Their wagers became known as 'cock and bull stories' – fictional anecdotes or tall stories. These and other coaching inns provided lunches or afternoon teas.

Some people managed to take photographs inside Bletchley Park, but it was strictly forbidden. Consequently, few inner visual records exist. Once outside, however, anyone with a Box Brownie was eager to photograph their excursions. Daisy captured a cold day with her Hut 7 friends. Their photo stage was a wooden fence by a picturesque field in Stony Stratford, a popular spot for off-duty Bletchley staff. Dot and her Block E friends took a similar pose close by in November 1944. Dot, Elsie, Tiny (Florence Wilks), Betty Allman, Sybil Golden and Pixie (May) Parker were all part of the fun. Mary Stoney photographed the scene, high on the top bar, then minutes later Tiny switched with her to snap another. They were probably at the bus stop for the old green Bletchley Transport bus. Sylvia Palmer, during a well-earned break from the message teleprinter of Colossus and the Newmanry, also ventured into the countryside with her friend Marjorie Cundall, known as Billie; they too posed by a similar fence.

When the buses returned to Bletchley's security gate an army soldier checked every pass right to the back of the bus. Security was rigid, nobody was getting into Bletchley who shouldn't. Daisy's pass slipped easily into her pocket avoiding the need for a handbag. Female drivers from FANY

1944: On the fence — a cold November day in Stony Stratford. Daisy (right), Paula Martin and "Winnie" (centre). (Daisy Lawrence Archive)

Dot (second from left top row) and her friends took similar photos, with Tiny (Florence Wilks), Mary Stoney, Pixie (May) Parker, Elsie, Betty Allman and Sybil Golden. (Dorothy Edney Archive)

Sylvia Palmer was snapped in a similar pose with her friend Marjorie Cundall—known as "Billie". (Fiona Ewers)

drove the buses and cars and Daisy enjoyed the luxury of a chauffeur driven car from time to time. Sometimes she used the train to and from her billet. The eight hour, three-shift system had taken a while to master, but after two years she was used to it. Summer months seemed easy, but in winter snow and ice often created problems for Bletchley Transport and the late shifts. When the vintage buses had to take Wrens to Woburn Abbey the journey was much longer, which infuriated those living in town billets; a detour was the last thing anyone wanted, especially after a late shift.

However, civilians, who sat all day, did not always realise the Wrens stood for long periods of time working Bombe machines. Indeed, some called the cranky buses Liberty Ships. But so-called freedom was not always evident when they returned to extremely cold rooms and the austere conformity of Woburn Abbey. The grand house, rebuilt by the Dukes of Bedford in 1744, was run like a ship and life for the Wrens was highly regimented. There was no carpet or heating in rooms, called 'cabins', and when they left the freezing temperatures through the front door, they were referred to as having 'gone ashore!'

Chapter 30

Winter of 1944

When the lake froze, Bletchley employees used the opportunity to ice skate. Daisy had learned at Streatham Silver Blades and rushed home for her boots – a present from Harry some years before. Tan coloured, the brass hooks and eyelets tightly held the long laces at the front of each boot, securely hugging her slender legs and protecting her thin ankles. Dot also fetched her accordion from home. She was a skilled

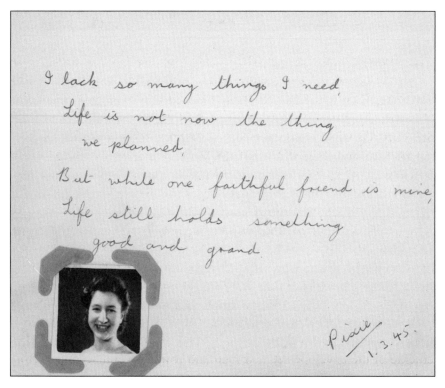

I lack so many things I need,
Life is not now the thing
we planned,
But while one faithful friend is mine,
Life still holds something
good and grand.

Pixie 1.3.45.

Kind words from friends — Pixie (May) Parker 1945. (Dorothy Edney Archive)

musician with a perfect ear, and able to squeeze out tuneful melodies without reading music, while Daisy in her fur coat and equally bundled-up-friend, Marjorie Stott, took to the ice. It was cold and foggy, but others had already tested the safety of the ice. It was fun as they gingerly skated around laughing and swearing politely in equal measures. Marjorie did not have the balance she needed and often found herself down on the ice, but gradually they made their way around the frozen mass. Twice around was as much as they could handle before two American officers appeared and offered to skate with them. The nice men from 'the North', knew how to skate.

Daisy knew the Allies were winning, but didn't know if Stan would live through his ordeal. She was frustrated and couldn't wait for the war to end, but when would that be? In the darkest corner of her mind it was her greatest worry, but when she read a short poem by Dot's friend, she had hope. Pixie Parker's words were a good omen.

* * *

The frosty conditions continued into February 1945, when Annie Lawrence called the emergency Leighton Buzzard telephone number she was given to speak to her daughter. It was an unusual form of contact for both, but she thought the message was urgent. A letter had arrived, not from Stan, but from the War Office. An envelope stamped RASC Records – Army stationery. She guessed it was important news about him and her daughter needed to know.

Daisy had just finished a night shift and was tired, but her heart seemed to stop when she heard her mother's voice. 'What type of news?' She stared at the telephone and a pain throbbed behind her eye, until she was jolted from her thoughts by her mother who repeated, 'Shall I open it?'

They both thought of how war-time families were notified after the death of a loved one. 'I think you usually receive a telegram,' said her mother, without further explanation. Daisy thought that was so, and besides any notification like that would be sent to Stan's next of kin. The crackle of the envelope seemed loud and it was several seconds before her mother cleared her throat and said, 'It's from The Colonel's Office, RASC, Hastings, Sussex.'

The butterflies in her stomach released as her mother read the letter:

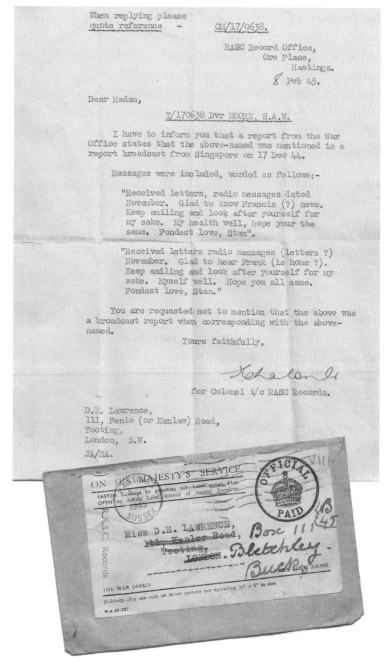

Letter from the colonel's office, RASC, Hastings, February 1945. (Daisy Lawrence Archive)

Stan was talking to her through a radio message! Broadcast from Singapore, he'd received her correspondence and the news about his brother Frank. Singapore! The message had been picked up two months before on 17 December 1944. Thank God for Listeners! With sheer joy and indescribable elation, she thanked her mother and asked her to send it to Bletchley. The same day, 11 February, she composed a reply. Meantime, her mother re-addressed the envelope, this time to B45, Box 111, Bletchley, Bucks, enclosing the original communication.

Daisy, however, sent her reply from her Tooting address; she couldn't reveal how she knew the right questions to ask, or how she knew what the consequences were of making such inquiries. For readers outside Bletchley's circle, it would seem poorly written, but reading between the lines a keen code breaker would understand. Elated, Daisy now had a good feeling. The atmosphere at Bletchley was positive and it was just a matter of time…she hoped.

* * *

The Yalta Conference in Russia had taken place with Churchill, Roosevelt and Stalin the week before. A stronger line was encouraged – especially on the question of Poland. Final plans were made for the defeat of Germany and future of post-war Europe. A date was set for a United Nations Conference and conditions laid down for Russia's entry into the war against Japan. However, it was to be the American President's last since Roosevelt died suddenly of a cerebral haemorrhage on 12 April 1945. Everyone was shocked; he had been president for twelve momentous years, and that day the armies he helped muster drove rapidly toward a final victory over Nazi Germany. 'Worn out at 63, he died as other forces, fighting in freedom's name, having foretold the doom of militaristic Japan,' newspapers lamented. At 7.09 that evening, Vice President Harry S. Truman took the Oath of Office as America's 32nd chief. Britain was stunned. Churchill found it hard to voice his extreme grief, but Roosevelt's legacy continued when the United Nations Conference on International Organization took place in San Francisco and lasted from April to June with delegates from fifty nations.

* * *

In the two months after Roosevelt's death, Europe saw Allied forces close in on Berlin and a platoon of victorious marines hoist the

American flag after a savage battle on Iwo Jima in the Volcano Islands, 750 miles south of Japan in the Pacific Ocean. Allies crossed the Rhine into the Ruhr, the industrial heart of Germany; Cologne was taken and Vienna liberated. Horrific sights in the gas chambers of German concentration camps became a reality for the world to see and never forget. Forces advanced into the territory to help refugees and bury corpses. Step by step, the Allies drew closer to Berlin and the final defeat of Nazi Germany.

Chapter 31

War's End

'It's Over!' an excited voice in the office shouted, the war's over!" The war in Europe was ending at last. Everyone glowed as they celebrated and reflected on their contribution to teamwork. The ecstatic staff of Bletchley Park felt theirs was not just a battleground but an entire war.

Headlines V – Day.
(Public domain)

For months and years, thousands of people behind the scenes connected and listened to world-wide messages. People from all classes, mostly women, pulled together to break codes – civilians, military men and women, and men of the professor type. Without them the West may well have lost the war. The next day, jubilant and proud newspaper vendors shouted from every street corner; people danced in the streets and flags flew from every window on 8 May 1945 – the official day of unconditional surrender by Germany. Adolf Hitler had committed suicide on 30 April and Admiral Karl Dönitz, agreed to authorise the surrender.

Victory in Europe

With advanced knowledge Daisy and Dot's supervisors had granted them leave. They were grateful for permission but didn't really care; they would have gone anyway. The war was OVER. They needed to be in London – close to home – to see and hear the important government dignitaries of their capital city, their country. Peggy Weston and Mary Goddard went too. The four, and several other Bletchley personnel, caught the next train to Euston to join other excited crowds rushing to Buckingham Palace.

The Bletchley friends hurried among the throngs filling London's Mall, as policemen, gates and barriers prevented them from getting close to the palace. But Daisy's group squeezed into a space opposite the gates, high on the steps of Queen Victoria's statue. The world seemed to be there, thousands of grateful people, including government officials and mixed uniformed personnel: men, women, sons and daughters, fathers, mothers, sisters, brothers, grandmothers and grandfathers, some with babies in their arms. London's atmosphere was electric and joyous in anticipation, as the country waited to hear the Prime Minister's wireless announcement and see the Royal Family that afternoon. Loudspeakers were set up in the palace courtyard for everyone to hear.

Eventually, the door onto the palace balcony opened and people jostled to see King George and Queen Elizabeth step out with their daughters, Princess Elizabeth and Princess Margaret. A loud cheer erupted as they waved to the crowd. Daisy felt her knees quake at the excitement, but soon recovered. Then quiet. The extraordinary hush seemed an eternity as the crowd waited only seconds for 3pm.

Then Big Ben's magnificent gong sounded. Three times it struck, followed by the voice of Winston Churchill. The Bletchley four glowed with admiration, deep in their secret; they couldn't speak of their proximity to this great man, or how they had helped, but enjoyed the afternoon camaraderie. In his usual fashion, Churchill's delivery was droll as his oration of the surrender and signing resembled a station master's announcement for the next train to Bletchley, until he almost sang, 'The evil-doers now lie prostrate before us.' At that the crowds gasped with enthusiasm as Churchill concluded with the words 'Advance Britannia! Long Live the cause of Freedom. God Save the King!'[1] This was Britain's finest hour. Radio stations around the world also transmitted the recording; everyone heard, including PoWs in Singapore eventually, via a covert receiver.

Others around the country listened to Churchill's short speech on their wireless sets at home, and the BBC ended with a bugler's solitary Last Post, followed by 'God Save the King' where all sang along heartily. After the broadcast, Churchill prepared to deliver his statement to the House of Lords in person. On any normal day the ten-minute journey from No 10 Downing Street to Parliament would have been quite straightforward, but this day fervent crowds delayed his arrival. Question time in Parliament usually ended promptly at 3.15pm, but MPs kept proceedings open with supplementary questions, so that by 3.23, when he finally arrived, 'the House rose as a man'.[2] After a standing ovation and congratulatory cheers, Churchill thanked the House for their 'noble support' throughout the war, then moved 'for the House to attend the Church of St Margaret's, Westminster, to give humble and reverential thanks to Almighty God for our deliverance from the threat of German domination.'

He added, 'This is the identical motion which was moved in former times.' Churchill had recalled Armistice Day, 11 November 1918, the end of the First World War. The motion was carried and in official procession the MPs filed out into the sunshine where mounted police forged a path through crowds of tens of thousands to a chorus of 'Winnie, Winnie'.[3] There was no one else the people wanted.

The Royal Family were cheered eight times that day and Winston Churchill was with them on the balcony at one point, but Daisy and her friends had missed that appearance. Instead they rushed to the Ministry of Health in Whitehall to hear him speak again. That afternoon from the Whitehall balcony, they heard him shout, 'This is your victory.' To which Daisy and the rest of the crowd roared, 'No, it is yours.'[4] He was their hero. Later that evening as bright searchlights beamed around London's buildings, the city was illuminated in peace, accompanied by the faint smell of celebratory bonfires and cries of cheering crowds. The searchlights that pinpointed enemy planes and rockets for five years, now created a carnival atmosphere as Churchill dined in London with family members and his publisher Lord Camrose. What a story he had to tell. At 10.30pm he was told the crowds still called for him, so he returned to the Whitehall balcony and told the assembly below:

> 'My dear friends, this is your hour.... There we stood, alone. Did anyone want to give in? The crowd shouted "No." Were we downhearted? "No!" The lights went out and the bombs came down. But every man women and child in the country had no thought of quitting the struggle. London can take it. So we came back after long months from the jaws of death, out of the mouth of hell, while all the world wondered. When shall the reputation and faith of this generation of English men and women fail? I say that in the long years to come not only will the people of this island but of the world, wherever the bird of freedom chirps in human hearts, look back to what we've done and they will say "do not despair, do not yield to violence and tyranny, march straight forward and die if need be – unconquered."'

He also told them that Germany 'awaits our justice and our mercy', and that Japan, 'stained with cruelty and greed', would likewise be vanquished. 'Britain would fight the battle hand in hand with America.'[5]

* * *

Throughout the night people celebrated: Soldiers, sailors, tinkers, tailors, everyone embraced the moment; some more intimately than others, some with complete strangers – the euphoria of peace was everything, and it was nothing to worry about who you kissed. Some couples fell in love on the spot and found a future husband. Peace at last; a moment in history never to be forgotten. They danced in fountains and the streets, well into the early hours of the morning. Alcohol had been restricted, but revellers found enough to share. The night was hot, the fountains cool; the law was low and everyone celebrated. The world joined in, including Moscow, Paris, Brussels, New York, Washington and Los Angeles. Germany was defeated.

* * *

That night was an enjoyable memory for many, including Daisy, Peggy, Mary and Dot – until they missed the last train from Euston to Bletchley and their only option was to wait for the 5am milk train. Somehow, they slept on the wooden seats in the waiting room; their clothes were damp but at least they were warm. A train pulled into the station and they woke with bleary eyes. As dawn approached at 4.45am, they marvelled at the dark blue sky and its splendid sunrise – the first full day of official peace in Europe for more than four and a half years.

But the unloading of clunking milk churns disrupted their reverie and Dot shouted for them to move quickly. They clambered aboard to find seats in a passenger carriage where they could spread out. Soon the slow steam train reached the countryside as it discharged a celebratory whistle. At Bletchley Station the rested codebreakers alighted and prepared for 8am shifts. They were jaded but happy to be part of such an historic occasion, a celebration they and the world would never forget.

An official message from Director General, SGM – Major General, Stuart Graham Menzies, Head of MI6, awaited each of them. On thin, almost transparent paper, the messages were one of hundreds re-typed or printed by Gestetner duplicating machines. All Bletchley employees received the important missive of unbounded admiration, gratitude and praise.

MESSAGE FROM THE DIRECTOR GENERAL

The following message has been received from the Director General:-

"On this ever memorable day, I desire that all who are doing duty in this Organisation should be made aware of my unbounded admiration in the way in which they have carried out their allotted tasks.

Such have been the difficulties, such has been the endeavour, and such have been the constant triumphs that one senses that words of gratitude from one individual are perhaps out of place. The personal knowledge of the contribution made towards winning the War is surely the real measure of the thanks which so rightly belong to one and all in a great and inspired organisation which I have the privilege to direct. This is your finest hour."

(Signed) S.G.M.

8th, May 1945.

Message of "unbound admiration" from the Director General, 8 May 1945. (Daisy Lawrence Archive)

Leaving 'Owing to the Cessation of Hostilities'

Packing complete, many codebreakers left Bletchley for good. Some had worked and lived there for two or three years, others longer. Where would they go, what would they do? A marked sense of loneliness and loss set in for some. This was home, a generation's university and seat of further learning, their chance to interact with a wider world. What would they do? Return to their normal mundane lives? But who knew the definition of normal now?

Time to leave Government Communications HQ, "Owing to the cessation of hostilities …" (Dorothy Edney Archive)

A strong sense of pride was instilled in everyone who worked in Intelligence. All knew their contribution was important, but many lives had been lost. The sad reality should never be forgotten. They couldn't talk about what they did or what they knew. They were simply to go back to their communities as if nothing happened; abide by the rules of the Official Secrets Act and quietly melt back into civilian life. Gradually the huts at Bletchley emptied; only skeleton staff for Japanese Naval Intelligence remained. There were a few parties, and friends who forged relationships exchanged wishful rhymes of thanks, with promises to meet again. Some gave addresses. Dot asked her friends and colleagues to sign the message from the Director General, but Daisy refused to sign. 'You shouldn't be doing that.' Nobody outside Bletchley Park needed to know where she worked during the war.

Would these people from afar see each other again? Was their wartime experience just a small chink of their life? Their work never to be revealed, or even understood? Only a few of the hierarchy knew the full story. The secret Work of National Importance was to be shrouded forever. Dot left Bletchley at the end of May 1945, after the end of the European War.

* * *

They could never tell what they knew, but some kept illicit souvenirs; a snapshot of their life in the Second World War, memories hard to leave behind. Poems were written and autographed; photo prints from auto-booths around Bletchley were saved and hidden, only to be found by another generation. As Bletchley graduates died, their offspring wished they'd asked more questions or understood more. But it was not the end of Daisy's war. She was needed at Bletchley to continue her area of expertise on Japanese Marus. The Allies were still at war with Japan and danger for PoWs in the Far East was imminent. She stayed earnest in her work on Japanese bookbuilding – coordinates, loads and Japanese Naval codes. It was her duty to Stan and the troops to see it through; they could not be forgotten. They had to survive.

Chapter 32

'We Also Served'

Germany surrendered at a schoolhouse in Rheims to Field Marshal Montgomery and Allied Supreme Commander General Eisenhower on Luneberg Heath near Hamburg. Not long after, the school children in Tooting celebrated the end of war. Mothers felt they too had served, keeping kids in line and occupied in the absence of a father figure. Some looked forward to normality, others didn't know what that was; some children didn't know their fathers. But everyone came to celebrate the end. Tables and chairs were brought into the streets, and yards of bed sheets were spread across scaffold boards for makeshift banquet tables and benches and, despite rationing, food appeared from all corners of the neighbourhood. Daisy's nephew, Ron Collingridge, the young evacuee remembered:

> 'When the war was over our dad didn't come home because he was on navy mine sweepers. But we still had a street party. It was organised with washing lines hung across the road, representing the Siegfried Line. We children called it the "Seed freed line".[1] We wore fancy dress and I was a vicar. The hat was one of Mister's old bowlers cut down; I also wore a white shirt collar back to front. Our father came home after he was de-mobbed and that's when we saw his bad side. Fortunately, soon after, he left.'

Even little children served and paid a price.

Ron's uncles, Harry and Bill came home, but his Aunty Daisy stayed working somewhere in the countryside. He didn't know what had happened to Uncle Stan until much later. After VE Day, Bletchley staff received a standard letter of reference from the Foreign Office to mark the end of their National Service. The letter was designed to assist future employment. Dot couldn't wait to leave; she'd had enough of Bletchley and wanted to be with her fiancé Albert Hodgson, a military policeman. Both were eager to celebrate the end of the war at home in London.

* * *

Toward the end of May, battered Europe prepared for recovery. In London the British Coalition government was dissolved and an election was planned. The question was: would Churchill survive to run Britain in peacetime? In June, the European Advisory Council apportioned sections of Europe to Russia – part of the Allies' deal with Stalin for Russia's help to defeat Hitler. Germany was divided, East and West. American troops moved back 150 miles westward, but not everyone agreed. As German citizens were forced to view the grim evidence of Nazi death camps, William Joyce, Lord Haw-Haw, the propaganda commentator, was captured in Denmark. In several recordings he'd said he was British, but later claimed to be American 'born in New York'. He was tried for treason in Britain and hanged in 1946.

In the Far East, 300 miles south of Japan, a vicious battle raged between 50,000 American troops and Japanese forces for the strategic island of Okinawa. On 21 June 1945, bloody hand-to-hand combat on land and in caves, culminated in full Japanese ritual when the enemy commander admitted defeat by committing hari-kari at dawn in front of his unit. The cost: 12,000 American and 110,000 Japanese killed. By 26 June delegates from fifty countries signed the World Security Charter to create the United Nations, as international peacekeeper.

In July, the Potsdam Conference was held in Cecilienhof, Germany, home of Crown Prince Wilhelm. The 'Big 3', UK, USA and USSR – Churchill, Truman and Stalin – attended with their aides. During the meeting landslide results of Britain's 5 July general election were announced – Winston Churchill's coalition-party lost and Labour's opposition party was now in control. Clement Attlee, suddenly the new Prime Minster, wasted no time in forming a new government.

In the five months since Yalta, a number of changes had taken place which affected the relationship between world leaders: Roosevelt had died on 12 April and Harry Truman became the American President, Hitler was dead and Germany had surrendered, Britain had a new Prime Minister and the Soviet Union had asserted its authority over Central and Eastern Europe. Roosevelt, before his death in the name of Allied unity, had brushed off (rather naively) warnings of domination by a Stalin dictatorship in Europe. At the time he explained, 'I just have a hunch Stalin is not that kind of a man,' reasoning 'I think if I give him everything I possibly can and ask for nothing from him in return, "noblesse oblige" he won't try to annex anything and will work with me for a world of democracy and peace.'

Churchill's Soviet policy since the 1940s, differed considerably from the former president's, as he believed Stalin to be a 'devil-like' tyrant leading a vile system. After Germany's surrender, Stalin repeated his promises to Churchill to 'refrain from Sovietization of Central Europe'. But in addition to rebuilding, Stalin pushed for rewards, 'war booty'. This would allow the USSR to directly seize property from conquered nations without limitation, quantitative or qualitative. A clause was added to permit this, but with limitations. Stalin's Red Army had control of the Baltic states, Poland, Czechoslovakia, Hungary, Bulgaria and Romania and, consequently, fearing a complete Stalinist takeover, refugees fled their countries. Stalin went on to set up a puppet communist government in Poland, insisting his control of Eastern Europe was defensive against possible future attacks and claimed it was a legitimate measure in the sphere of Soviet influence.

* * *

When Vice President Harry Truman, became the American President, his succession saw changes in the platform of war which aimed to forge a passage to world peace. Soon after VE Day Japanese victory was on the horizon and he warned, 'If Japan doesn't surrender, atomic bombs will be dropped on her war industries.' The world watched and waited when he promised 'a rain of ruin' from the air.

Chapter 33

Rain of Ruin, Rain of Tears

Early in August 1945, the Royal Navy task force joined the American Third fleet in a dawn assault on Tokyo and four other Japanese cities. It was the strongest fleet ever assembled in the Pacific. On 6 August the US Army B-29 super-fortress aircraft *Enola Gay*, carried and dropped the world's first atomic bomb on Hiroshima, the capital of Honshu, Japan's largest island. A second bomb fell on Nagasaki three days later. Both obliterated their targets, thousands of Japanese civilians died and tens of thousands would die later of radiation poisoning. The bomb's plumes of smoke lasted days as they hovered over the dead and dying and complete devastation. No longer secret, the British-American led Manhattan Project was the team product of 100,000 international scientists who produced the most devastating weapon of mass destruction of all time. The targeted areas were vaporised. Silence. Death. Destruction. Tears.

> 'In January 1944 I went out to Colombo, where I stayed for two years working on Japanese decoding. I came home in December 1945. The war was over, and our work dried up completely after the atom bomb was dropped on Hiroshima. I remember not really understanding what atomic meant until we were shown the first aerial photographs and I saw the utter devastation.'
> Alison Gibson (neé Densham) WRNS Bombe Operator.[1]

Conversely, it is said the Atom Bomb saved many lives and shortened the war by at least two years. But that wasn't the end; through intelligence reports the Allies had to act quickly to halt enemy repercussions and to prevent a certain massacre of all prisoners of war.

* * *

At Bletchley, Daisy heard news of a massive bomb, as a rumour trickled through. Then a message was received in Hut 6 (Hut 16 as it was by then). Five women from CMY (Cover Management Y section) were on the day shift, when their supervisor Mr Williams – known as 'Bungy' – congratulated them saying well done and that an intercepted signal from Tokyo to Geneva revealed the Japanese were about to surrender. As he smiled the girls sat shocked and silent. This was huge news, made in a rather matter-of-fact way. He then shuffled from one foot to the other, not knowing what to do next, and said, 'Well…, bloody well get on with your work!'

In the melée of whispered secrets, Bungy later confirmed the information had been sent to King George VI and the Prime Minister, but Bletchley couldn't announce anything before the message had gone from Geneva to London. 'Otherwise they'd know we're listening.' Marion Graham (Lady Marion Body) was one of the girls in that room with twins, Valerie and Mary Glassborow.[2] 'It was a great moment, one I've remembered all my life.' she commented seventy years later.

The rumour spread quickly, as Daisy listened to tenuous reports; she was relieved the bomb was nowhere near Singapore and she was one of the first to hear about the surrender. Overwhelmed, she felt sick – incredulous, happy and sad, but she didn't know who to turn to next – she couldn't say anything to family until news of the surrender was public. The war with Japan was ending; Stan would be home soon.

Emperor Hirohito surrendered unconditionally to the Allies on 15 August 1945. Victors in Europe and around the world celebrated VJ Day (Victory over Japan). Like VE Day, after more than 2,000 nights of blackouts, London and the rest of the country lit up in a carnival-like atmosphere. Piccadilly was filled with RAF and American forces celebrating in uniform. Children with families enjoyed street parties. Bonfires blazed and over 7,000 lampposts were re-flamed in Croydon alone. The heavy veil of darkness had lifted and bells of peace rang out again.

On 28 August Supreme Commander of Allied Powers, General Douglas MacArthur, led the occupation of Japan. Under his leadership formal signing of the Instrument of Surrender by the Japanese Empire took place aboard aircraft carrier USS *Missouri* on 2 September, the official VJ Day in America. The deadliest and most costly war in history was finally over. Affecting over sixty countries, with more than 60 million people dead.

VJ Day

When the news was eventually confirmed, a rush of relief hurtled toward Daisy. Everyone was jubilant. After years of worry coupled with long late-night shifts of toil and stress, the war was over, and Stan was probably safe. Tears flowed as excitement raced through the corridors. A celebration was swiftly prepared and with the release of generous portions of food, beer and spirits the Victory Ball was held in the mansion. Relief and happiness was infectious as codebreakers prepared for one final fling of camaraderie and merriment. Records played, and speeches were made. Soon their special relationships would stop and become just a memory. Someone sang the sombre Bletchley anthem. Those who knew the words joined in with their version of Joyce Kilmer's melancholy poem, 'Trees', written especially for the Victory Ball and set to Oscar Rasbach's music.

During the speeches Stan Sedgwick recited the BP rhyme he had adapted for the end of the Japanese War. The long poem featured friend and foe and made everyone laugh. It was a vivid picture of Bletchley and their plight; the way they handled their predicament, their positive attitude, teamwork and the secret tasks they undertook. Daisy kept her copy. Some lines are serious, some are amusing, but overall it is clear the codebreakers made the best of their unusual situation. Couples gathered for a last dance and, perhaps, a final kiss. There was even one last

```
                "TREES"

I think that I shall never see
A sight so curious as B.P.
This place called up at war's behest
And peopled with the queerly dressed
Yet what they did they could not say
Nor ever shall, till Judgement Day.

For six long years have we been there,
Subject to local scorn and stare:
We came by transport and by train;
The dull, the brilliantly insane!
What were we for, where shall we be
When God at last redunds B.P.?

The Air Force types who never fly,
Soldiers who neither do nor die,
Landlubber sailors, beards complete,
Long-haired civilians, slim, effete:
Why they were there, they never knew:
And when they told, it wasn't true!

If I should die, think this of me:
I served my country at B.P.
And should my son ask: "What did you
In the Atomic World War 2?"
God only knows, and He won't tell,
For after all, B.P. is HELL!!
```

"TREES," Joyce Kilmer's melancholy poem for the VJ Day Victory Ball. (Daisy Lawrence Archive)

A — Is for Anthony, our nominal head,
At least until the country went "Red"
We're Bevin boys now and through Ernies capers
Poor Eden has had his redundancy papers.

B — Is for Budd, the head of Hut 2
Who hands out the wallop to me and to you
When the Park closes down, the last man to go
Will be Mr Budd- at least we hope so.

C — Is for Crawley- our own dietician
Who serves up our grub like a mathematician
It's round stodge or square for the rest of your life
And eat the darned stuff without even a knife.

D — Is for Denny, whose nickname is stoker
We think 'cos he peps up his pipe with a poker
He issues the 'Blonce' and beer in a cask
If it's not in window come in and ask.

E'S — for Sir Edward, the governor upstairs
Who pinches our clubroom for Christmas affairs
He passes our transport times without number
In a pre-war upholstered beige-coloured Humber.

F — Is for Foss 6ft 6" in his shoes
Seen in a kilt but not tartan trews
If on a Friday a stroll you will take
You'll find him dancing a reel by the lake.

G — Is for Griffiths who finds us our digs
Some live like princes, some live like pigs
It's no good protesting, your wasting your breath
If you find your own billet he's tickled to death.

H — Is for Howgate deceiver of Wrens
He lures the poor creatures to dimly lit dens
He twirls his moustache is manly and curt
But spoils the effect with an A.T.S. shirt.

I — Is Intelligence the boys in the Park
They all need a hair cut but please keep it dark
The question I hope is to be answered one day
Is how can a corpse be intelligent, pray

J — Is for Joan the sec. of the club
She chases you up for an over due 'sub'
She books you the gatehouse and looks up your trains
Then gets her flowers pinched for taking such pains.

K — Is for Kevin with hair slightly red
A crescent shaped scar on the side of his head
You may think he got it from some ancient dirk
But he says his mother was scared by a Turk.

L — Is for Lowe, a clanking occurs
Handlebar Harry is out with his spurs
He doesn't claim to be much of a dancer
But what can you hope from a Bengal Lancer.

M — For John Moore, whose fingers 'tis said
Allows him to carry on drinking in bed
A slight overstatement his friends all retort
For when fully loaded it holds but a quart.

N — Is for Nenk the Major in F
When staff wanted leave he used to be deaf
Now that his number is not far away
He took them all out for a picnic one day.

O — Is for Owen, that's Dudley I mean
When the curtain goes up he's not to be seen
But if it comes down in quite the wrong place
It's Dudley the stage boss who losses his face.

P — Is for Parker, the check-suited dope,
Who thinks that his acting surpasses Bob Hope
We know that his fortes a bullocks pack pins
Imagine a fan mail to father of twins.

Q — is for tea it is only a penny
If there is cake it stretches to Penny
If work is a bore I'm sure you'll agree
Let's on the T.Q.

R — Is for Reiss who can always be found
With a large coloured brolly and two feet of hound
When he goes up to heaven and his name they record
We hope they will ask "Is it down on the board".

S — Is for Sedgewick who ran all the "hops"
In the tough old days of American cops
Hush, hush whisper who dare
He faintly resembles that chap Fred Astaire.

T — Is for Tiltman just one of the boys
Red tabs he won't wear with brown corduroys
When billets were scarce Dame rumour doth say
He lived in the States and flew over each day.

U's — Uncle Sam who sent us some chaps
3,000 miles to Bletchley perhaps
They came for the fashionable season
We're glad to have had them whatever the reason.

V — is the visitor- distinguished Brass Hats
Came snooping around to see what we're at
We sweep the place clean with dustpan and broom
And move all the empties to some other room.

W — for Wallace the colonel you know
His name's at the end of a B.P.G.O.
He works in a room that looks out on the grass
And forbids you to prop your bike on the glass.

X — Is the name of our perishing station
The board at the gates gives you no indication
Of what we are up to, for all that it states
Is "Go very slowly through our Secret gates".

Y — Is for you, folks in the hall
As time passes by I hope you'll recall
The dances you've been to here- above all
Tonight the Japanese Victory Ball.

Z — Is a stinker, I think you'll agree
I can find a name that starts with a zee
That is the end of this scurrilous rot
I hope that my friends who are mentioned will not
Take offence, or yours truly for slander will sue
I must say I liked it and hope you did too.

STAN SEDGEWICK.

A is for Anthony our Nominal Head.... Stan Sedgwick's Bletchley Park rhyme adapted for the end of the Japanese war. (Daisy Lawrence Archive)

hurrah for the Gay Gordons! They were the first graduates of Bletchley Park, Churchill's 'Geese that laid the golden egg and never cackled,' the second-best kept secret of the Second World War, after the Manhattan Project's devastating Atom Bomb, the bomb to end all wars.

* * *

Daisy stayed at Bletchley as machines and files were packed away. There was no mass bonfire as some would suggest, though papers were burned because they were rubbish. Typex, Colossus and Bombe machines were dismantled and removed; possibly destroyed. She didn't know exactly

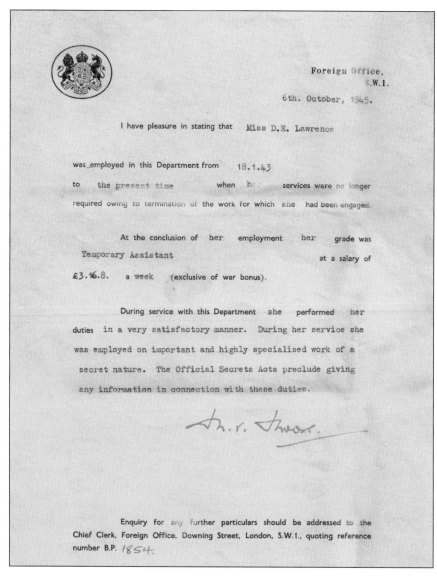

Foreign Office,
S.W.1.

6th. October, 1945.

I have pleasure in stating that   Miss D.E. Lawrence

was employed in this Department from   18.1.43

to   the present time   when   her   services were no longer

required owing to termination of the work for which   she   had been engaged.

At the conclusion of   her   employment   her   grade was

Temporary Assistant   at a salary of

£3.16.8.   a week   (exclusive of war bonus).

During service with this Department   she   performed   her

duties   in a very satisfactory manner. During her service she

was employed on important and highly specialised work of a

secret nature. The Official Secrets Acts preclude giving

any information in connection with these duties.

Enquiry for any further particulars should be addressed to the Chief Clerk, Foreign Office, Downing Street, London, S.W.1., quoting reference number B.P. 1854.

Daisy's Foreign Office release and reference letter from Miss V. M. Moore confirming her position, final pay and employment reference BP 1854. (Daisy Lawrence Archive) where everything was going but Eastcote seemed likely. She cleared her dues at the billeting office in Hut 9, via Robert Foster Corby. Her dismissal letter allowed her to leave in October, but she was paid to 1 December. Her Foreign Office letter confirmed her position and final pay of £3.16s.8d. per week; reference BP 1854. Her immediate boss wrote a glowing personal handwritten reference, calling her his Leading Clerical Assistant.

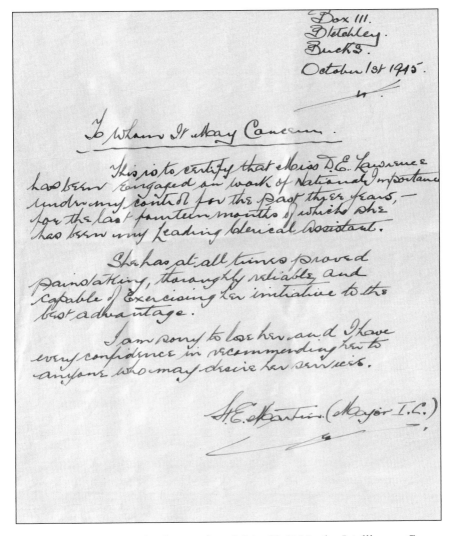

Daisy's glowing personal reference from Major H. E Martin, Intelligence Corps. (Daisy Lawrence Archive)

It was the end of Daisy's temporary employment and time to leave. How would life be now? She already knew she would miss her colleagues and Tooting may not necessarily offer her what she wanted. Her dismissal letter arrived, PO Box 111, that omen again – 111 Kenlor Road. Which 111 was really home? She said goodbye and made plans to keep in touch including Mary Goddard,[3] Peggy Weston and Muriel Gotzheim. She also looked forward to seeing Dot again, and her best friend Peggy Johnson, but most of all she would be glad to be back with Stan. She just needed to know he was safe and coming home. When would that be? She had already contacted the War Office.

Olive Humble also received a similar reference from Major Martin. She was on leave when Japan surrendered and on her return was told she was superfluous to requirements and should depart immediately. Back in front of the commander for formal dismissal, he repeated the warning that if she ever said anything, she would get thirty years in prison, but this time added 'or the firing squad'. With one week's pay she said goodbye to Bletchley and went home. Her father asked what she did at the Foreign Office. She replied, 'I'm sorry I can't tell you, please don't ever ask me that again.' Sadly, her parents went to their graves never knowing about the important work their only child did in the war. Olive emigrated to South Africa with Bletchley friend Doris Ward from the Japanese section, though neither knew what each other did. Olive married two years later and went on to have three children and several grandchildren.

* * *

As Daisy prepared to leave Bletchley for the last time, she reflected on the years and months since her arrival. From that cold January morning in 1943, she had evolved as a young woman, seen life from different perspectives and met many interesting individuals she now considered friends. She was part of an amazing team of intelligent and trustworthy people who knew how to work together and keep a secret. She recalled the first nervous moments meeting Barbara Abernethy[4] in the waiting room of the mansion on 18 January 1943. Barbara knew everything about everybody. At 18 she had become Commander Denniston's secretary before the war and continued working at Bletchley for Commander Travis. Now she was responsible for personnel records of thousands at GC&CS and would soon be the one to lock Bletchley's doors for the last time.

Daisy said goodbye to her and took the train back to London and Tooting Junction. It was a sunny but cold October day; same coat and boots, same suitcase and handbag; just her rounders bat and several newspaper cuttings as additional items to her clothes, her ice skates slung over her left shoulder. It seemed only a few weeks had passed since she'd walked along icy Longley Road to catch the early train. But it had been nearly three years; three years of secrets and three years of her life – all to be erased.

* * *

When she arrived home, she plumped her suitcase on to her bed and pulled off her boots. Nothing had changed. She glanced at the Christmas card on the mantelpiece from her brother Harry and picked up the photo of Stan. She wondered if it was really over; had it all been a dream?

Harry was the only person to welcome her home. He had returned from Palestine and was about to be de-mobbed. Her parents would soon return after visiting relatives in Gloucestershire. They already knew better than to ask what she did at Bletchley. Harry made tea. She noticed he could make it for himself now and smiled. Had he heard if Stan was still safe, or when he would be home? She hoped they would marry soon and cycle off into the sunset…perhaps 'on a bicycle made for two!'

Part III

Secret Burden

Chapter 34

After the War

The Second World War was the most devastating conflict in human history. Its global destruction affected many countries under the primary focus of Allied and Axis powers. Distinctions between military and non-military were blurred, as vast resources – human, economic and technological – allowed brutal assaults on civilians. More than sixty million people lost their lives (some estimates state 70-85 million from all causes) and over a trillion dollars were spent on the conflict. A seismic shift in the international status of new age superpowers emerged in the years that followed, along with disagreement between the USA and Soviet Union, and the accelerated decline of the French and British empires. Japan and Germany nurtured new democratic governments and communists led by Mao Tse-tung ruled the People's Republic of China from 1949, after defeating the Chinese Nationalist Party of Chiang Kai-Shek.

No Recognition

In Britain, compensations, post-war training in various trades and industries was offered to those who fought and came home. Medals were awarded but no training, awards or compensation were given to wartime employees of Bletchley Park. The clandestine operation disappeared from British public records and was forgotten; simply erased from history without any recognition. David Kahn's mid-1960s book, *The Codebreakers: The Story of Secret Writing*, is evidence of this where most references to British codebreaking and Bletchley's successes were removed before publication. In later years Churchill only referred to his secret source as, 'The Geese that laid the golden eggs, and never cackled!' But codebreakers knew who they were and never did cackle; not until they had permission to do so.

Wren Ruth Henry confirmed that women in Britain were not offered a medal or workplace re-training, equivalent to America's GI Bill, for their wartime service, whether they were military or civilian employees. 'When I was decommissioned from the Navy, I married and still worked with knobs, dials and drums; I kept myself busy – I managed a launderette! We were just expected to blend back into society, with little or no recognition.'

Only a small war pension of pennies was offered which Daisy found distasteful. She tried to be involved with Bletchley Park's revival in 1995 but felt nobody was interested in her story. Bletchley historians only wanted famous people; a sad reflection of British society which claims to be inclusive, but is not. Sixty-three years later a form of recognition came in a badge, but then for just a few. By then it was too late for Daisy, as it was for many.

A Mysterious Interval

Little is known about Daisy's life in the nine-year period after VJ Day 1945. She did not keep a diary. Stan came home from Singapore a few months later. His ordeal as a Far Eastern PoW was a horrendous experience, but he survived, albeit his body wasted and fatigued. He did keep a secret diary, written in fading pencil; now the subject of another book. They waited six months for his strength to improve and for him to acclimatise to 'normal' life. After he was de-mobbed they married on 29 June 1946. Daisy didn't wear white, she said she couldn't afford a wedding dress, purchasing fine fabric was not an option after the war, but all seemed happy from the wedding photograph and they did have a two-tier wedding cake. There was a short honeymoon on the Isle of Wight, before returning to live in Daisy's small apartment in Deal Road, Mitcham with her black kitten, Tinker. The only wedding presents were a large earthenware pitcher, a clock and two white linen tablecloths, though there must have been other family gifts. Money perhaps.

Apart from marriage, there are few post war photos, but one in her secret wartime hoard sees her returning to central London. The date was Saturday, 19 October 1946, Leicester Square. She is with her Bletchley colleagues from the north, Peggy Weston and Marjorie Stott. All were

Reunion in London, 19 October 1946. (Daisy Lawrence Archive)

smartly dressed for an important reunion to celebrate their war days; research also reveals it coincided with the day the Strategic Services Unit (SSU) officially dismantled. Was there a connection? Was this a final goodbye to American personnel at Bletchley? The London office was in Grosvenor Street, less than a mile away.

The SSU was an American Intelligence agency created from the wartime branches of Secret Intelligence and Counter Espionage, it existed in the period immediately after the war, created from the Office of Strategic Services (OSS)[1], and was pre-Central Intelligence Agency (CIA). Formed in 1942, OSS was for joint chiefs of staff, of all branches of US Forces, to coordinate espionage activities behind enemy lines. The US Army and Navy codebreaking departments, SIS and OP-20-G, however, were separate. Up until 1929 a version of the US Bureau, similar to MI6 and called MI8, was founded by Herbert O. Yardley, but his department was closed by then Secretary of State, Henry Stimson, who claimed it inappropriate for the diplomatic arm because 'gentlemen don't read each other's mail'. Yardley, a First World War veteran and pioneer in US cryptology then openly published *The American Black Chamber* after the closure. He was one of the first to write of such covert operations and his 1931 indiscretions were instantly popular but embarrassing for the US government.

During the Second World War he specialised in Japanese codes and was a frequent visitor to Bletchley Park as director of the Examination Unit (XU) of Canadian Signals Intelligence, a counterpart to GC&CS in Ottawa, Canada. It is unlikely Yardley was at the close of SSU, but other former Bletchley staff known to Daisy and her friends, probably were. In August 2008 names and documents of personnel involved with the OSS were released by the US National Archives. Among them are Julia Child, Arthur Goldberg, Arthur Schlesinger and Boston Red Sox baseball player, Moe Berg.

* * *

Daisy continued to work for the Foreign Office after Bletchley, though she rarely mentioned this or where exactly, apart from the name Great Smith Street (also not far from Grosvenor Street). If we caught reference to this period in her life, it was Uncle Harry leading the discussion about the India Office. We thought he worked there. She once said she, 'used to work in the library, in the Map Room, and helped foreign office diplomatic personnel with their leave allocations.' But it seems she had more of a connection to India than was obvious, when her department was discovered to be connected to the Westminster Library from late 1945 until Partition in 1947 – India's independence from British Empire

Another secret posting? On the roof of the Westminster Library – India Office 1947 with Beryl Rogers who also worked at Bletchley Park during the war. (Daisy Lawrence Archive)

rule. A group photo was found in her Bletchley treasures. She is with other India Office personnel on the roof of the library building in Great Smith Street. It is inscribed: 'India Office Leave Section Staff – 1947.' Her words now make sense. Only one other person is mentioned in the photograph of seventeen people – Beryl Rogers – she was also at Bletchley Park and her BP Roll of Honour confirms: Naval Section, Block A, decoding Japanese codes.[2]

At the same time a postwar newspaper cutting regarding a Mr Pickles and a Mr A. Mostyn provokes curiosity. Daisy's friend, Peggy Weston, found the article in a Barnsley newspaper and sent it to her. Was this the same Leonard Pickles who worked in Singapore and Bletchley Park?

* * *

During the fifties it was time to start a family, and Daisy used some of her free time to volunteer at the baby clinic at St Barnabas' Church, Mitcham. As far as we know she did not work after the India Office. It was in this setting of mothers' random chatter and nursing babies, she learned of four new houses being built on the edge of Mitcham Common. Mary Hudspith, a young mother, was involved with her husband's small post-war-funded building project. Daisy told Stan who was immediately interested and after discussions the couple agreed to buy their first house for £2,000 from Mary and Jack. It was to become their family home for more than fifty years.

Chapter 35

Memory

Children

I was six when I first heard about Bletchley Park. A teacher encouraged us to ask about our parent's Second World War experiences, the war with Germany and Japan. I learned my father had been a prisoner, a grim discovery for a child, to hear that your father had been in prison. I was embarrassed, but a short account of his wartime voyage and captivity seemed to explain this period in his life, though he spoke little of his ordeal after. 'It was a sad and difficult time, long ago; you don't need to worry yourselves. War is a terrible thing.'

Despite this, his Sunday afternoons, were often spent watching old black and white war films on our small walnut-cased Philips television. We were lucky to have one; our cousin's husband worked for the TV company. The films were dark and dismal, but this was how he learned of other peoples' war – winning and losing – suffering. Fact or fiction, fighting, killing and certain death – history seemed bad and Singapore was just a far-off land. At that age my twin sister and I had no real concept of distance, time or the lasting emotions caused by the horrors of war. His brief story was unimaginable, but he was safe and had returned with a few souvenirs. He revealed his cream woollen army socks, Japanese money, a wooden toothbrush and a cut-throat razor he'd made in captivity. The collection was just enough to revisit his time of incarceration in Changi jail, under British administration and the cruel guards of the Imperial Japanese army. We learned he was not a prisoner, but a prisoner of war. It was different, but he refrained from saying more, and we changed tack to ask our mother what she did during that time.

Her reply was, 'Oh, nothing really,' or 'I can't really remember.' Then feeling she should say something she said she worked as a clerk in an office at Bletchley Park – figure work and filing, nothing important.

It was the first time we heard of this place in the English countryside and Dad didn't know much about it either. But our innocent questions led to despair. Remembering the war for Mum opened a hornets' nest of forbidden stories – secret memories locked in her mind that she could not divulge to anyone – not her family, her parents, her husband or her children. They had to be hidden, self-erased.

* * *

Memory. Information compartmentalised and held in a brain, a 'filing' cabinet waiting to be recalled. Random notes coded for future use; mind mapping, a useful search and find tool, a universe, a constellation of snippets of information, life events, ideas, maybes and sometimes falsehoods. I can recall that time in clear detail. We had a new 1960s Ford Poplar car, Oxford Blue. Dad kept it in the garage at the end of our garden with his precious tools. It was reserved for Sunday visits to relatives or special excursions. Other days, including Saturday mornings, Dad cycled to his carpentry job home at Marcos the shopfitters in Rowan Road two miles from home. Mum couldn't drive so without Dad we walked everywhere or caught a bus.

Around that time Mum planned a fun weekend excursion to a zoo near Dunstable, north of London. This was unusual because we normally travelled south toward the sea, but this time there would be no sea, only countryside in the middle of England. Dad showed us the route on his map. The new adventure meant we'd drive through the middle of London, something we'd not done before, except partially on a bus. He also pointed to Bletchley, the town where Mum worked during the war, and Leighton Buzzard where we would stay overnight. Both were close to the zoo.

Mum bought durable black and white speckled covers before our trip to protect the new car seats. They stretched perfectly over the original grey hide but did little to prevent the overpowering smell of pristine leather. This, mingled with petrol fumes, was stifling. Dad always filled the tank which meant we breathed the pungency of petrol and car seats the whole journey. We often felt sick as we rolled around in the back; no seat belts or air conditioning then. Usually, our summer journeys were hot, with our blonde curls stuck to our sweaty faces, but not that day. It was cold and raining and the windows were firmly closed to keep us warm.

MEMORY

We were woken by Dad at four-thirty in the morning and left Mitcham soon after. It was exciting to visit the zoo with the funny name, Whips… something, but we were not looking forward to the long car ride. One of us was sure to start a chain reaction of throwing up. The night before we had loaded blankets and pillows to make the journey more comfortable. We also had our puzzle books, colouring pencils and Enid Blyton stories from the library. 'Are we there yet?' we moaned after what seemed an age. It had only been thirty minutes. The weather was miserable and there was talk of turning back, but we continued; Mum insisted, the B&B was already booked. The journey, south to north via central London, could take three hours back then, especially with one or two stops en route. Early-morning Mitcham was free from hustle and bustle and we saw, in the dark, familiar outlines of places seen only before from the top of a red double-decker bus. In Tooting the buildings seemed dreary with black terraced houses polluted by coal fires. Coal-dust resolutely stuck to everything.

We rarely drove at night, but main roads were well lit, some with gas lamps. At the Broadway the memory of a Salvation Army lady, by the Wesleyan Methodist Church, hall flashed through my mind; we used to give her a penny and she gave us a small flag or pink rose to pin to our lapel. In winter, we often had bright red poppies from the British Legion. All were there to help us remember the war, though we had no idea why that was necessary. Dad kept to the main road through Balham, but soon we crossed Clapham Common and drove by Battersea Park where we once visited the Easter Bunny. That day we had worn our Easter Sunday dresses and bonnets for the splendid Easter Parade but now the trip seemed sinister. Large, blocks of flats loomed in the darkness, their boundaries edged with low walls and narrow black metal fences. I later discovered these were re-used stretchers from the First World War.

We crossed the River Thames at Westminster Bridge. At dawn, twinkling streetlamps blended into grey daylight as we drove into central London. There we saw grander buildings and monuments only seen in newspapers and the cinema's Pathé News. Through the raindrops, Mum pointed to the Houses of Parliament and toward a place where she worked after the war, Great Smith Street. Soon we were in Trafalgar Square where we marvelled at statues of lions and Lord Nelson standing on top of his column, but it was the pigeons that fascinated us most. They flew around in droves, heading to the next out-stretched hand of dried lentils or breadcrumbs. We'd not seen so many birds before. 'Can we stop to feed them?' But Dad said there was no time and we pressed on. Soon the pigeons and our capital's grandeur were behind us. By 6.30 the rain and traffic increased and Dad continued to navigate the less-travelled territory of north London.

After an hour, and through London, we stopped in a lay-by next to a field to eat breakfast. Mum had made a picnic: orange squash for us, hot tea for them, cold egg-and-bacon sandwiches. But the rain poured and we remained inside the car to eat. After a toilet break in the bushes, when the rain was lighter, we set off again on our journey. It seemed endless, but eventually we arrived at Whipsnade Zoo, one of Britain's original Safari Parks. It was 9am.

* * *

Mum said it had become a refuge for Regent's Park zoo animals in 1940, after the Blitz. Celebrity giant pandas, Ming, Sung and Tang were evacuated there, but later returned to London to boost morale. She explained the Blitz was the war with Germany, enemy bombs, but we didn't want to listen. I remember feeling sad when she said a young giraffe had died. He was 3-years-old and had been literally frightened to death when bombs fell on Whipsnade. His name was Boxer. The bomb craters later became ponds.

As we drove through, Dad slowed so that we could take photos of misty animal shadows with our cameras. Lions, zebras, elephants and giraffes perhaps; the animals enjoyed their freedom in the green hills of the once-derelict Hall Farm on Dunstable Downs. We could hardly see a thing but remained hopeful our film might reveal something when developed. Mum had her new Kodak Instant and we had our two second-hand Box Brownie cameras. One used to be hers, the other was once Aunty Doris's, Dad's sister. Our photography experiment was abandoned when all we could see were grey murky forms through rain-speckled lenses. We all felt trapped inside the car but it was too dangerous to get out. Small animal movements in the shadows were of no consolation, though I still retain a misty memory of a tall mother giraffe encouraging her calf to stretch her long neck upward to chew leaves from a tree.

Chapter 36

Bletchley Park

The zoo visit was curtailed and we continued our journey through Bedfordshire to Leighton Buzzard. Mum map read and we detoured to Bletchley. She was a good map reader and wanted to see the place she worked during the war. Jill and I were curious too. Dad was not keen but went along with her plan. 'This is it,' she said as we reached a leafy area with a fence. The barbed wire boundary led to a pair of large gates secured with padlocks and chains. NO PUBLIC ADMITTANCE read the sign. It was Sunday and Bletchley Park was closed. Mum was disappointed, but we continued to drive and found a nearby pub for lunch. The rain had stopped but British law forbade children in public houses, so we sat outside the Eight Belles on damp wooden seats. Dad went inside to buy a beer and ginger beer for Mum and us. He also ordered a plate of ham and cheese sandwiches. Mum expected the usual pub offerings of stale slices turned up at the corners, but they were surprisingly tasty with fresh white buttered bread.

After lunch we continued to Leighton Buzzard and spent the afternoon looking in tiny shops and driving around, before taking up our lodgings at 4pm. From the car Mum pointed to the front of a terraced house in Queen Street, where she was billeted during the war. When asked about 'billets', she explained it was a place she slept when she worked at Bletchley Park. Her employer had arranged for her to stay in the house as she was far from home. The owners were a young couple, Muriel and Jack Gotzheim; she shared a room with Aunty Mary. She explained Aunty Milly, whose real name was Muriel, and Aunty Mary were her wartime friends. They often sent her letters, and birthday cards and presents for us, but they were the unrelated 'aunts' we never met.

The Gotzheims no longer lived on Queen Street, and our B&B was in a different area; Mum had booked half-board, to include dinner. We took our overnight bags upstairs to a room with one double bed and a sink.

She said we would all sleep in the same room, which seemed odd. Where were our beds? Dad was grumpy and tired from driving and wanted to rest, but Mum asked him to get the collapsible camp beds she'd packed from the car. He grudgingly retrieved them, set them up, told us to be quiet and fell asleep. Mum napped too. Puzzle books kept me and Jill busy. Dinner was at six.

The fire in the room helped dry our damp clothes while we waited to go downstairs for our meal. We liked the B&B lady. She said we could sound the dinner gong, but it seemed an age before the hands on the clock ticked closer to six. Eventually Mum woke and we had a quick wash. At five to six we sat with her on the bottom stairs, waiting for the lady's signal. At six o'clock sharp, she gave us permission to bash the huge copper gong with the heavy padded baton. The loud noise hurt our ears, but we were eager to take more than one turn. Dinner was served! Dad and the four other guests in the house appeared slightly shaken but laughed at our noisy antics; soon we were all at our tables in the dining room. The lady's daughter served roast lamb with mint sauce, roast potatoes, gravy and spring greens. Everything was tasty, but Dad grumbled.

He never complained about anything usually, but the gravy was cold and so he asked for hot gravy. Mum was embarrassed, Dad seemed cross, something was wrong, they were silent. The lady's daughter brought hot gravy. Throughout the meal, we kept our eyes averted in the silence until dessert – Libby's canned fruit and ice cream – a favourite. Dad noticed the rain had stopped and said we should go for a walk before bedtime. We went to the park, but not for long. Everything was wet, we couldn't use the slide or the swings. We all went to bed early.

After a good night's sleep, we ate a hearty English breakfast of eggs, bacon and beans, mushrooms, grilled tomatoes, toast with butter and marmalade, all washed down with cups of hot tea. Everyone seemed happier, but it started to rain again. By ten o'clock, we had packed our belongings while Mum and Dad argued. Mum insisted we go via Bletchley on the way home, even though it was the opposite direction. Dad's anger was brewing, he didn't want to go, he was fed up with Mum's wartime talk, the drive and the weather. He just wanted to get home. We hadn't heard them shout before.

But Mum retorted. She hadn't gone all that way to be disappointed, Bletchley Park was all she wanted to see. 'Can't we try just one more time? When am I likely to return?' Hearing the sense in her last question,

Dad gave in. She wanted to see, and for us to see, where she worked during the war. It was true: we couldn't travel that far and not try. We wanted her to be happy and were interested enough to see where she worked, though we weren't sure why. Dad just wanted to forget the war and couldn't understand why Bletchley Park was so important.

* * *

It was a typical rainy Monday morning. Dad had arranged to have the day off work. We left the B&B and after twenty minutes arrived back at Bletchley Park, peering once more through the steamed-up windows of our car. This time we stopped closer to the NO PUBLIC ADMITTANCE sign on the gates. It resembled the factory entrance near our home, with a barrier and a sentry box. To the right was a factory building with many windows and a flat roof. We could see a car park in the distance, trees and bushes. 'Well, this is it,' Dad said disparagingly. 'This is where your mother worked during the war.' He was being sarcastic.

'Where are the swings and slides?' Dad confirmed it wasn't a playground, 'It's called a park, but it's just offices, I think.' Mum, deep in thought, stared out of the window and announced that she couldn't see the mansion, whatever that meant, and stepped out of the car toward a man wearing a heavy rain-proof jacket and dark flat cap. Its blue and white chequered band meant he was a policeman. We knew because he looked like the policemen on TV's Z-Cars. He guarded the gates and the barrier. As she approached, the black and white wooden bar lifted to let an unmarked vehicle through. We watched as Mum continued toward the man. She wore her grey coat and carried a small beige umbrella to shelter from the rain. Black plastic galoshes covered her shoes. The barrier came down quickly as the policeman stopped her. After a couple of questions and shaking his head, he eventually pointed toward the main road. After they exchanged more words, she came back and banged on the car window, indicating to Dad to wind it down. She said she couldn't get in there but was going to try the back entrance. 'Okay,' he agreed with a sigh, indicating that we could park across the road in front of the station. 'Don't be long.' Dad rolled his eyes as slowly as he rolled up the window, and with his approval, she ran across the road and disappeared around the corner.

As we drove past the place where she vanished, I could just make out a hole in the bushes leading to a small pathway. It was surrounded by high barbed-wire fences, overgrown elm trees, brambles and vines. Raindrops dripped from the dark-green leaves, but she was nowhere in sight. It was as if she had fallen into a rabbit hole. Dad pulled into the station parking area. After reading the sign and peering at his watch, he announced, 'We can stay here for twenty minutes.' Then he closed his eyes, rested his head on the back of the seat and fell asleep. We tried to be quiet, but that didn't last long, our puzzle books were full.

Soon we asked, 'When's Mummy coming back?' The car was dreary and steamed up, despite air from a slight gap in the window. Dad didn't answer. We waited and eventually he looked at his watch again. Fifteen minutes had passed. We fidgeted most of the time, trying to sleep. 'Where is she?' Jill whined impatiently. Mum had been gone for so long that we both started to cry. It was nine-thirty. More minutes crept by and eventually we wound down the windows to clear the condensation. The rain stopped and the sun started to shine. Dad pointed to the gap in the fence. 'She should come through there.'

The small black pathway bending to the right, narrowed to the size of a pin prick. The tall fence and mass of trees and bushes still looked scary, a hole in the woods where goblins and large spiders lurked. She still hadn't returned, and we continued to whine. 'I don't think she'll ever get in,' Dad said, frustrated. 'This is high security. She must be mad,' he concluded as he pointed to another sign on the other side of the road: NO PUBLIC ADMITTANCE – HIGH SECURITY. Then he expressed another thought saying that if she did get in, perhaps they should keep her there! With that, our whines turned into uncontrollable sobbing. Longer, louder and harder; now we knew we'd never see her again.

Not long after, she re-appeared from the undergrowth and the fenced-in forest pathway. Her umbrella was closed. Dad questioned her as he looked at his watch. She'd been gone twenty-five minutes. 'I didn't know the password,' she whispered. She opened the car door and sat next to him. After a long pause she said, 'I can't remember.' Tears streamed down her face, and she bit her lip as she looked back at her puffy-faced, tear-stained children. At that point Dad's anger reached its tipping point. 'I've had it!' he said and jammed the car into first gear and sped out of the car park. He'd had enough of his crying family. The three-hour journey home was mostly silent. We were happy she was back, but she seemed disappointed. She had wanted to show us Bletchley Park but couldn't.

Chapter 37

Hospital

Jill and I pushed the weekend-washout to the back of our minds and concentrated on happier things, like playing with our dolls, puzzle books and games in the sunshine, but Mum's mind was left stirred and confused leading to serious deterioration in her mental well-being. Looking back, there were other times before that contributed to her moods. I remember sitting on her lap in the kitchen; Jill was there, too. She asked if we would like a baby brother. We said no, but a sister would be okay. We didn't like boys much; they were naughty. The boys next-door were proof and so were our younger boy cousins. We never knew the reason for her question until years later. Once on a wet Monday morning just after Dad had gone to work, Jill and I went with her to the Church of the Ascension. She wanted to see the vicar. It was November, Guy Fawkes night was imminent. She wore a long green plastic mac and a folding see-through rainhat tied tightly beneath her chin to protect her hair. We had pink Snow White umbrellas. Usually we continued past this church to the Baptist Sunday school, but today we went inside the gates to a quiet entrance porch. 'Stay here. I won't be long,' she murmured as she settled us on a wooden seat at the front door. 'You'll be OK.' She took off her rainhat and went inside.

The porch seat was cold and uncomfortable as we waited. I felt vulnerable, she had never left us alone like that before in a public place. Jill stood on the bench to try to read the notices on the board above. A firework display, a cup of tea, words that didn't make much sense, but we recognised Jesus, Mary, crosses and angels from Sunday School posters. After a while she reappeared wringing a damp handkerchief in her clammy hands, as she nervously took ours again. It seemed long to be left alone for a young child. She had been crying and I asked what was wrong. 'Nothing,' she replied sorrowfully, and gazed ahead in the direction of home. We continued our short and silent journey in the rain.

All seemed sad and drab, but we were glad to be home near a fire. Using old newspaper and smokeless coke from the coalscuttle, Mum rekindled the flames mindlessly with a long metal poker. As she prodded the embers she slipped deeper into thought. We asked what the vicar said, but our simple questions went unanswered.

When she lay on the sofa, tears ran down her face. We offered comfort but, feeling useless, Jill and I turned helplessly to each other, shrugged and made a beeline for the biscuit tin. Mum was too preoccupied to notice the treats were disappearing as we stood munching by the guarded fire. Steamy vapours from our clothes produced an aroma of burned woollen fibres, and the damp atmosphere created rivulets of condensation on the windows – perfect drawing boards for sad wet matchstick men, rabbits and other finger-doodles. Distracted we happily devoured the remaining contents of the tin, until Aunty Ciss arrived.

Another day, the house was cold because the fire in the dining room had not been lit. Mum asked us to keep warm with her by the oven. There was a strange smell in the kitchen, but we could at least be warm with her. She gave us pillows to put on the oven's open pull-down door. It was an uncomfortable way to sleep and the smell became stronger, but with Mum's arms around us we started to drift off. I dreamed about getting a new kitten. Suddenly, a green head-scarfed figure appeared in my dream. It was banging on the glass at the back door. The rapping was urgent as Mum didn't move to answer. But it wasn't a dream. Jill and I looked up, dazed as glass shattered, and Aunty Ciss's hand turned the key on the inside to quickly unlock the door. 'What's this smell of gas?!' she shouted as she turned off the oven taps. She grabbed our hands and pulled us out of the kitchen into the garden. She was shouting at Mum, as she gave us our coats that conveniently hung by the backdoor. It seemed an age before we could go back inside. The neighbours and the doctor came. Dad fixed the pane of glass in the kitchen door.

There was more angst when her younger brother and his family emigrated to Australia. Uncle Bill and Aunty Cath applied for a 'once-in-a-lifetime opportunity' promising a new start, job and warm weather in a growing country via a government assisted passage migration scheme. They were selected and with their four children, under six, set off on a two-year adventure – the minimum stay for a free passage home. They sold their furniture to family and friends, and their motorbike business in Tooting Junction to Bill's partner Les Cocks. Their top floor apartment at 109 Kenlor Road, which they now owned, was rented to other family members. For their leaving party our seamstress 'Nanny', Emma Moore, made us cute blue twist dresses with patterned aqua blue Bushbaby fabric, edged with strips of brown fur from one of Mum's coats. The party, on 13 September 1961 was full of jokes, speeches, games and laughter, and someone played the piano. The next day, when it was time to bid farewell, a large hired coach transported everyone to Tilbury. Mum worried and cried for those two days. Bitter-sweet moments. Between the tears and smiles we sang 'Waltzing Matilda' and sombre Roy Orbison or Elvis songs – favourites of Aunty Cath and her best friend Jean Fennel – and waved our Union Jacks alongside the Australian flag.

On the dockside at Tilbury, flags and handkerchiefs fluttered as the young Lawrences boarded SS *Orion*. We watched and waited until we could just see them in the crowd waving back from the highest deck of the cruise ship. Our lavender-coloured duster coats that Mum made, flapped in the cool September breeze, as the ship's horn bellowed its signal for departure. The deafening noise filled our ears, which we quickly covered with our hands, and in the eerie peripheral silence we held our collective breaths to capture the intensity of a life-changing moment.

Bon Voyage. The massive vessel, free from its gigantic rope tethers, engaged its engines and thrust away from the dock. It seemed over-crowded and precarious with hundreds of families and children. Somebody said many on board were orphans, leaving for a better life. We continued to wave toward the top decks looking for the place where we thought we could still see them – Uncle Bill and Aunty Cath, Gary, Ian, Jayne and Lee – four small children dressed in white sailor suits, waving flags and shouting goodbye. Mum believed they would all drown. We didn't know why she thought their boat would sink. Dad said Mum was just being silly. 'Something about the war.' The voyage took several weeks. Letters were written to describe their many days at sea and Mum showed us every port of call in our brown leather-bound atlas – a recent jumble sale acquisition. Portugal, Spain, Africa; after North Africa they sailed through the Suez Canal to Aden and the Maldives.

Their journey was interesting but arduous; they could rarely leave the ship and the worst was yet to come – the Indian Ocean. The vast expanse of water with no sight of land for many days, made Aunty Cath seasick and homesick; the children were sunburned and bored. It was unsettling and challenging. Only in Fremantle, Western Australia, could they disembark, refresh their sundrenched bodies and recharge their enthusiasm for the final voyage to Adelaide, South Australia. Mum said Aunty Cath would be on the first plane home if she could afford the fare.

* * *

We were seven during this family event; conversation between adults was of little else. Mum worried about her brother and his family's safety, but other family, friends and neighbours thought she was crazy talking about ships being bombed, as if the country was still at war. They couldn't understand why she was so upset. Neither could we. Sixteen years had passed since the end of war, but why was she so concerned? The crying and hopelessness worsened. Adults assured her they would be safe and attributed her strange outbursts to increasing psychological problems and an inability to cope. But when family, friends and neighbourly visits became daily, we realised a serious situation was evolving. It was probably the first time we heard she was seriously unwell. Dad said she couldn't be left alone for long periods of time. We tried to help, but not long after she was sent away.

* * *

We didn't know where exactly and weren't allowed to see her. Dad said she was in hospital. He had become increasingly more irritated and couldn't deal with her worrying and crying all the time. He said her stories about the war were hallucinations and couldn't possibly have happened. 'How would she know? She was just a filing clerk!' She was 'away' for nearly three months and we later discovered she was in Tooting Sanatorium. Dad had reluctantly signed the papers for her to be committed to the mental institution, a course of action recommended by our local physician, Dr Silver.

Mum's ability to cope with anything, including us, had gone. Even watching black and white films on TV made her worry. Dad had to console her and explain that what happened in a fictional thriller wasn't her fault. They said she would be 'away' for a while, until she was better. She was in hospital 'because of her headaches'. We were young and what caused these was not our concern. Dad said she worried too much. We didn't know she was plagued by a constant state of unease; near-suicidal thoughts caused by inexplicable worry and immense grief for a lost past; memories she was not permitted to recall, memories that would linger in the future. Her life was a burden. She was committed for her own safety, and ours.

* * *

As time passed Dad continued to work; we cried when he left. Relatives and neighbours came but it was Aunty Ciss who was there most of the time, cooking, cleaning and helping him with laundry. We were used to Mum's sister coming to take care of us – it had happened before when Mum needed a gallstone operation. That time, when we were four or five, Dad said she had gone to hospital for 'Anaesthetic', a big word for us then. He explained it would be injected into her body with a needle to make her sleep, and the doctors were going to cut her open with knife to remove a stone! It sounded frightening but our toy doctors' and nurses' kits helped explain the suturing process. After three or four days, we were allowed to visit her in St James' hospital, Balham. I was scared to visit, but happy to see her sitting up in bed in her pink robe. The operation was successful and a week later she came home.

Now she was in another kind of hospital for special treatment and headache medicine. We later learned this was her third time away not the second. The first time was when we were nine months old, when we stayed with Auntie Molly and Uncle Frank for three months. The large black and white photo of us as babies was taken at their house.

* * *

Aunty Ciss indirectly blamed us for our mother's condition. It seemed everyone was on a short tether during that time and all had to do the best they could. During one of her stays she tried to teach us how to knit. We did well to a point, lined up on dining chairs facing 'the teacher', but Jill was frustrated with purl one, plain one, wool and knitting needles, and quickly revealed a raging temper. The episode resulted in many woollen tangles which resembled the knots in our hair – another problem for Aunty Ciss to tackle, once with scissors – Jill and I began to throw the needles at each other like javelins. With tears cascading down our cheeks we fought, and hair was pulled out in handfuls. The stress of missing our mother and the stark discipline of sitting in line at home was not a good experience for us. 'No wonder your mother is in a mental hospital!' shouted Aunty Ciss. 'You two are enough to drive anyone mad!' Shocked by her loud words and the sudden silence we wondered what she meant. We didn't understand but calmed down quickly by crying silently together into the sofa cushions. Neither of us were used to this strange outburst from our usually quiet aunt.

Dad said Mum would be in hospital for several weeks that autumn. Most mornings our neighbours, Mrs Mawby, Mrs Cooper and Mrs Hudspith, kept us in their homes when Dad left for work, until schooltime. Sherwood Park Primary was only a five-minute walk and a welcome distraction from missing Mum. The Headmistress, Miss Horsburgh, was informed of the family situation and our teachers seemed to be kinder.

When we arrived at school, we hung our coats on designated coat racks outside the classroom; our gym kits were stored in bright blue, newly painted, cubby baskets underneath. Everything in our brick-built modern school was constructed after the war. Only two nursery classes remained in the original wooden huts, Red Class and Purple Class, where a strange aroma of heated oil and wax crayons emanated from paraffin heaters. Each morning we had to drink government-supplied milk. Nobody could decline except for medical reasons. The free nourishment came in small one-third pint milk bottles with silver aluminium caps. We had to be careful not to slice our fingers on the sharp foils – blood in milk did not taste nice. As we supped through waxed paper straws, all was quiet for a while. But some boys didn't follow form, preferring to gulp straight from the bottle, though they had to be extra careful not to cut their lips. Pulsating, bleeding lips were worse than cut fingers. As we all tried to avoid accidents and spilt milk our Green Class teacher, Miss Glasscock prepared us for pre-lesson morning assembly. She was plump with spectacles which made her look old. Her grey hair and hand-knitted cardigans with pockets either side did nothing to put her into the higher realms of fashion. We lined up in alphabetical order and marched a short distance to the gym-cum-assembly hall.

We hated Assembly and wanted to be like the Shapiros, the Jewish brothers who could miss the daily Christian ceremony. Cross-legged on the floor, we sat and listened to the headmistress for what seemed like hours. Respite from boredom only came when we stood to sing hymns. Like Miss Glasscock, our headmistress, Jessie Horsburgh was short and rotund, but with grey hair protruding from her round ruddy face. The hair on her head was also grey which she tied in a tight bun. Her large silky dresses were belted at the waist, resembling smoky blue parachutes. Sometimes a draught from an open window caught her skirts, as we stifled our laughter, she struggled to maintain her dignity to not reveal her silky cream underwear. She wore sensible brown shoes or sandals we called 'Jesus sandals'. For a small woman, she had a booming voice and must have been super intelligent to hold such an important teaching position. Miss Horsburgh later received an MBE from the Queen. Sherwood Park was one of the first primary schools in the country to use her all-inclusive modern teaching methods, which we later discovered were something of an experiment.

After prayers the slightly slimmer figure of Assistant Head, Miss Buttress, played the piano. Often the hymn was 'For those in Peril on the Sea', a dirge which made our sad situation even sadder. On other days, she enthusiastically played the cheerful version of 'Oh Thank We All, Our God…with hearts and hands and voices'. The rousing tune was invigorating, and on those occasions, we left happy and ready to take on the day; the words of composer Martin Rinkart still ringing in our ears.

PE was a time when we could burn off excess energy, and during break we huddled with friends to play games and eat our snacks. Dinner money of 1/6d was paid each week for ghastly lunches, but Dad or Aunty Ciss made corned beef or cheese and pickle sandwiches for playtime. The white bread snack was always accompanied by a packet of Smith's Crisps, the type served with salt wrapped separately in a tiny twist of blue waxed paper, and an apple usually saw us to the end of afternoon playtime. Some lessons were interesting and informative. I liked stories and clearly remember the first time a student teacher read *The Hobbit*, mainly because her short black and green tartan skirt over thick black tights was so shocking. As other teachers, Mum's and Aunty Ciss's skirts were always calf length. Classroom story time was always great, but by late afternoon when the sun shone unrelentingly through the enormous windows, most pupils had dozed off.

* * *

Weeks passed. Adults said Mum was improving and would be home for Christmas. We were excited to see her. She spent most days in her pink dressing gown, but we were permitted to comb her thin hair. There was little left of her long blonde curls; they said the medicine she took caused her hair to thin. During those few days, she seemed constantly distracted, her mind in a different world. She wept often. Aunty Ciss helped her dress in her new brown suit and peach sweater for Christmas Day. Dad bought her the clothes as a present. The new outfit matched her demeanour, sombre with just a hint of a bright smile when we tried to make her laugh. I gave her a gold-coloured brooch with a huge green stone, bought from the post office store with my pocket money. Mum pinned it to the collar of her new suit, but two days later Dad drove her back to hospital.

Chapter 38

Mental Health

Mum was gone for several months and returned home in March 1962. Dad helped her assimilation and aided with the necessary medications. Gradually, things returned to normal, as she began to assist us again with schoolwork and started to exercise. 'Down with a bounce; with a bounce come up.' Eileen Fowler became her favourite instructor with her no-nonsense routine. The BBC's fitness guru appeared on TV every morning at 6.45. A year later, Mum's recovery seemed complete. She worked for a while in the school dinners kitchen and then applied to be a bookkeeper at Smiths, an automated clock manufacturer – numbers, calculations, dials, switches and codes. She enjoyed figures and was hired.

But after a week she left. Dad eventually explained Mum had to leave because of her headaches, and because everyone in the office wanted to know more about her work during the war. At the time we didn't know about the confidential Foreign Office reference letter – the one she showed to her new employer, the one that was hidden, the one that was, just once, brought out of obscurity only to become headline news in Smith's finance department. Her confidentiality shattered and mind in tatters, she couldn't fully explain to Dad either. Everyone wanted to know: what was the 'Work of a Secret nature; Work of National Importance? All she wanted was to hide, find a safe place, where no one would ask questions. It seemed that everyone wanted her to explain her wartime past. She couldn't lie but she couldn't tell. The only solution was to resign – a nervous wreck. The letter was never referred to again. Her signed acceptance of the Official Secrets Act's rules meant her precious references were useless for any position beyond the Foreign Office.

Mary Hudspith, our neighbour, worked in the MD's office of Mitcham Maid, the margarine factory opposite – often referred to as the Creameries – and through her Mum was hired there for a while. She didn't like packing cheese triangles, but it was all she felt she could manage, nobody questioned her about the war. All was fine for a while and Dad even entertained the idea of emigrating to Australia. He showed us the forms, but Jill and I loathed the idea and so we didn't go. In any case, Uncle Bill and his family were on their way home on the SS *Orsova* by September 1963. Then Nanny, Dad's mother died. Emma Moore had moved to live with Dad's sister, Doris and her husband Vic Hicks, in the Channel Islands, where they owned a small private hotel. Uncle Frank and Aunty Molly had followed in the late fifties as part of Jersey's continued repatriation after five years of German occupation. We were lucky enough to spend our summers there and life was grand. We were in awe of the rich side of our family, especially when they returned to England in the winter months bringing huge tins of Quality Street and other duty-free gifts for Mum and Dad: cigarettes, liquor, jewellery, Nivea and Tampax.

Dad heard the news of his mother's death from Uncle Frank via Mr Cooper's telephone; we didn't own one then. That evening when he came back from our neighbour's house, he rested his head on the front door latch and sobbed. It was the only time I saw him cry – Armistice Day, 11 November 1963, eleven days before President Kennedy's assassination in America. We knew all about sadness and death at that point. Aunty Ciss stayed while he went to the funeral in Jersey. We were nine. Soon after Mum was struggling again; the news of Nanny's death and Kennedy's assassination seriously affected her. I asked Dad what was really wrong with Mum? The headache answer was wearing thin by now. 'Silly war stuff,' he said. 'She believes she's killed people.' The shock on our faces prompted him to continue: 'Of course she didn't, she was nowhere near the war.'

Mum appeared permanently sad. Her pained puffy eyes and pasty pallor indicated her mood and she seemed incapable of speaking or caring for herself. Her hands shook often as she wandered around aimlessly swathed in her own thoughts. We trod carefully around her. 'Don't upset your mother,' Dad uttered regularly, especially before he left for work. He was the one who made sure we were awake, had our cereal and milk, and that we were ready for school with our books and snacks. We behaved as best we could. There were days when we tried to make her happy by copying down words of meaningful songs she wanted to remember. Every word of 'I Believe', by The Bachelors had to be correct. Wrapped in her world with our loving arms around her, we often stood together as she silently wept by the gas cooker recalling distant memories that made her cry. Until the day she decided to return to hospital.

***

The following Monday, as Dad left for work, she shouted for him through the closed bedroom window as if he could hear her. 'Stan, Stan, come back, ...please come back.' Her voice was cracked and weak, but loud enough for us to hear from our rooms. We ran to find out why she was calling him.

It was a foggy, wet morning. 'He's leaving.' Her sobbing was uncontrollable, as she stood, steadying herself by the side of the white wicker chair in the bay window. Our parents' room was at the front of the house and faced the long lane leading to the tree-lined road of Mitcham Common. The main road often seemed far, across the large expanse of wild grass, and in the early morning mist we could just see the outline of the tall brick chimney and old workhouse wall by the margarine factory. As Dad walked up the lane toward the iron gates, a barrier lifted to allow a milk lorry through. Mum continued to call him. It was 7am and usual for Dad to walk the 200 yards along our muddy lane to meet his work friend, Wally Hammerston. Both had left Marcos and now worked for Jacksons, a shop-fitting firm in Tonbridge; their commute was an hour. Every day, the white company twelve-seater van arrived at the top of the lane in front of the factory gates. In the grey mist we could see Dad in his heavy grey overcoat and greeny-grey worsted cap carrying his lunch and tool bag along the track. His black Wellingtons splashed in the puddles, his head bent. Was he upset too, or just sheltering from the rain? Had they argued? We didn't know what was happening, but we knew he had to go to work. We pulled her back from the window, with assurances that everything would be okay.

Wally's punctual white van arrived and Dad climbed into the passenger seat. Then it pulled away and he was gone. He would return for dinner at six. We made her go back to bed and made more tea. She managed to finally compose herself as she sipped Co-op tea from a white china cup that rattled as she set it on the matching saucer; she now accepted he had gone for the day. 'Don't worry, I'm okay, Aunty Ciss will arrive soon.' She was sorry we had seen her so upset, and acknowledged we had to get ready for school.

Within moments, we heard Aunty Ciss opening the backdoor, downstairs. She had her own key. How she always knew when to come at a crisis point, we will never know. She didn't have a telephone either. She was perhaps clairvoyant, but probably an arrangement had been made with Dad over the weekend. Perhaps Mum's turbulence was because she knew she wouldn't see him for a while. As we left for school, Mum said she had a doctor's appointment and might need to go to hospital for a test, but not to worry Aunty Ciss was going with her and she would be at home for us after school. We were used to her doctor's visits. It was 8.15am. We collected our satchels and left.

* * *

Mum wanted to go to West Park Hospital, Epsom, which was the reason she wasn't home after school. We knew little of the psychological attention she needed, but adults said she needed to be there because she suffered with her nerves, a general feeling of helplessness and inability to cope, a 'nervous breakdown'. It was a term we heard often. Dr Silver had arranged the necessary papers. In medical jargon this translated to Neurasthenia which originally meant a mechanical weakening of the actual nerves. Neurasthenia was the psychopathological term used to denote the metaphorical idea of 'nerves', such as symptoms of fatigue, anxiety, headache, heart palpitations, high blood pressure, neuralgia and emotional disturbance creating a depressed mood. The term appears in the World Health Organization's International Classification of Diseases; another term was 'nervosism'.

The nineteenth and twentieth century condition was explained as exhaustion to the central nervous system and its energy reserves, the cause of which was 'modern life'; stress of urbanisation and business. Typically, it was associated with the upper classes, particularly those in sedentary lifestyles or occupations. A variety of physical symptoms were highlighted by Freud, including dyspepsia with flatulence, indications of cranial pressure and spinal irritation which, as well as lack of movement, he believed was due to infrequency of emissions or to non-completed coitus. Cultural pressure confusion was also to blame. In short, bodily functions and sexual desires should not be inhibited for long periods, nor should surrender to impossible social and educational pressures be desirable or advisable. Neurasthenia was also a common analysis for 'shell shock' during the First World War.

Once diagnosed the solution was rest, particularly for women; though men were often prone to dizziness and fainting more than commonly thought. The 'modern life' disease became an epidemic and drug companies capitalised on their medicinal elixirs claiming to be soothers for bouts of neurasthenia. In Japan therapy for neurasthenia involved mandatory rest and isolation, followed by increasingly difficult work and a return to an important role in society. Alternative experimental treatments such as Electro-convulsion Treatment (ECT) were controversial. Freud declared it a 'pretence treatment', while some considered it a cure for their suicidal thoughts.[1]

But this diagnosis is sometimes used as a smoke screen for more serious mental illnesses such as schizophrenia and mood disorders. The term 'neurasthenia' was abandoned in the twenty-first century, as it is seen more as a behavioural condition than physical. The World Health Organization (WHO) now classifies this under 'other neurotic disorders'. The modern thought on neurasthenia is that it is actually 'dysautonomia', an imbalance of the autonomic nervous system. Today for people dealing with the trauma of war, we talk of Combat Stress Reaction (CSR) and Post Traumatic Stress Disorder (PTSD), two different reactions to often dangerous and upsetting conditions.[2]

With PTSD, mum needed drugs, ECT and occupational therapy.

Chapter 39

Believe

Each day Aunty Ciss was there to feed us after school and prepare Dad's dinner. He seemed worried most nights and smoked more cigarettes than he should. We tried to make him happy with knock-knock jokes, our schoolwork and made sure we were on our best behaviour. One evening he said we could visit Mum. Dad and Aunty Ciss had visited her in the special hospital several times, but it was our cousin Pam, Mum's niece, who accompanied us. Pam was 30 and heavily pregnant, but the journey was easy, just two buses; the 118 for five minutes, then the 93 from Mitcham Fair Green to Epsom. We stopped by the sweetshop on the way and chose Opal Fruits for our treat. The 93 buses were infrequent, which meant we waited a long while at the bus stop. The route also had many stops and took more than an hour, but we had more puzzle books for the journey. Our Opal Fruits, however, did not last long.

We alighted just outside Epsom village and followed the bus driver's directions along a narrow pathway between two fields. It was raining slightly. Eventually we reached an old double-fronted Edwardian house. It didn't look like a hospital; we questioned but Pam thought we were in the right place – West Park.[1] It had an eerie feel and seemed different from hospitals we'd visited before. This was a big residence with unusually quiet surroundings. In the shadow of the doorway we felt cold and damp and stood looking at the large dark green front doors. Pam was uncertain too, but after a few seconds, she pushed one side and the door creaked open. As we stepped into a yellowing cavernous hallway a single bell tinkled far away.

The grand foyer had a large winding staircase and a round oak table in the centre. Before too long a figure in an old-fashioned nurses' uniform appeared in a distant corridor. Her dark blue calf-length dress was tapered in the middle with a wide black elastic belt around her waist. Her skirt swayed as she padded softly toward us. But her most striking feature was the white pointed hat she wore, reminiscent of a Dutch milkmaid.

She was not wearing clogs, but sensible flat brown lace-ups. Mum would have approved, she always made us wear shoes like that. This is Matron whispered Pam. The large Dutch-looking lady had a sharp nose and appeared angry when she asked if she could help. Pam explained we were there to see Mrs Moore. 'These are her daughters… and I'm her niece.'

Apparently, we were a day late. The sudden expectation of not seeing Mum was quite upsetting but Pam asked if it was still okay to visit. Matron breathed in deeply and looked as if she would suddenly take off, like a fairy in Sleeping Beauty. Was she a good fairy or bad? Evil? She looked at our inquiring faces and motioned for us to follow. We walked toward the staircase but instead of going up we went behind into a long, narrow corridor with more yellow stained walls. The passageway seemed endless. On either side multiple brown doors remained closed, except for one. It was a parallel perspective I later observed in an ochre painting of Salvador Dali. Everything seemed surreal, almost down to the distortion and the dripping clock. Gesturing to the open door on the right, she motioned for us to enter the small room. The door closed abruptly behind us as we started to hear screams from further down the corridor.

Matron told us to wait. 'I'll be back soon. Are you ready to see your mother?' She asked jovially. Jill and I nodded yes. However, in the uncertainty, we were not sure whether to be happy or cry. She left and firmly closed the door behind her, but not before we heard more screams in the corridor. 'Who is that?' we asked. Pam replied that it was nothing, adding her usual nervous giggle. She probably felt unqualified to explain the habits of mental asylum patients to a couple of 9-year-old girls. She sat down, clearly hot and uncomfortable from the weight of her baby. It was a cool autumn day, and she wore her red fuzzy long mohair coat, sixties fashion. Jill and I were hot too. The room had a single table with two wooden chairs, utility supply. Uncomfortably, Jill and I shared a chair. The heat was unbearable and we all removed our coats, while a light pendant hung from the middle of the stained ceiling; its dingy bulb barely illuminated the walls. The windows had shutters with no obvious sign of natural light. I imagined we were in a prison cell, like those on TV. Weird shadows appeared as we moved around, but Pam tried to lighten the atmosphere by making rabbit silhouettes with her hands. We laughed and joined in, glad for the playful distraction – though at nine we thought we were too old for such folly and wondered why we couldn't just go to Mum's hospital bed.

We had both spent a few days in hospital after our tonsils were removed and visited Mum after her gallstone operation years before. Back then she shared a ward with other patients, and we sat on her bed. This was our expectation. Why did this feel strange? Breaking the awkward silence, Pam tried to explain that Mum was there because she needed more special treatment and medicine to help her forget. We didn't understand why there were no other people in the room or why she needed to forget. Pam didn't answer our questions. Instead a chill filled the room in the uneasy atmosphere and Pam repositioned herself on the chair while feigning a pronounced shiver. Then, as she rubbed her hands together the door opened, and the silhouette of Mum stood in the doorway. She looked different.

As a 9-year old child, I couldn't adequately explain then the immense rush of emotion. It was something far more than I'd ever experienced; feelings of love bottled up in a vacuum – a popping cork. Looking back, it was overwhelming for all of us. Jill and I ran to hug her. She bent to kiss our heads and wrapped her arms around our small bodies. Pam watched, clutching her handkerchief; everyone cried. Even the stern matron had tears in her eyes. We hadn't seen Mum for a long time. Her blonde hair was now almost gone and any wisps that remained were thin. 'Don't cry,' she said, gently wiping our eyes with her handkerchief. 'It will soon grow back. It's just the special medicine.' She seemed thinner but wore the same brown suit and peach sweater as the day we saw her crying in the kitchen. The greenstone brooch was still pinned to her collar. We still didn't really understand why she was there. We heard the front doorbell ring and Matron left saying she would soon return. We were glad to be alone without the stranger and pleased Mum was able to see us; we talked about our schoolwork and answered her questions. 'Who's looking after you? Are you being good? What are you learning at school?'

Our main question was when would she be home? She said her occupational therapy was helping and she had made nice things in her pottery and basket-weaving classes – mosaic plates with tiny pieces of coloured tile, and woven tea trays mostly. 'I'll bring them when I come home.' She didn't reply to our questions about when that would be or why she was ill, but said it was not our fault. Looking to Pam for further answers, the conversation turned instead to her baby. Mum was happy for Pam and her husband Alec; they thought they were having a boy.

But then Mum's gentle demeanour abruptly changed as her mind seemed to wander and she started to whisper in a deep voice about losing a lot of blood in hospital; with tears in her eyes she seemed upset and frightened.

Pam stood aghast just as Matron re-entered the room in time to hear Mum's deep and worried far-off tone. We didn't understand what she meant, but clearly Pam did. Suddenly it was time for Mum to leave and with some force, Matron started to pull her out of the room. We were told to quickly say goodbye. 'But when are you coming home?' 'Soon,' she said. But we didn't believe her. She had been gone far too long. We hugged her waist, not wanting to let go; we'd had only five minutes with her and now she was being torn away. Matron and Pam shared their physical strength to detach us from her body. And so, we released her and tearfully waved goodbye as she was led along the yellowing corridor by other nurses to a remote room. She didn't turn to wave. The door closed. Numb, the large hall now seemed even more cavernous. We put on our coats.

Rays of late afternoon sunshine bathed our faces as we stepped through West Park's double doors, out of the oppressive atmosphere into fresh air. Pam wiped our eyes, 'Don't worry she'll be home soon. Now, if we hurry, we'll catch the next bus, instead of waiting another hour.' Finding our feet and breathing freely again, we ran. Towering beech trees lined the narrow path between the fields and, sure enough, we could just

West Park Mental Hospital, Epsom, Surrey. (Wellcome Collection)

see the red single-decker bus arriving. Pam struggled with her additional baby weight and bulky red coat, but we grabbed her hands and made her run. Pulling her along, we just caught the bus in time.

* * *

The days passed slowly, but within a few weeks Mum returned. She seemed happy and healthier and Dad was glad to return to normal. Then early one Sunday the doorbell rang. I ran downstairs to unbolt the front door. It was Aunty Ciss. She had been crying. Mum came down in her nightdress to see why she was there at 7am on a Sunday. Soon she was crying too. Two months after visiting Mum in West Park, Pam's baby had been stillborn. I remember thinking it was our fault for making her run. But what did a 9-year-old know of pregnancy risks and miscarriages then? Baby Andrea was buried a few days later and Mum referred to the words written in the front of the birthday book Pam had given her earlier; the words to The Bachelor's song meaningfully underlined. Did she believe or was her hopefulness in ruins again? *'Everytime I hear a newborn baby cry or touch (a leaf), or see the sky, then I know why I believe.'*

Chapter 40

Recovery

During one of her 'moments' – a nervous breakdown – it was often Mum's friends, Aunty Dot and Aunty Peggy, who came to talk with her. Generally, she was uplifted by their visits. As time evolved, we discovered these local friends had also worked at Bletchley Park during the war. A problem shared was a problem halved; they understood. She was unable to speak of this past era with others and therefore reluctant to expand her friend or work base. Lies within lies, she just wasn't good at lying. Did she worry about conversations with others before her first breakdown in 1955? Before she married in 1946? Before leaving the India and Commonwealth Offices in 1948? Churchill died on 24 January 1965, nearly twenty years after the war; Mum was indelibly depressed. What was this attachment? We were 10 years old then.

There were interludes of happiness: day excursions to the beach and longer vacations to Jersey, or simple occasions involving rounders or badminton. Sometimes we played in a field on Box Hill, a grassy patch at Frensham Ponds, or after a picnic in Morden Park where we often met Aunty Dot and Uncle Albert with their children, John and Sally. In summer, when the grass in front of our house was newly mown, we flattened the straggly patches to play there. Mum kept her rounders bat in the garden shed. It was one of her wartime mementos from Bletchley, along with the old black bicycle she accepted when Bletchley Park closed in October 1945. She rode it for many years.

As we finished junior school and entered secondary education in 1965, we still didn't know why Mum worried about everything, or what she needed to forget. To some extent we ignored her predicament; we only knew we should not make her worry, and that the pills and treatment she received in hospital stopped her headaches. Dad said she was unable to cope. But what or who was she unable to cope with?

* * *

Following her second breakdown, third if you count the one when we were babies, we all somehow coped with our family needs. During that time we went to Wimbledon Theatre with Aunty Dot and her children, to see somebody perform as Widow Twanky in Aladdin. We were 12 by then, too old for pantomimes, but it was a significant event for the adults, as one of the actors was with them at Bletchley Park. Jill and I both did well at secondary school, though not Rowan Girls as Mum had in mind. Instead we insisted we attend Pollards Hill, the modern co-ed institution. Looking back this was a low point for her, as she believed the all-girl's school superior in education. She might have been right, but she was accurate about one thing – boys were a distraction! During the late sixties there was more freedom in almost anything, especially liberation for women. Our parents, however, enforced the usual parental restrictions for young girls and arguments often ensued: hormonal moods, curfew, boyfriends, clothes, make-up and money!

Throughout that time, they kept us on track for our education within their means; but it was Mum who worried most. Dad only worried about Mum worrying all the time. She was happy we were on a business studies course, where we learned how to write in code with Pitman's Shorthand, how to type fast, accounting, balance sheets, profit and loss statements. We learned market research and marketing, as well as the usual cooking, needlework and geography (though no mathematics or history). We were both quite sporty and Jill was particularly good at art. We learned new technology, faster versions of punched card systems and electric typewriters! Computers, as we now know them, hadn't been invented...or so we thought. Perhaps Mum knew different.

Our weekend jobs provided additional pocket money. I helped Uncle Bill and Aunty Cath on Sundays in their new sweet shop – Lawrence's Corner, in Tooting – and Jill worked Saturdays at a hairdresser on Mitcham Lane, close to Pam's. She and Alec had a new baby boy by then and I sometimes babysat Neil. Mum made us stay at school and not leave too early, as she had done to earn money for her family decades before. Some of our friends' families, however, needed their offspring to leave at 15; a tempting notion as they earned 'real' money. But Mum put her foot well and truly down to ensure we completed the extra year to avoid shopwork and filing.

At 16, after passing all our exams with flying colours, Mum encouraged us to apply to the Halifax Building Society in Wallington a few miles away. The savings bank had an automated punched card system. She considered this the way forward, but we couldn't see why we should spend our precious time with huge machines and coded cards locally, when the bright lights of London offered well-paid office work. If only she could have explained exactly what she did during the war. Instead, Pam was our role model. Before her pregnancies she worked in London as a successful PA and this was our aim. There was no talk of attending university back then. If only Mum could have said more about her Foreign Office work and her Bletchley 'university', a crucial time in her life with a panorama of enlightenment. Instead she was prohibited from describing her war work, a constraint which affected her in many ways – her health, her future and ours.

* * *

Dad encouraged us to drive as soon as possible. That was his thing. We both had good employment and saved enough money to each buy a car by the time we were 17. Mum appeared to be well and held a good clerical job. After the margarine factory and recovery from her 1964 breakdown, Aunty Ciss found her a position at the company where she worked: Freeman's Mail Order Catalogue, 'filing', she said. Her hair had recovered, and friends and family commented on how well she looked. She was happy for the most part, but when David Kahn's book was published, with little or no mention of Bletchley Park, she felt the steel barrier to her secret was in danger and again began to worry. A fourth nervous breakdown took her back to West Park. We were 17, asking adult questions and expecting adult answers.

'What is wrong with Mum?' We didn't know about the book. We only knew we weren't supposed to make her worry. It seemed the slightest thing would push her off the edge into a harried world of hopelessness; though not suicidal this time. She just seemed to need attention. If she wanted to tell us anything it wasn't obvious; but now, looking back, if only we'd known which questions to ask. Would that have helped? Dad started to answer with comments like 'things in the past'. In other words, don't ask. Did he know? I wondered why she always went to West Park and not Banstead – the other local psychiatric hospital was closer. 'It's best for her there, and that's where she wants to go.' But as a young adult he also felt I deserved more information. 'She needs to talk to somebody about her war work, and that's where she feels safe.' He didn't know why, but she thought someone was coming to arrest her, or a spy was going to kill her, all because she might have said or done something.

'She also thought she'd killed people during the war.' As he recounted her predicament, his voice reached a high pitch. 'Sounds crazy, right?'

Angrily, he went on to give his own views, saying, 'She gets caught up in all that silly stuff. She wasn't even 'in' the war!' His burning words went on to provide a poignant account of his own wretched incarceration. 'She never got her hands dirty, saw blood and guts, dead people and beheaded soldiers.' He choked back his emotions to wipe his eyes and blow his nose. 'Those Japanese bastards, they slaughtered my friends and fellow PoWs.' He stopped to swallow, unable to resume. His eyes were tearful and red. The experience he was reliving was too painful. It was 1970 and the truth of war and Japanese atrocities was beginning to be revealed. Only those in secret places knew more, they had known for years. Did Mum know this too?

The Sook-Ching Massacre in 1942 was a mile from his Singapore prison at India Lines, Changi. The disturbing details were indeed horrific. Guards under Japanese command had slaughtered more than 70,000 Malay-Chinese on the beach. They were dissenters of Imperial Japanese reforms, and were marched at gunpoint to the sea, where they were blindfolded and bound, pushed into the water and systematically executed. Wading and waiting in knee-high water for the guns to fire, the injured were left to drown. If they tried to leave they were shot again; men and women, some just children. Their bodies washed out to sea or back to the beach depending on the tides and the weather. The eeriness of the barbaric massacre still lingers on Changi Beach – ghosts of despair, their spirits still crawl across your skin as you walk across the sand to the sea. 'No, she never did anything in the war; I don't see what she is worried about,' Dad concluded in frustration.

* * *

In West Park, Mum underwent further electro-convulsion treatment and doctors experimented with new calming medication to help her cope and forget. Did the mental hospital have first-hand knowledge of what was in her mind? Was West Park the selected place for military people suffering from CSR or PTSD? Was this part of the cure? Was she really a threat to national security? If in America they had the Bureau of Medicine for military veterans, did Britain have a similar department? The Defence Health Agency? Did Trevor Silver, our family doctor, know her full story? He was often the first person she turned to. What was the specific secret she kept?

Chapter 41

The Seventies

Still we were told Mum just worried about everything and needed to forget. Again, her blonde hair thinned noticeably, along with memories of the past – her own life, her relationship with her husband and children – erased or at the very least masked. All was calm for a while. The treatment was mostly effective and Dad had kept Mum stable on a cocktail of prescribed drugs, carefully administered to the best lowest dose to prevent her from completely flipping until the spring of 1974, when further cracks in the wall of Second World War secrets began to appear.

It was a significant and credible source, that was not just a scant comment from my mother or aunts. The subject of Bletchley Park was suddenly in my workplace; not only in the publishing company where I worked, but in my office. At the time I worked for Macdonald Educational, a publishing division of the British Printing Corporation. The scene is still carved in my mind, of a discussion between production director Stephen Pawley, and a young editor, Christi Campbell, regarding a special thirtieth anniversary edition of *The History of World War II*. Christi also worked on a monthly Second World War part-work, an off-shoot collaboration between our sister companies Phoebus, and Macdonald & Jane's, publisher of Jane's Fighting Ships.

That day, my ears pricked up as they mentioned the morning news regarding MI6. The headline had caught my eye too, as I travelled into London on the Tube, but I hadn't expected to be connected to the exposé until I heard Christi's reference to Bletchley Park, which now had to be included (officially) in his manuscript. 'My mother worked at Bletchley,' I interrupted. It was, I thought, a casual reference of little consequence, after all I'd never needed to mention this to anyone before. In the echoing silence that followed, they both stared at me incredulously, then in unison belted out: 'Your mother was at Bletchley Park!' Eyes agog, Christi demanded, 'What did she do?' Stephen asked, 'How was she chosen?'

My answers, of course, were feeble, 'I don't know,' or 'I think she was a filing clerk, at least that's what she said.' With that their interest waned, her role was way too minor. But Christi told me to watch out as there would be more about Bletchley in the future. A warning? Did they still need to be careful? Mum thought so. I told her what had happened and she was interested to hear about the book.

Little by little, more revelations of the government's clandestine Bletchley Park operation began to emerge. It was astonishing! Britain and America could read all enemy secret messages during the war, and much of the intelligence was instrumental in Allied strategies! These were serious and stunning revelations of previously tight-lipped security – wartime secrets concealed by more than 10,000 wartime employees for nearly thirty years! Mum said she wasn't surprised but felt betrayed by the publicity and continued to comply with the Official Secrets Act. Others were relieved they no longer needed to censor every conversation about the war and their specialised Work of National Importance.

During this time, Mum didn't think she fitted into the codebreaker category because she hadn't operated a machine. Authors and reporters simply did not know enough about the work there, and people who said they did figure work and filing simply weren't that important, or so they thought. Their Foreign Office title of Temporary Assistant also camouflaged their roles – TA could also mean 'traffic analysis'.

Back in my London publishing office, an older but trendy man, appeared. David Cook wore his straight blonde hair long, just below the collar of his stylish sage-green corduroy jacket. His face was chiselled and always tanned, but unfortunately he smoked profusely and his yellow nicotine-stained hands matched the colour of his face and hair. Cook's official title was book designer, but another colleague, Philip Hughes, said I should be careful around him, 'He's a spy with connections to MI6 and GCHQ.' He was joking and serious at the same time. After, I noticed David Cook's hands always shook, but why I needed to be careful was a mystery to me – I hadn't done anything wrong, worked for the Foreign Office or signed the Official Secrets form. Not until 2016, when I received a National Archive document regarding my mother's name appearing on a Bletchley list, did I wonder if its compiler was the same person. My list of GC&CS WWII records was compiled in 1996 by D.W.J. Cook, GCHQ Consultant.

* * *

When the previously mentioned first history of codebreakers appeared, American author, David Kahn, was neither at Bletchley or Washington's codebreaking establishments. He had, however, close ties with William Friedman and was chosen to tell his story twenty years after the end of the war. The book claimed to be a complete history of codebreaking, but there was no mention of Bletchley Park. In 1965, at manuscript stage and with CIA verification, the British government had forbidden any mention of its wartime operation. Their interpretation, to comply with the Official Secrets Act, was for life, not thirty or fifty years. The governments, GCHQ and the CIA, then agreed that all references to Bletchley Park would be removed. Ultimately, America took most of the credit for Second World War codebreaking when the incomplete book was published. Naturally, this provoked some Bletchley employees to set the record straight with their own accounts.

Publications about the secrets of Bletchley, MI6, spies and codebreakers started to trickle out. Books were written by Bletchley people who wanted to tell what they thought was true, and those with vivid imaginations believed their information was correct. Perhaps their part was, but that is where it ended. Nobody had the full story. Individual war experiences were only part of the massive chapter in history – the part they knew from the section where they worked. TV dramas piqued the population's interest including our aunts' and mother's. Whether read or viewed the reaction from them was always the same: 'That didn't happen like that.' In 1974, Frederick Winterbotham published *The Ultra Secret* with Weidenfeld & Nicholson, but the book was later denounced as 'an unreliable source of information', especially by American historians. Nonetheless, even with its flaws it was the first full account on signals intelligence (SIGINT) and remains an important part of Bletchley's recorded history.

* * *

Now Aunty Dot and Mum talked more about Bletchley but still only snippets of information. We saw less of Aunty Peggy, but occasionally both would visit for tea. Dot would boldly mention Bletchley Park; Peggy and Mum less so, but with no elaboration on their office work. Usually discussions centred around war-time friends, family members, the Co-op, life and death, general matters and their offsprings' struggle or success in the developmental programme of nurture and nature. If they elaborated too much about Bletchley their conversation would end abruptly when we walked into the room, sometimes mid-snippet, with 'Well, we shouldn't be talking about that, should we?' One weekend Dot and Albert came for coffee and the conversation soon turned to the news and more revelations about Bletchley Park. Their previous truncated conversations had revealed little, apart from 'clerks and mundane figure work'. Now Dot felt she could talk more openly.

She disclosed she was in the Typing Room, but her typing machine was not a regular typewriter. The name she used was Typex. For me that sounded like Telex, and I imagined long strips of ticker tape with lines of coded holes. She also brought with her a file of names and small photographs of her many friends and colleagues from that time. Her victory message from the Director General, Stewart Graham Menzies, head of MI6 on 8 May 1945, included sixty-five hastily scribbled signatures and their heartfelt messages. Dot reflected on the day she left Bletchley Park as a time of happiness and sadness, but Mum treated the keepsake with disdain; she always followed the rules. 'Throw it away!' she cried. But it would have been sad if this historic document had not survived.[1]

Mum said she was in a different department and didn't dare keep such information. All she had was a maroon address book containing a few contacts. Her job she said was figure work, indexing and filing. Still neither divulged full details, accept to confirm they handled wartime coded messages, 'High and Low code Diplomatic messages,' she said. I asked if they were enemy messages, to which her reply was yes. She was surprised by her honesty.

Dot questioned this. She knew Daisy's work was also secret, connected to military messages, but didn't know where they originated. Her Typex Room in Communications saw only coded messages re-enciphered into other coded messages. I asked if they were spies, to which they both laughed and said no, with a knowing glance to each other. 'No, we weren't spies,' echoed Dot. Mum went on to explain she had never heard of Enigma; she worked on another type of machine code. But they had both heard of the Bombe and confirmed, 'Only Wrens were allowed to go in that room.'

When asked, Mum replied she didn't really work on a machine, apart from one that relayed messages to another room. Most of her work was manual, pencil and paper. Though she said later there was a larger and faster machine somewhere at the back of another building. The codes had strange names, like Fish, Tuna or Tunny. She couldn't quite remember, but thought the code's name was Lorenz, and the machine was Colossus.

Bletchley talk sounded alien and not at all in line with current chatter. Their grade levels were also discussed, and whether Dot recommended Mum for the job at Bletchley. Mum was Grade III at the end of the war, and always thought Dot was higher because she could type. Dot was Grade II. Mum was also vehement that her actions alone led her to apply to the War Office in 1943. She insisted her recommendation came from someone else, not Dot, but perhaps she didn't remember. Still guarded by the Official Secrets Act, they shared only names of public figures such as Roy Jenkins, Ian Fleming and Alan Turing. Winston Churchill of course was their chief commander and everything they did was for his victory.

* * *

As the morning continued, we had a surprise visit from the Coopers, our former neighbours. It was a day to remember. We were all stunned by Mr Cooper's memory of wartime events he'd kept secret from our family for twenty years. In the mid-sixties the family had moved to Taplow near Slough in Buckinghamshire, due to Mr Cooper's relocation as head cashier at P.B. Cow and Co., Streatham.[2] The rubber textile manufacturer was mostly known for inflatable beds – Lilos. Mr Cooper – Ray – had once given Dad two sub-standard samples which we used for seaside camping trips. The mix of Oxford-blue cotton and rubber created a thick and durable fabric, but in our case Lilo weak spots were patched with Dad's bicycle tyre repair kit. He also made sure to tether these with several yards of string to prevent us from drifting out to sea. Cow Gum and other industrial adhesives were also P.B. Cow's products, as well as lifeboats and lifesaving equipment for the war and, it is said, fake inflatable tanks and weapons to fool the enemy for Operation Fortitude.

Mum corresponded with Peggy Cooper via Christmas cards and we once visited their new home near Beaconsfield Model Village, though our parents visited them other times without us. It was Kitty Mawby

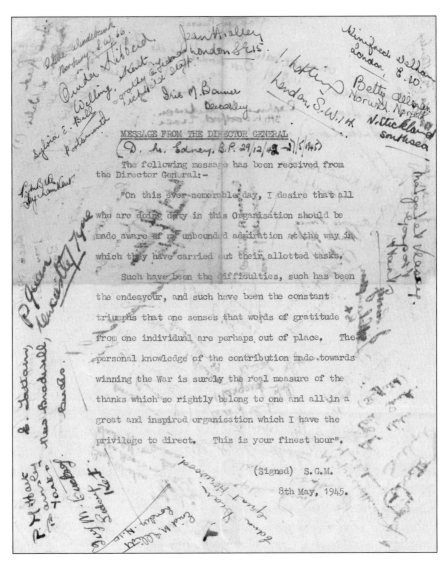

The following message has been received from the Director General:-

"On this ever-memorable day, I desire that all who are doing duty in this Organisation should be made aware of my unbounded admiration at the way in which they have carried out their allotted tasks.

Such have been the difficulties, such has been the endeavour, and such have been the constant triumphs that one senses that words of gratitude from one individual are perhaps out of place. The personal knowledge of the contribution made towards winning the War is surely the real measure of the thanks which so rightly belong to one and all in a great and inspired organisation which I have the privilege to direct. This is your finest hour".

(Signed) S.G.M.

8th May, 1945.

Above and opposite: Dorothy Edney's secret wartime keepsakes from Bletchley Park. (Dorothy Edney Archive).

our other next-door neighbour, who organised their visit to Mitcham in 1975. Dot and Albert stayed for lunch too. That day Mrs Cooper, a bubbly brunette, asked how Mum and Aunty Dot knew each other. 'We worked together at the Co-op and then Bletchley Park,' they said in unison. 'Really?' said Peggy, 'Bletchley Park? Ray's older brother was there too. I never knew you were there, Daisy.'

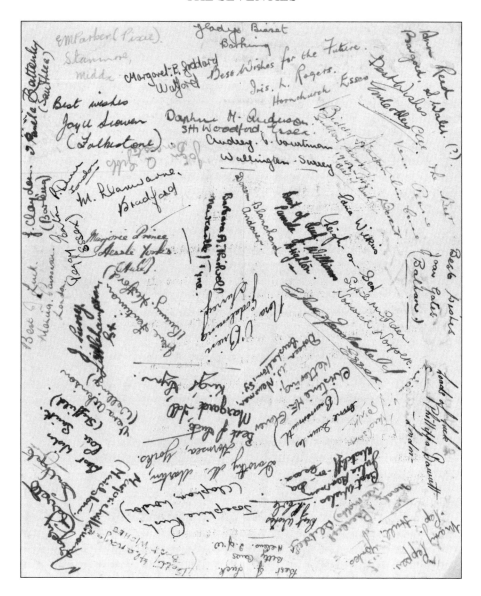

An element of mistrust hovered for a few seconds, mainly because Bletchley people were unsure what to say or to whom. They were guarded in their replies. After a pause Mum asked his name and where he was in the military. The name she provided was unusual but sounded similar to Joe. 'He was Air Force; Ray too. Oh yes, he's is very involved with Bletchley and writes reports for the government, GCHQ, doesn't he Arthur?' She shouted to the other end of the room. Mrs Cooper sometimes used Arthur, his first name, though we knew him as Ray. As I watched the scene play out, I thought it odd how we had known them for years, but my parents had never discussed their former lives with them.

The cloak of secrecy was still down in our living room when Mum confirmed they shouldn't talk about their work, but Peggy Cooper was more than exuberant to contribute to such a hot topic. It was fascinating for her and of course she had not signed the Official Secrets form. Answering his wife's call, Ray (Arthur) strolled over from the other end of the room. He had been admiring our garden with Dad and Albert. As he sucked on his ebony and walnut pipe, his black moustache twitched on his top lip; Mr Cooper's stoic personality and upright appearance now suited a man from the Air Force. 'That's right,' he confirmed taking in a deep breath, 'My brother was at Bletchley, we were both Air Force; he had an important job connected to Bletchley Park. I didn't know you were there, Daisy,' he echoed cautiously. Mum said nothing, still terrified of being caught talking about her work, and so the conversation stalled until Dot asked him where he was stationed in the war. Ray re-lit his pipe and took in a long draw. 'I was in Singapore,' and blew out a large swirl of smoke.

If there was any talking in the room at that point all was suddenly silent and time seemed to stand still. Everyone paused to take in what he had just said. 'You were in Singapore!?' Dad asked incredulously, breaking the silence. Everybody knew that Dad was there as a prisoner of war. Why hadn't Ray Cooper, in the twenty years he'd known him, mentioned this before? Ray said nothing, knowing what Dad was thinking.

'Really, you were in Singapore, when I was there?' repeated Dad. 'No, I was there before the Japs came. We got out in time. I went to Melbourne.' Dad was flabbergasted and sat down heavily in the chair; tears welled in his eyes. 'You were there and never told me!?' Ray Cooper couldn't look at Dad, his eyes averted to the floor, gaze fixed firmly on the swirling beige, brown and yellow carpet.

'Yes. I didn't mention because I felt guilty, and besides I couldn't speak about the work I did, which was connected to Bletchley.' Mum confirmed with him that he was part of Japanese codebreaking, but for the codebreakers that was enough reveal for one day after thirty years of silence and everyone left. I never saw the Coopers again.

Dad pulled out his handkerchief and blew his nose. 'I can't believe he never told me.' At that point he was not party to any of the secrets of

Dot, Daisy and the Cooper brothers.[3] Nobody except the codebreakers understood and only a few knew the full story. 'He fled and left us there to die,' concluded Dad.

* * *

A delicate net of secrecy continued until 1982 when Gordon Welchman published *The Hut 6 Story*. The new tell-all book had a far more serious effect on the British authorities, including MI6, and the author was considered a criminal under the Official Secrets Act. The publication was halted and warehoused copies were ordered to be destroyed by Margaret Thatcher, then the British Prime Minister. After the war, Welchman had taken his computer knowledge to assist MIT (Massachusetts Institute of Technology) and the Mitre Corporation and, later, from the relative safe haven of America, he felt compelled to tell his own story, following the earlier accounts of Kahn and Winterbotham. But the US National Security Agency (NSA) also disapproved and Welchman lost his security clearance and his job. He was banned from discussing anything about the war or the methods he and Turing had progressed (Turing died in 1954). He avoided extradition from America to England, and a jail sentence, and by 1983, in a major and intriguing publishing event, all further copies of *The Hut 6 Story* were 'pulped' by major booksellers. Even though freedom of speech was a hot topic, the government had stepped in to limit the supply of classified Bletchley Park information… but not for long.

Chapter 42

Reunion and the Sales Time

'What would the government do? Surely they couldn't put us all in jail?

Good question. News was widespread and everyone wanted to know the true story of Bletchley Park. How did the 10,000 employees, mainly women, help win the war from a country estate in the middle of England? But national security protocols were upheld. Kahn's book told the codebreaking story from America's point of view, omitting details of Britain's important role, and Winterbotham's and Welchman's accounts provided more fodder for the British public. Masterman made everything seem fantastic and fictious, but now the truth was called for.

Next came Peter Wright's *Spy Catcher*, published in Australia to avoid British law, and Mrs Thatcher reeled once again from its exposé of classified information once cocooned in National Security; this time the publication covered far more than just Bletchley. She was supposed to protect the secrets of the Crown, but all she could do was cry 'treason!' The government had no choice but to gradually de-classify the history and release some of the information to the Public Records Office, the National Archives.

Meanwhile, the grounds of Bletchley Park were left to rot. The shoddy facilities were utilised for government training – telephone engineers, air-traffic controllers and schoolteachers, some of whom went abroad to teach British forces children after the war. Attempts to update the crumbling structures using modern materials – white paint, plasterboard and cheap Formica laminate – were made in the 1960s, but trainees were unaware the location was still part of the post-war GCHQ, where a clandestine staff worked in dilapidated huts. Bletchley Park was now even more of a dreary place to work or learn new skills. The once-manicured lawn tennis courts were asphalted to become a car park, the maze was destroyed and roofs sprouted weeds. The blast-proof cement walls, once protection from enemy attack, disintegrated and every room smelled damp; flakes of paint and plaster speckled wooden floors. Inside the blocks, the metal frames of their Crittall windows stood strong against blue sky in stark contrast to the dank interiors; daylight filtered through the broken unwashed windows, as dust particles danced in warm rays of sunshine and a smell of gas dominated the air. The once lively estate was all but dead.

* * *

During the mid-1980s, I discovered a machine in my parent's garage. I'd left home and when I visited for some reason I can't remember, I had to go to Dad's garage at the end of the garden; maybe for a hammer to hang a picture. I don't know where Dad was, but he didn't go, I did. The cumbersome mass on his workbench opposite the door caught my attention immediately. When we were young, we would often snoop in there, to see what he was making us for Christmas. Whatever it was – a sewing box, a dolls house or chair – it was always in the same spot covered with a white dust sheet. Now, pushed toward the back was something else with a black heavy rubberised cover laden with dust. I thought it was odd and couldn't resist a peek. To my surprise it was a typewriter. But was it? It was much larger than a normal typewriting machine. Mum never learned to type so it was strange they should have anything like this.

The keyboard resembled a typewriter. It was old and dusty with black and reddish fabric-covered wires leading to a set of small lights, an unusual feature for even the most modern of typing machines. The whole thing was squarish and heavy. I pushed down the keys trying to type, just to see if it would work. I knew it probably needed to be plugged in, but they were stiff and difficult to push, and did not follow the usual QWERTY pattern. Unusual spools and a contraption to the side made the machine broader and deeper than any typewriter I'd seen before. It had a platen roller, perhaps where paper went in? I could only speculate. Something about it wasn't right. Electrically, it looked quite dangerous.

I went to the house to question Dad. He said it was an old machine from Mum's office, something to do with the war, and the Foreign

Typex Machine, likeness found in the garage decades after the war (By kind permission Director GCHQ)

Office. But 'It's taking up too much space, and Mum wants to get rid of it anyway.' She said someone had given it to her and didn't seem to know much about how it worked. He didn't want to plug it in; afraid the whole place would fuse, he just wanted it covered up. The cover was specially designed for the large machine. But where did it come from? How was it transported? It wasn't in the garage when I left home in 1977. It could have been there for ten years.

My belief is that it was a Typex machine[1] Aunty Dot used, and in later years she asked Dad to keep it in his garage. Several months later Dad gleefully announced he had sold the machine for £50! 'Somebody came by and asked if I had any old machines?' I asked him if the purchaser was Mr Sparrowhawk, the rag and bone man, but he said no, just someone interested in old machines, 'he was quite excited to find it!'

* * *

After *Spy Catcher, The Hut 6 Story* and the machine – which we didn't think of again – we heard little news of Bletchley until 1994, when another friend sent Mum an article from *Saga Magazine*. It reported that a reunion had taken place in 1991 as the Bletchley Mansion was to be destroyed to make way for multiple housing. Mum was upset she hadn't heard about this and checked with Dot to see if she knew. Of course, she didn't, she would have said. The local Bletchley people, some of whom were former Bletchley Park employees, had decided to hold a final event to celebrate their war days. 'The Last Party', 3 October 1991 had rounded up as many former employees as possible. Invitation was by word of mouth with no comprehensive list; it was all about contacts, who you knew, who was still living etc.

Around 400 attended, but unfortunately the chatter did not reach Daisy and Dot in South London. Feeling disgruntled they resolved to find out more. Now they really could start talking and maybe reunite with war-time colleagues. But it was difficult for Mum to visit regularly as she didn't drive and her eyesight was also failing. We wondered how this new freedom would affect her, but she seemed happy to remember and slightly more at liberty to speak about her war days. Before long she wrote a letter to her grandson, then aged 8½, who was learning about the Second World War and its fiftieth anniversary at school. Note: Grandma never actually told Christopher what she did at Bletchley.

* * *

Using the magazine article, Mum searched further. This was a rare period in her life when I saw her independently animated. She wrote letters with purpose claiming her part of history. She was sad to miss the reunion, but glad to delve into the past; this time without worry. She checked the local library, pre-internet, using references such as Enigma, Typex, Cipher and Colossus. The librarian provided little except the Bletchley Park phone number, where she discovered the next set of weekend tours would be 21-23 October, 10.30-5pm. There was one each hour. She was galvanized to become an active member of Bletchley Trust.

The drive from Surrey took Mum and Dad about three hours. This time Indian summer skies delivered a better journey, no misty rain or whining children! As they approached Bletchley, the familiar wide expanse of countryside she once loved, suddenly became a mass of roads, roundabouts and tightly packed houses. Disoriented, she remembered only trees and fields around the estate, so-called modern progress had destroyed the Park's beautiful surroundings. It was fifty years since she'd left, excluding the miserable weekend trip when we were six and the time she faced fierce GPO security. But the trip was another disappointment,

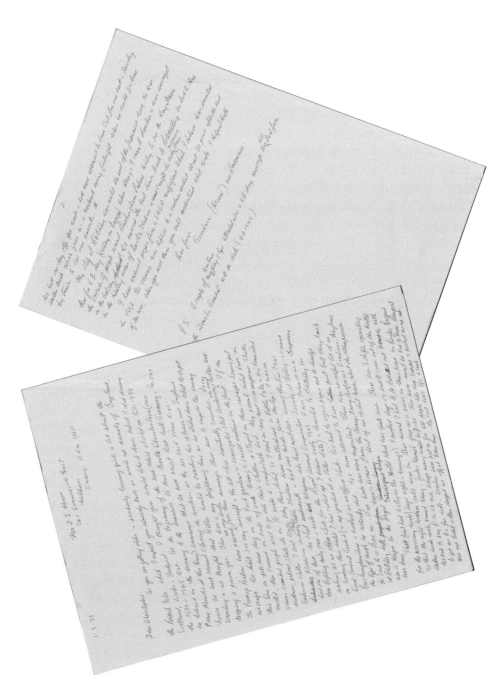

Grandma's letter to Christopher, 1995. (Christopher Robertson)

coupled with the fact that nobody seemed interested in her story. She wrote to The Bletchley Trust, whose founders were Tony and Margaret Sale, saying the estate had become shockingly derelict and not at all how she remembered, '…the beautiful lake; now clogged with debris.' Her letter went on to praise the tour revealing that, 'I learnt things I didn't know while working there.' Tony Sale, who previously worked for MI5 under Peter Wright, (author of *Spycatcher*), was also instrumental in the rebuilding of Colossus from 1993.[2]

Mum uncovered her Bletchley mementos, hidden in Harry's old wooden trunk at the end of her bed. Under blankets and other items, she had saved old newspapers and photos, including three or four Bletchley play programmes tucked between pages of other important papers. All were wrapped tightly in a green folder. She once said they were things from the war, 'but you won't be interested,' and had placed her old worn ice skates on top saying. 'I last used these on the lake at Bletchley Park.'

Now she wanted to talk more about her treasures and donate the four drama group programmes. Margaret Sale replied on 27 October saying she was interested, but still Daisy thought there was an edge of snobbery in the air which saddened her: 'It wasn't like that during the war; everyone was friendly toward each other.' She sent the drama group programmes to Margaret on 11 February 1996, who confirmed receipt nine days later, saying 'The Museum is growing all the time, but the expansion into Block D is still some way off.' Mum never returned to Bletchley. She said nobody was interested, and at that point, even her daughters were not keen. 'One day perhaps we could all go,' she suggested, 'but the place is such a dump, why would you want to?'

Around this time I considered being an indexer for my publishing company; I could work from home and bring up my family. Mum recalled part of her job was indexing, but hers was a different type of indexing. Was this when she worked alone, back to the camera, sitting at a table with a file box? Then late in 1999, another letter arrived but not on Bletchley Park Trust paper. Now Margaret spoke of changes at Bletchley Park Trust and their struggle to keep control to preserve the site.

Chapter 43

Still No Recognition

For decades they couldn't show or tell. What was written in the messages and on the laborious index cards my mother decoded and categorised? Examining records at the National Archives indicates further information for Hut 7, but this must be the subject of a future publication as the study continues to be of some length.[1] Records at TNA, despite denials of being involved with strategising and perhaps running the war, reveal that Bletchley hosted a small office of dedicated employees who met weekly as the Western Front Committee. In Block B, Room 149, a collection of filtered, intercepted messages and derived intelligence, was used for war strategy and recommendations were presented to commanders who made decisions based 'on the best information available'. This was especially true for the Normandy Landings in 1944. Perhaps without advance knowledge of the enemy's plan from Bletchley Park, Britain would have lost to Hitler.[2]

* * *

Japanese diplomatic signals were the main route to highly confidential messages from German and Italian High Command – though by 1942 that knowledge was too little and too late for Singapore. If methods in analysing Japanese messages were employed earlier the situation might have been different for Stan. The teams in Hut 7 and other huts, manually analysed, classified and annotate each message ready for immediate or future reference and 'story' completion at an elevated level. Both at Bletchley and Washington, their codes were broken and information was collated, providing a manual base that led to faster electronic processing machines crucial to all codebreaking successes.

It must not be forgotten therefore that the methods, programmes and efficient inventions were designed by hard-working humans from

Room 40, Polish Intelligence and forces Signals Intelligence – both in Britain and America – then input and expanded on an industrial scale, first at Bletchley Park and later in the Washington DC area. Indeed, its unprecedented development of mass information storage and retrieval became the basis of the internet we know today. But sadly, its secret nature prevented most of these vital humans from being properly recognised. At the end of the war, anyone in British uniform was awarded a medal for their service, but not for the science they used, though some inventors received MBEs or OBEs, however, most Foreign Office Civilians received nothing for the important work they undertook.

Even Commander Alastair Denniston who retired from Berkley Street, in London, as head of the 'civil' side of GC&CS on 1 May 1945, left with a modest annual pension of £591. The government may not have been very appreciative of everyone's efforts, but codebreakers indirectly congratulated themselves. American codebreaker, William Friedman, for example, wrote to his friend Denniston saying: 'I do want you to know that there are many of us here who realise the exceptionally valuable contribution which you made toward bringing the war in Europe to a successful conclusion. This added to what you did in the last war makes a target for those who will follow you to shoot at, and it will take some very good shooting to come near it.' (Bletchley Park's Facebook page 1 May 2020)

* * *

In 2000 a new guard protected Bletchley Park's history and wartime achievements. Inroads were made to expand and curate the museum at a higher level for visitors in general, military historians and veteran codebreakers. But by 2008 Bletchley Park still struggled, and government funding was lacking, despite its important role in history.

'The work here at Bletchley Park…was utterly fundamental to the survival of Britain and to the triumph of the West. I'm not actually sure that I can think of very many other places where I could say something as unequivocal as that. This is sacred ground. If this isn't worth preserving, what is?'

The late Professor Richard Holmes, Military Historian.

Enter Sue Black

It took a single mother to rouse the Bletchley population and its followers, to bring further awareness to the fated grounds. Dr Black first visited Bletchley in 2003 for a British Computer Society networking event for women. She had a PhD in software engineering and Bletchley's story captured her interest, after all 10,000 people had worked there during the war, and more than half were women. Their combined efforts had saved millions of lives.

Black's personal story of family and struggles leading her to become head of computer science at the University of Westminster and later University College London, is at the least compelling.[3] But the fate of Bletchley lingered with her: 'It was a goldmine of history with amazing women who carried out most of the day to day communication analysis during the war.' She decided to be pro-active and involve her computer networking community, including BCS Women, the first on-line support for female IT professionals.

After discussion with Bletchley management and director Simon Greenish, the 'Women of Bletchley Park' project was launched in March 2008. But Bletchley still had no financial support from government or industry, despite GC&CS being a government department and that British industry had benefitted from its incredible science and systems developed there during the war. Funding depended solely on visitor tours and entrance fees which meant the grounds and wartime buildings were never far from demolition. The historic site teetered on a cliff edge trying to keep visitors interested, while Simon Greenish knew that if numbers fell the park and museum would close. It was a crucial time and difficult to balance; the future was bleak.

Three months later, Greenish informed Dr Black of a petition on 10 Downing Street's website and the British Prime Minister, Gordon Brown and his government were asked to help save Bletchley Park. A government petition can be set up by anyone and, provided there are over 100,000 signatures, Parliament must debate the issue. This was Black's chance to announce Bletchley's plight to the world using her network of computer science colleagues. She lost no time in emailing everyone, including all members of the Council for Professors and Heads of Computing (CPHC), asking them to sign.

The exposure was staggeringly successful, even the royal family showed interest. Bletchley Park was now on most people's radar, but the threat of closure was still an important battle to win. A Badge of Honour was finally issued to all surviving codebreakers, but it had taken sixty-four years for the government to issue formal recognition. Sixty-four years! All wore with pride, but Daisy never had that pleasure as she died in 2006. Sadly, the accolade was not awarded posthumously. She would have been 92 in 2009 and proud to wear one. In her later days the question was still: 'Who will save Bletchley Park?'

Daisy waited, but nothing was forthcoming in her lifetime, and she never saw the transformation she hoped for. In 2011, a successful bid to the Heritage Lottery Fund was won by the Park's directors, and funding was secured close to £4m. Dr Black should be proud of the impact she made. Soon after Queen Elizabeth II unveiled a new memorial in grey polished granite adjacent to Block B. It stands eight feet high with twelve dark circles the size of a small plate. Each bears a letter: W E A L S O S E R V E D.

Further recognition was not forthcoming until 2016 with Bletchley Park's Commemorative Wall, where Daisy is honoured by her daughters. Perhaps in time all Bletchley veterans will be honoured by the government as an important part of the victory and development where machines, we must still remember, are the result of human brain power and hard work.

Chapter 44

Conclusion

There is no doubt that the work of Bletchley Park and the intelligence gathering systems that evolved were instrumental in winning the Second World War. There is still more to uncover, but the codebreakers' story is incredible, and, as more information is declassified, we wonder to what else did their work contribute?[1] Bletchley Park's preservation is a fitting monument to the memory of our mother, all codebreakers and their diligent work. The Government Code & Cypher School played a crucial role, relaying information where it was of best use. From a small government room in London to a massive organisation in a remote area of the British countryside, the most astonishing aspect was the thousands involved who managed to keep details of their work secret for so many decades. The codebreakers' profound loyalty is unprecedented.

Signals listeners, who seemed to be late in receiving recognition, were the important group who intercepted messages. Often stationed at draughty outposts in remote areas around the country, abroad and at sea, some were inadvertent targets for the Luftwaffe, some Bletchley-trained codebreakers died at sea en route to Colombo.[2] A whole raft of people gathered enemy message signals in various forms of encipherment via military personnel and selected civilians who secretly listened. The coded messages were collected and sent to Bletchley Park by teleprinter, scrambled telephone or special motorcycle dispatch drivers, where they were decoded, analysed, disseminated and indexed for future use to be ahead of enemy plans.

Despite the various ciphers and many codebreaking processes, the procedure was virtually the same for all. Only the presentation and secrecy make Bletchley seem mysterious and confusing. The simple path for each strand of cipher was to intercept the enemy message, work out the seeds of the code via manual mathematics and logic by decoders and translators – do this faster, via sheets with holes, then with new and faster machines; read and analyse the information in the message, prepare reports, paraphrase and re-encode via Typex to divert the enemy who also listened, so they couldn't discover we read their messages, send the resulting intelligence report to those in charge of the war via teleprinter, Typex and the SLU, then categorise and store details of used and unused intelligence for future reference. This was ULTRA, and as Field Marshal Montgomery's chief pointed out, 'very few armies ever went into battle better informed of their enemy,' and, 'What we should have done without it is idle to linger over. Yet, it must be made clear that Ultra and Ultra only put Intelligence on the map.'[3]

Daisy Lawrence and her colleagues were just small cogs in this very important wheel. It is their lives during this time and the intelligence process – collection and analysis – that is so interesting, along with the pursuit of a deeper understanding of the intercepts and campaigns. The codebreakers' secret work affected everyone's future, but for some, their knowledge and hidden secrets were a burden for many years. The women were chosen because they tested high for intelligence and aptitude. And their ability to keep a secret is certainly proven; competence, trustworthiness, logic and diligence – today we all want to know their tasks and discover how they felt. Could they have dealt with the reveal thirty years ago? Would codebreakers' children's lives be different if they'd known earlier about their mothers' (and fathers') roles in the war? Would their children be interested? Our mother tried to guide us to better things without revealing information, but she was aware of future possibilities in technology, and she knew how to spot the difference, read between the lines and did her best to keep this incredible secret.

* * *

Now I have researched the various compartments of my mother's war, I understand why she sometimes behaved the way she did, and why her 'moments' were intermittent. Working at Bletchley Park had a profound effect on her. Until now, nobody realised the keen loyalty she possessed and conversely, the lasting damage caused by her keeping even the smallest of secrets, secret. To be sworn to secrecy for life in compliance with the Official Secrets Act, with no safety cushion or purpose in a similar environment, was an obstruction for her. There was no outlet for re-training or counselling or access to another profession to protect the burden she carried – unlike America's GI Bill which offered further training and financial compensation to obtain a college degree. British non-military codebreakers, mostly Foreign Office civilians, were restricted far more than other government employees or the Armed Forces.

With her Work of National Importance expertly hidden in a trunk – release papers and references – Daisy was restricted in talking openly about a time she clearly enjoyed. Questions from those outside her Bletchley circle led to further questions, but any mention of the Foreign Office had to quickly morph into other interests, such as cooking, the weather or gardening. Bletchley had been her university; her time of intellectual growth. She built relationships with others from all walks of life and quickly learned that life away from South London and her Tooting friends could be different and possibly more exciting. Perhaps she didn't miss home at all.

When she did return, her relationships changed with family and friends, especially if they didn't have a similar wartime experience. Her inability to divulge details of her war work and relationships with new acquaintances, some in higher places, remained secret. This made her appear aloof and snobbish. 'Our evasions were seen as rudeness, not respected,' recalled one codebreaker. Neither did Daisy's Bletchley Park reference letter help as intended. After the war, she continued employment with the Foreign Office in a subsection of the India Office in Great Smith Street. There is no reference from this department, only a recently discovered good luck message in 1948 from Clarence House which confirms she worked in The India Office – Commonwealth Relations Office 1945-1948. The message of well wishes was hidden in the paper lining of a drawer until 2018! Why did Daisy feel she needed to keep these documents concealed? And was her Bletchley letter supposed to be the ultimate in prestige?

Obtaining other employment was hard for Daisy as she couldn't explain her 'previous experience'. Her attempt in the accounts office at Smith's Time Pieces was disastrous. Her confidential Foreign Office letter became headline news and everybody wanted details, 'What exactly did you do in the war on Work of National Importance?' Outside government circles the letter was useless. Any enquiries made to the Foreign Office by a post-war employer about her work only revealed everything was 'classified'. It was a unique wartime experience to play

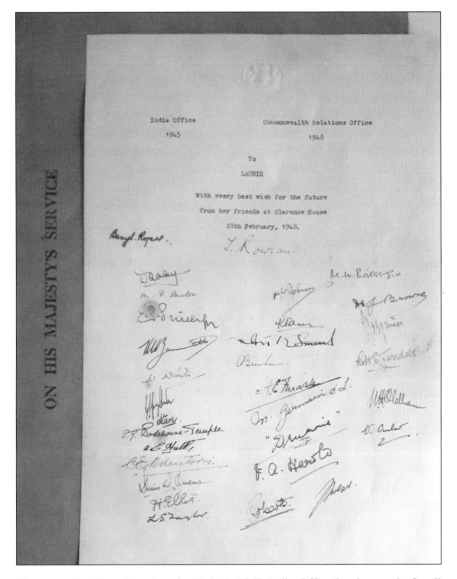

Known as Pat, Lawrie or Laurie, Daisy's 1948 India Office leaving card of well wishes was hidden in a drawer until 2018. (Daisy Lawrence Archive)

a major role in defeating Hitler and the Japanese. 'We rubbed shoulders with brilliance, and we did our bit to win the war, but who would believe you?' It was a profound and pivotal time for them to accelerate their brain power, if only they could take advantage of their new skills and wider knowledge. Some did, but many didn't.

Remaining Silent

As years passed, turmoil ebbed in Daisy, and silence became her best ally. Trapped in seclusion, she was lonely but safe. She didn't want to lie, especially to her husband and daughters. Obscuring her secret life was hard and interaction with adults, apart from Dot and Peggy, was difficult. To a degree, children were easier and on good days her gift to us was additional reading, writing and arithmetic, puzzle books and games we could complete alone. We were taught how to 'spot the difference' on duplicated black and white cartoons that looked the same; but were they? We were taught that not everything is black and white and to read between the lines, how to play Battleships and Boxes, guess what was on the tray, after one item was removed. 'What's missing now?' There was one less object. The brain and eyes were trained to notice something different. Whether this particular memory game and other visual tactics were used in training at Elmers School is yet to be determined, but brain stimulation, spotting differences, varying letters, numbers and positions are important skills in the art of codebreaking – finding operator error or repetition in German or Japanese ciphers could open a floodgate of clues leading to successful decoding and important intelligence information. Who would think that such childhood games could be so important? Reminiscent of her Bletchley work, she encouraged us to learn at arms-length with some skills simply explained as a party game on a tea tray, with items masked by a tea towel.

Hugs and Kisses

In few shows of emotion and nothing discussed in detail, Mum rarely interacted with us conversationally. I believe she loved us but her personal expression of this was hard. She bought us presents and wrote 'love from Mum xxx', but that was as far as love went. Sometimes there was the odd hug. Did she suffer from what we now know as Depersonalization disorder?[4] The little discussed mental condition, where a sense of disconnect prevails and everything appears in a haze or fog, or even in 2D, is brought on by trauma or acute anxiety. Sometimes it is life threatening with suicidal thoughts. To understand, imagine having to undertake something you really don't want to do, you are uncomfortable or extremely nervous of, for example taking a test, being on the stage or divulging forbidden information. How do you face the situation? Do you step into Alice in Wonderland's magic mirror and let it flow or STOP, to produce a barrier to hold it back? Keep it in; prohibit the information from escaping – as Daisy did? Many years later, she talked about being in West Park during one of her breakdowns. That's when she remembered: 'There was a lot of blood.' We discussed miscarriages at the time, and she thought this happened to her the first time she went to West Park. We attributed this to the time when she asked us if we wanted a baby brother. Was 'he' shocked away through drugs and ECT to cure her psychological condition and help her forget? After the procedure, strapped into electro-convulsion treatment where they didn't always provide anaesthetic back then in 1960 – she was left empty. We trod eggshells around her; she seemed hollow like a dead tree. She was trapped in a cell, a metaphorical straight-jacket, from which she could not entangle herself without feeling she had committed treason.

There were other times she wanted to return to Bletchley. She often reminisced with Dot about good times 'during the war', but she couldn't just jump in a car to go there; she never learned to drive. Perhaps such a learned skill at Bletchley, might have provided her with the freedom to take-off when needed. She was always trapped, but eventually, her Bletchley bicycle kept her pedalling to her local post-war filing job.

Growing up Dad's wages paid the mortgage, bills in general and food. Mum used hers for presents, clothes, holidays and other small luxuries. My sister and I were not as outgoing as we might have been, had we more interaction with our mother's past, but we eventually developed our own group of friends and became skilled at school: English, art, business studies – where we wrote in code – Pitman's shorthand, and typed like our cousin Pam and Aunty Dot, something Mum insisted we do. As young working adults, we also started to contribute to household expenses, including central heating and, finally, a telephone! We were not permitted one before we reached 16, and then we had to pay for it ourselves. Mum said no, 'People listen; they might raid our house.' This seemed crazy spy-movie talk but makes sense now. When asked 'Why,' she elaborated: 'Men with hats in dark coats, they'll come to take you away.' Especially if you said or did something wrong. 'They did that in the war.' She really believed we might be spied upon. Was she right? 'They know; they watch and listen,' she continued. One of her greatest fears was being caught for small misdemeanours, like taking a paperclip!

In the 1980s, our parents spent retirement travelling Europe, and other parts of the world. Ultimately, they visited Singapore as well as Hong Kong and Australia, but they didn't go to Japan. Dad would have nothing to do with anything Japanese, not until much later in their lives. He was aware of the return to Japan of the PoW, Louis Zamperini. Dad said he was mad; he would never do that, forgive them; but something later inside said it was time to let down the guard when he bought a Datsun car and let Mum buy a Japanese sewing machine. All the while she never admitted to knowing Japanese or working on Japanese intercepts.

Meanwhile, in a regular doctor's visit and neurological assessment she was told all her problems probably stemmed from an accident she had when she was young. Could this be true? A bump on the head from the motorcycle accident, in a sidecar? We didn't believe the analysis, but Mum found peace with this alternative explanation. Now she could blame the accident instead of the war. At the same time and toward the fiftieth anniversary of the start of the Second World War, Dad recorded his own PoW story using his hidden diary to revive his memory. I asked him many times to do this and eventually provided him with a hand-held tape recorder. Four small tapes were completed but now it was Dad who suffered with PTSD after remembering the dark episodes of his incarceration. He went into a depression for a few weeks and fortunately recovered, but the reality of this time for him was extremely painful.

With her small pension, frugality, careful saving and dexterity in handicrafts, Daisy's retirement years were comfortable despite being registered blind. She sewed patchwork squares, knitted sweaters and crocheted coasters, until the effect of this, and perhaps close figure work through code checking under dim lights, took her eyesight. She succumbed completely to macular degeneration in her late seventies, but she could still do crosswords! Dad was the pillar of strength, who kept the peace – in his desire for a quiet life – mostly in his garage or garden. We know our parents were incredible, but Mum was an extraordinary woman that we are only now just discovering; a beacon of hope on good days like a mother should be, but at times skating on thin ice to retain the secrets she could never tell.

Dad kept her on a track with a remedy of pills at just the right mix (everyone said he was amazing, now we know why). Her special friends, Peggy and Dot, also checked on her welfare, with the two aunts we never met, Mary and Milly, who wrote often. Both our parents needed rehabilitation in one form or another for post-war stress – Dad had Mum committed to a mental institution for his own sanity, while trying not to succumb to the horrors of his captivity. PTSD, Post-traumatic stress disorder, or CSR, Combat Stress Reaction. We had a double dose in our household. I sometimes feel it's a miracle we all survived.

* * *

How many others were affected by the shackles of Bletchley's secrets? How did Bletchley cope with mental illness? How did it affect the codebreaking? There was no system at the Foreign Office; no confidential safety net for employees to share wartime experiences or involve loved ones to help spread the burden of keeping such important secrets. For most of the codebreakers, intelligence work was not their career choice. They simply signed up for war work not knowing what to expect.

How different life might have been if our parents had been able to better explain their war, a pivotal moment in their lives. In conclusion, they were not given the chance to shine. There was no recognition or adequate compensation for the pain and burden they endured – sometimes horrific episodes of war that remained on their conscience. They had to keep quiet; forget. Dad tried to be part of his local Burma Star group but found he didn't 'fit'. Too much time had passed; he felt his 18th Division was inadequately recognised. Mum tried to be involved at Bletchley Park in the 1990s, with a similar response. The younger generation wasn't interested either. Obtaining the deserved recognition seemed problematic and awkward.

* * *

Despite Mum's condition, past secrets and hidden work, we came through successfully. We prospered but wished we'd known more earlier. Their history is important, and everybody needs to be aware of the past to prevent future mistakes. Our hope is for an enlightened, less troubled world. Mum's post-war employment at the mail order catalogue in Norbury, twenty years after the war, was a place where the past didn't matter. Aunty Ciss understood Mum's problems better than anyone, but whether she knew everything is uncertain. Mum was good at her job: analysing, searching, organising, filing and keeping quiet about the contents; she didn't need to reveal a thing. But she could have done more. Each day, she cycled up the steep hill of Northborough Road and down again six hours later with tough rubberised bags of grocery shopping on the handlebars. 'Feel the wind in your hair!' she shouted to no one, freewheeling downhill, homeward bound. Her legs were strong, but her mind was perforated. She lived to be 89 years old, the last of my children's grandparents, outliving Stan by five years.

* * *

Then the tan ice skates; tucked away in the trunk under a blanket. We used to pull them out from time to time, but never delved deeper into the box. She said she ice skated during the war at Bletchley Park. It sounded wonderful; we liked to ice skate. A few years before she died, I remember her intensity to pass on ownership. 'Will you take these?' I couldn't think of a reason why I should have them. They were tan, not my favourite colour, and they were very old. I still wonder why I said no.

Where are they now? Did she give them to Bletchley or a jumble sale? Are they hidden in another box? The trunk is in America, they are not there. I hope to find them one day. Her name is scratched inside with black indelible ink in her familiar hand: Daisy E. Lawrence. The ones that hold the secret memories, the ones that were there; the ones that might tell her story, written perhaps on thin yellowing paper hidden under the inner sole of the boots in which she once stood and twirled around the ice on the lake at Bletchley Park.

Epilogue

Codebreakers reunion 1996. Daisy Lawrence (left), Dorothy Edney and Peggy Skinner (right). Christine Slimming (next to Daisy) GCHQ commissioned to Wilhelmshaven after the war. (Author)

In 1996 our parents celebrated their fiftieth wedding anniversary, which presented an excellent opportunity for the three codebreakers to reunite. But the big surprise for all was when my mother-in-law announced she and my deceased father in-law were vetted at GCHQ Bletchley Park in 1946. They did not meet each other then, but romance blossomed during their independent postings overseas to teach Allied Forces' children at Prince Rupert School, Wilhelmshaven, Germany.

* * *

Soon after their anniversary Mum was officially registered blind. Dad continued to control her weak and tearful moods with just the right cocktail of coping drugs, the safety line for the rest of her life. But then he died suddenly on 18 October 2001. He thought he was healthy and would reach a hundred, but a clot in his leg resulted in an aneurysm. He was 84. Mum accompanied him in the ambulance, but Dad was unresponsive at the hospital. The shock of his death, and her own acute osteoporosis breakdown, led her to be hospitalised the same day. Jill, thirty miles away, was there immediately. I flew to England that evening.

When I arrived, Mum was sedated for shock, but I was concerned about her medication. She had collected her pill box before entering the ambulance, a habit spanning five decades, and inside we saw an earlier doctor's prescription: 'Stelazine 1mg at night, in place of 2mg Stelazine tablets, for four weeks, then alternate at night for 2 weeks, then stop.'

We waited for her to come around the day after his death. She'd understood my sister and knew Dad had died but couldn't speak properly or express her thoughts clearly. The only sounds we heard were gobbledygook. The 'stop' in her brain was not there and her slurred speech seemed to be in some unreadable code that nobody understood, much like letters of a typewriter…or the gobbledygook of a wartime message. Her brain – her computer – was mixed; something had to be done. I looked at the dosage on the pill bottles:

Stelazine x 1 in the morning and one in the afternoon for depression, schizophrenia or schizo affective disorder.

Dispel x 1 in the morning and one in the afternoon for depression

Continue with 2mg Sparmite Stelazine in the morning, every morning

Trithoperazine 2mg od

Orphenadrine 50mg od, one in the morning

Navispare- od x 1 in the morning for hypertension (blood pressure) and depleted salt level (119 instead of 125)

Atenold (cyleopenthozide? 1 tablet 250mg-2.5mg100mg od x 1 in the morning or night for hypertension (blood pressure)

Castor Oil Pill x 1

Peggy Weston's letter remembering the day Daisy's news arrived. With her daughter, Pamela Hill, after the war. (Daisy Lawrence Archive)

I knew exactly what had happened and asked the nurse to stop all medicine immediately. They had not administered the perfect low-dose cocktail Dad agreed with the doctor, but the higher dose prescribed on each bottle, which affected her speech. It was alarming, but after a day of no drugs she was back to herself. The hospital diagnosed the episode as 'hyponatraemia (lack of sodium in her blood), an incidental finding and chronic, but secondary to her antipsychotics'. As such further investigation was not thought necessary.

She survived another five years until January 2006, when she died at the age of 89. Peggy Weston wrote:

> 'What memories you have stirred. I still think of your mother
> as the slight, naturally wavy, blonde-haired girl I first met,
> who asked us to call her "Lawrie" as she didn't like the name
> "Daisy". The time your father was missing, the explosion of
> joy in the office when she heard from the Red Cross that he
> was a PoW. The years of waiting and hoping....'

Bletchley Park Today

If only Daisy and her friends could see Bletchley Park's success today, as a museum and heritage site, saved by many volunteers, donations and grants. The nineties threat of destruction was happily thwarted through the great efforts and early intervention of Bletchley Park veterans, and foresight of Tony and Margaret Sale. If their group had not convened in 1991, and Dr Black had not intercepted, we may never have realised the full history of the codebreakers and their achievements.

This fulfilling work of more than eight years has led me to understand far more about the Second World War than I ever thought I needed to know, and to better understand my mother, Daisy Lawrence. I hope it will help others. By piecing together as much as possible of her role and those of her Bletchley colleagues, I feel this is one small contribution to the history of Bletchley Park, and goes some way toward recognition of Hut 7. Though the actual hut may only have existed for a brief time, the activities of Hut 7 – multifarious in many buildings – needs deeper analysis.

The snippets of information Daisy occasionally let slip, and research so far, reveals that Hut 7 was the precursor to the first manual 'Google' search engine, and central to Bletchley Park's naval intelligence operation. In 2014, when I asked Bletchley Park's Director of Learning and Collections about this area, she indicated that little was known about Hut 7. Others said it never existed. However, she was excited to say it was mentioned on a new interactive map in Block C's foyer. Through a secret backdoor, she went on to show me the area of the former site and its remaining electrical sub-station – which can also be seen from the National Radio Centre room, a small but separate section at Bletchley. But a dot on a map and the equivalent of a modern-day fuse box is hardly a serious representation of Hut 7's central role in Bletchley's operation. At a recent Veterans' Day presentation, I questioned if lack of funds was the reason this crucial area is left to the imagination. Iain Standen, CEO, replied: 'An outline of the building's foundations might be indicated on the ground, but there would be no building since it was demolished in the 50s – long ago.' Let's hope that at least will happen.

Last thoughts: Regarding the strain of keeping the secret for forty years, and the effect on codebreakers' mental health. As far as we know there was no back up for them or their families; no guiding support system for repatriation. If such a support system existed, we were unaware. Perhaps that will change.[1]

Regarding the Bletchley Badges of Honour and those denied simply because they died too early; all others in military service were rightly acknowledged, why not all the codebreakers? My request is for my mother and others to receive their official badge of recognition posthumously.[2]

Acknowledgements

My sincere thanks for the motivational push to write this book go to Dave Barasoain at NPR Atlanta, WABE 90.1 FM and Steve Goss, whose velvet voice in the mornings introduced me to Janice Martin Benario, an American codebreaking WAVE, whose own story – in a separate publication – provided the foundation for this work. Without all three, I would not have investigated the intricacies of my mother's life during the war, and neither would I have understood my parents' pain in coping with this fraught time in their lives.

In the end it is a memoir of self-discovery, as well as the memoir of my mother. She was a small cog in a huge wheel of many who performed their duties diligently and admirably to help the Allies defeat the Axis powers. I am grateful to be able tell her story. Thank you to everyone, especially my husband and our three children, for their patience in helping me complete this project, which sometimes presented more questions than answers. My sister Jill Robertson and her family, my cousins Patricia Franklin and Ronald Collingridge, Aunty Dot's daughter, 'cousin' Sally More and Jack Dart re Mary Goddard. All my friends, who have encouraged me to finish, especially Gaye Belkin who discovered David Kahn's original 1967 book *The Codebreakers* in her husband's library (I felt I was holding a million dollars!). Thanks to Anna Williams, Fiona Ewers and Laura Thomas for help with Wren information and photos, and a huge thanks to my nephew, Chris Robertson, for scanning the photographs to a higher quality. To Connie McKee for her help with the mental health aspect, thank you; the Atlanta Churchill Society, Atlanta Writers Club's many critics, and all my editors for their advice. And finally, my editors at Pen & Sword, the staff of GCHQ and Bletchley Park, oral historian Jonathan Byrne, and our veteran codebreakers. Special thanks also to Sir Dermot Turing for writing the Foreword.

ACKNOWLEDGEMENTS

'Certa Cito'
Discovered in Daisy's box of discarded broken pearl necklaces 2020.
The badge given to Radio Signals personnel.
Their motto is 'Swift and Sure'.

"Certa Cito," Royal Signals cap badge found in a box of Daisy's broken jewellery 2020. (Author)

List of Names from the signatures on Dorothy Edney's VE Day message (Chapter 41)

Front Page:

*Betty Allman (Ramsay), Norwich, Norfolk, FO Civilian CIII, BP Nov.1943-August 1945

*Sylvia Eileen Ball (Langford), Portsmouth. FO Civilian, Bletchley Park February 1944-August 1945. Probably Typex Operator in Communications Centre

Iris M. Baumer, Bletchley

Guy M. Bucksey, Sidcup, Kent

*Edna E. Dean, Great Harwood FO Civilian, BP 1942-1945. Block D Typing deciphered messages

*Enid Myra Elliot (Penrose), London N.10. BP. Block E. Communications Centre

P. M. Hart, Barnsley, Yorks

Linda Hibberd, Welling, Kent

P. Juan, Newcastle/Tyne

I. Lofting, London, SW14

P. McBeth, Feycham, Kent

Jean A. Olley, London SE15

E. Tattam, New Bradwell, Bucks

Dorothy E. Tedman, Lichfield, Staffs.

LIST OF NAMES

N. Stickland, Southsea

Margaret Veasey, Gosport, Lancs.

Winifred Welham, London E.10

Olive Winderbank, Norbury SW16

Back Page:

E.M. Parker (Pixie), Stanmore, Middlesex

*Gladys Bissett, Barking. FO Civilian BP probably Block E, Communications Centre, Typex Operator

O. Pamela Batterly, Southsea

*Margaret Brenda Goddard (Davis), Watford FO Civilian BP May1943-August 1945. Block E, Communications Centre, Typex Operator

Iris L. Rogers, Hornchurch, Essex.

Ann Reed, Bargoed, S. Wales

Emcerbley

Joyce Liowen, Folkstone

*Joan A. Gibbs (Storey), Doncaster. FO Civilian BP April 1944-August 1945. Block E, Communications Centre, Typex Operator

*Jessie Vera Claydon (Cooper), Barking, Essex, FO Civilian BP 1942-1946. Block E. Communications

*Peggy Eaton, Essex (M. Eaton - probably Margaret) FO Civilian TA BP. Block E. Communications Centre

*Daphne M. Anderson, Sth. Woodford, Essex. FO Civilian. Bletchley Park c.1944. Probably Block E, Communications Centre, teleprinter operator

*Audrey C. Courtman, Wallington, Surrey. FO Civilian. BP Probably Block E Morse-slip reader

Biddy Hagdon, Sutton, Surrey 1942-1945

Vera Pease, Lulworth(?) Cove, Dorset

Edna Wilkins, Leigh-on-Sea

Pamela F. Williams, Brighton

*Doreen Blanchard (Brown), Andover. FO Civilian. BP from September 1943. Probably Block E, Communications, Typex Operator

Barbara A. Thirlwell, Newcastle-upon-Tyne

Marjorie Prince, Hessle, Yorks (Hull)

*Irene Amy Fentiman (Davey), Burney, Hertford, BP

*Patricia Theresa Dunn, London. FO Civilian, TA - BP Jan 1942-Aug 1945. Hut 14 & Block E, Cipher Office

M. LLanwarne, Bradford.

Joan Gates, Balham

Sybil M. Golden, Norwich, Norfolk

*Eileen (Goodchild?) (Morris), Essex. Eileen M. Bletchley Park

Nora O'Brien, Godalming, Surrey

J Curry/Surry/Percy) Littlehampton, Sussex

Monica Parsons, London

Phillippa Barrett (Barnet), London

Vivien V. Hudson, SW4

Anne Saunders, Bournemouth

Christine M.E. Glover, Kettering,

Doreen W. Newman, Carshalton, Surrey

Margaret Hall (Fall), Kings Lynn

*Vera Atkinson (Boniwell), Welling. FO Civilian, BP 1943-1945. Block E, Communications, Typex Operator

Rose Smith, Sheffield

Dorothy M. Martin, Hornsea, Yorks

*Julia Elizabeth Anne Bearman, (Noakes) Westcliffe-on-Sea, Essex. FO Civilian, CII, BP May 1944-June 1945. Probably Morse slip reader

LIST OF NAMES

Nora Peerless, née Mobbs, Bletchley

Mary Pepper 'Pep', Hull, Yorks

J. P. Cole

Josephine Rush, Clapham, London

Betty Laws, St. Helens, I.O.W

*Betty Flanagan, FO Civilian BP. Probably Block E, Communications Centre, Typex Operator

Marjorie Chalkmore, Maidstone

*Margery Garrett, Southgate. FO Civilian. BP. Block E, Communications Center, probably Typex operator

*Additional information as appears on the Bletchley Roll of Honor 2020.

Abbreviations

ARP	Air Raid Precaution Service
ASDIC	Anti-submarine division/sound experimentation using quartz
ATS	Auxiliary Territorial Service
BEF	British Expeditionary Force
BFPO	British Fleet Post Office
BP	Bletchley Park
BRUSA	British and USA agreement 1943
CBE	Commander of the Order of the British Empire (Royal Honours award)
CCM	Combined Cipher Machine
CIA	Central Intelligence Agency (USA)
CII – CVI	Clerk Grade civil servant
CMG	Companion Order of St. Michael and St. George (Ambassador award)
CMY	Cover Management Y Station
COMINT	Interception of enemy communications
CSR	Combat Stress Reaction
D/F	Direction Finding
DNI	Director of Naval Intelligence
DTC	Defense Telecommunications Control
DTN	Defense Teleprinter Network
ECM	Electric Cipher Machine
ECT	Electro-convulsion Treatment
ENSA	Entertainments National Service Association
FANY	First Air Nursing Yeomanry
FECB	Far East Combined Bureau
FO	Foreign Office
FRUMEL	Fleet Radio Unit, Melbourne

ABBREVIATIONS

FRUPAC	Fleet Radio Unit Pacific
GC&CS	Government Code & Cypher School
GCHQ	Government Communications Headquarters
GI	Government Issue (USA)
GPO	General Post Office
HMSO	His Majesty's Stationery Office
HMV	His Master's Voice, gramophone and record company
HUMINT	Human Intelligence
IMINT	Imaginary aerial intelligence
ISOS	Illicit or Intelligence Services Oliver Strachey
ISSIS	Inter-Service Special Intelligence School
Jafo	Japanese Forces – Japanese Army and Airforce Intelligence
JMA	Japanese Military Attaché
JN	Japanese Naval codes and ciphers
JNA	Japanese Naval Attaché
MI	Military Intelligence
MIT	Massachusetts Institute of Technology
NID	Naval Intelligence Department
NSA	National Security Agency (USA)
NSIJ	Naval Section Intelligence Japanese
OBE	Order of the British Empire (Public service award)
OC	Officer-in-Charge
OP-20-G	US Naval Communications Signals Intelligence Operation (Section G, 20th division)
OSS	Office of Strategic Services
OTP	One-time cipher pad
POWs	Prisoners of War
PTSD	Post-Traumatic Stress Disorder
RACS	Royal Arsenal Co-operative Society
RAF	British Royal Airforce
RASC	Royal Army Service Corps
ROC	Royal Observer Corps
RSS	Radio Security Service
R/T	Radio Telephony
RVS	Royal Voluntary Service (WVS)
SCU	Special Communication Unit
SDX	Special Duty, Station 10

SIGINT	Signals Intelligence
SIS	Secret Intelligence Service
SIXTA	Hut 6 at BP, Traffic Analysis
SLU	Special Liaison Unit
SOAS	School of Oriental and African Studies
SOE	Special Operations Executive
SSU	Strategic Services Unit (USA - post OSS and pre-CIA)
TSAO	Temporary Senior Administrative Officer
ULTRA	Top Secret Intelligence
VHF	Very High Frequency
WAAF	Women's Auxiliary Air Force
WFC	Western Front Committee
WHO	World Health Organization
WRNS	Women's Royal Naval Service (Wrens)
W/T	Wireless Telegraphy
WTS	Women's Transport Service
WVS	Women's Voluntary Service
XU	Examination Unit
Y	Wireless Listening Service

Endnotes

Chapter 2: War

1. 1935 revisions to America's Neutrality Act, affected their future decisions on Europe. The first Act was issued by President, George Washington, 22 April 1793, when he declared the nation would abstain from conflict between France and Great Britain and threatened legal proceedings against any American who aided any country at war. The Act was formally passed in 1794, outlawing military operations against nations at peace with America. The 1930s amendments to The Neutrality Act were passed in Congress in response to repeated tensions in Europe. The amended 1935 Act sought to ensure America would never again become embroiled in other foreign conflicts. An embargo on all war item shipments was enforced, Americans were not allowed to travel on belligerent ships, and no belligerent countries were permitted loans from the USA. https://en.wikipedia.org/wiki/Neutrality_Acts_of_the_1930s Accessed January 2017.
2. *DK Millennium 20th Century Chronicle* 1999, pp507-510.
3. Daisy's letter to grandson © Christopher Robertson, May 1995.
4. Stanley Moore's tape recording made for the author. ©Jan Slimming 1990.
5. James Phinney Baxter III, Official Historian of the Office of Scientific Research and Development.

Chapter 3: 'Manoeuvres'

1. Roosevelt signed the 1941 Lend-Lease bill to aid Britain and China. In a subsequent period, America also supplied provisions to the USSR and other Allied nations, including warships, warplanes and weaponry. The aid was free though some hardware such as ships, were returned after the war. In exchange land was to be leased for US bases in Allied territory. The program effectively ended the United States position of neutrality and was a decisive step away from non-interventionist policy. https://en.wikipedia.org/wiki/Lend-Lease

Chapter 6: A Letter and a Telegram

1. Modern-day Taiwan

Chapter 10: New Surroundings and a Friendly Face

1. Ruth Bourne (née Henry) and Bletchley Park Trust.

Chapter 11: Room 40

1. *The Codebreakers: The Story of Secret Writing* and *Seizing the Enigma* pp17-27, both by David Kahn.
2. The Citadel held Operational Intelligence Centre; built 1940-42 in London's Horse Guards Parade. Churchill considered this a harsh monstrosity, but it was built to withstand enemy attack with bomb proof walls, firing stations and corridors to other Admiralty departments. Today the eyesore is softened by the encouraged growth of Boston Ivy.
3. https://military.wikia.org/wiki/William_Montgomery_(cryptographer, *The Bletchley Park Codebreaker* by Erskine and Smith p.14 and p.383, *Seizing the Enigma* by David Kahn p.117.
4. GCHQ Director Iain Lobban said in 2012 at Leeds University, that Knox visited the manufacturing company in Berlin in 1926 and bought an Enigma machine. Mavis Batey (neé Lever), also Room 40, confirmed in her biography that GC&CS was in possession of one in 1929 when Foss's codebreaking work was completed on Enigma. *Gordon Welchman: Bletchley Park's Architect of Ultra Intelligence* by Joel Greenberg pp 266.
5. A regiment formed to protect Edinburgh during the 'Glorious Revolution' of William of Orange, in the seventeenth century.

Chapter 12: Enigma and the Polish Bomba

1. *Seizing the Enigma* by David Kahn, pp39-43.
2. *Gordon Welchman: Bletchley Park's Architect of Ultra Intelligence* by Joel Greenberg, p.21.
3. Stewart Menzies had a distinguished career after Eton, fighting in the First World War in the Grenadier Guards. When he joined the counter-intelligence section of British Commander Field Marshal Douglas Haig, he found the chiefs of department fudged their intelligence estimates. Consequently, heads rolled and Menzies was promoted. He entered MI1b/SIS and was part of the 1919 delegation at the Versailles Peace Conference, and when Admiral Hugh Sinclair became director-general in 1924, Menzies became his deputy in 1929; he was promoted to full colonel soon after.
4. *Seizing the Enigma* by David Kahn, pp268-9.
5. Combining three Enigma rotors from a set of five, the rotor settings with twenty-six positions, and the plug board with ten pairs of letters connected, the military Enigma had nearly 158,962,555,217,826,360,000 different settings. Easily explained as 159 million, million, million (eighteen zeros).

Gordon Welchman: Bletchley Park's Architect of Ultra Intelligence by Joel Greenberg, p.204.

6. The concept of American-built Liberty ships came from Britain in 1940 to replace wartime merchant ship losses. A simple low-cost US design was made with a single 2,500 horsepower steam engine. Contracts were placed with eighteen US shipyards for sixty cargo steamers of Ocean class and mass-produced on an unprecedented scale at a cost of US$2 million (US$36 million in 2019). 2,710 Liberty Ships were built between 1941 and 1945. The Second World War Home Front Museum.
7. *Seizing the Enigma* by David Kahn, p55.

Chapter 13: Bletchley Park, the Prime Minister and a Letter
1. *Hut 6 Story* by Gordon Welchman.
2. Preface to Turing's *Treatise on the Enigma - The Prof's Book*.
3. David Kenyon. p.55. Letter from Denniston to Peters December 14, 1936. TNA HW72/9.
4. Ditchley Park is now owned by Ditchley Foundation, an Anglo-American educational trust created in 1964, Cyrus Vance, former US Secretary of State was an early Chairman.
5. The National Archives and *Gordon Welchman: Bletchley Park's Architect of Ultra Intelligence* by Joel Greenberg.
6. *Introduction; Organization Studies, History and Bletchley Park, Decoding Organization* by Christopher Grey, Cambridge University Press 2012.

Chapter 14: Living in Digs
1. The BRUSA Agreement was joint co-operation and regulations for handling and distributing highly sensitive and secret material between Britain and America. Its security procedures and protocols formed the basis for all SIGINT (Signals Intelligence) of the US National Security Agency (NSA) and British GCHQ.

Chapter 15: The Workings of Bletchley Park
1. *Bletchley Park and D-Day*, by David Kenyon, 2019. Chapter 4, p.99.
2. *Gordon Welchman: Bletchley Park's Architect of Ultra Intelligence* by Joel Greenberg, p.25.
3. Fleming was posted to Asia by the Director of Naval Intelligence, according to *Ian Fleming* (1996), p.154 by Andrew Lycette. Most of the trip was fact-finding, to identify opportunities for 30 AU in the Pacific, but the unit saw little action as the Japanese surrendered. 30 Assault Unit, aka No.30 Commando, was formed by Fleming in 1942.

4. *Gordon Welchman: Bletchley Park's Architect of Ultra Intelligence* by Joel Greenberg, pp.71-76.
5. *The Poles Reveal Their Secrets* by Ralph Erskine, *Cryptologia* 30(4), December 2006, pp294-305, *Wikipedia* John R. F, Jeffreys, March 2016.
6. BMP included Squadron Leader William Millward, RAF, 1942 to 1945, Hut 3 and Block D (3) Air Adviser, German air defence, and later Deputy Head of Hut 3A. Flight Lieutenant Frederick Seaton Prior was Air Section from 1940 until 1943, Hut 10 and Block A working on Luftwaffe air defence activity. He was in the Middle East from March 1943, but later returned to Bletchley Park.
7. The British government reviewed communication circuits of all armed services. The RAF – which had a defence network of radar installations – and the Royal Observer Corps (ROC) with other defence infrastructure, needed to meld with other departments. The GPO started the DTC (Defence Telecommunications Control) around the country, but there was a demand for voice communications as well as telegraphic facilities. The result was the DTN (Defence Teleprinter Network), installed by Standard and the GPO. The DTN had the same capacity as the public or civil network, which tripled by 1944. Its network of five large switching centres were discreetly positioned around Britain, with smaller switchboards and teleprinter terminals (as at Bletchley) at other military and government buildings. At its peak DTN comprised over 12,000 individual telegraph circuits, 10,000 teleprinters and associated equipment. Many large teleprinter rooms had 200 machines. *Bletchley Park and D-Day by David Kenyon,* p.28. Reproduced with permission of The Licensor through PLSClear.
8. Tiltman was well decorated and worked with William Friedman again in 1951 deciphering the Voynich manuscript. As well as the Military Cross, he received the OBE, CBE, CMG and Legion of Merit. He died in Hawaii August 10th, 1982, aged 88. In 2004 he was inducted into the NSA Hall of Honor. The first non-US citizen to be recognised this way. The NSA commented, 'His efforts at training and attention to all the many facets of cryptology inspired the best in all who encountered him.'
9. *Gordon Welchman: Bletchley Park's Architect of Ultra Intelligence*, Joel Greenberg, p.47.
10. Derived from 'Googol.' The number 10 raised to the power of 100 (10100) = 1 followed by 100 zeros. Its name represents in this case masses of information categorized many times over. The word 'googol' was first coined in the 1920s by Milton Sirotta, the 9-year-old nephew of America mathematician Edward Kasner.

Chapter 16: Working and Waiting
1. *Seizing the Enigma* by David Kahn Chapter 19, p.283
2. BBC interview, *Desert Island Discs*, 5 June 2015. Susan Pamela Rose (née Gibson)

3. The *Scharnhorst* escaped with the *Gneisenau* via the English Channel in 1942. They were nicknamed *Salmon* and *Gluckstein,* by Listeners in Falmouth. Known as *'Lucky Scharnhorst,* she was described as one of the most beautiful warships ever built, with a flared 'clipper' bow, able to reach a record-breaking speed of 33 knots. But her luck ran out when she was sunk by *HMS Duke of York*, 26 December 1943. Intelligence from Norway and Bletchley Park, and two Royal Navy convoys as bait, the vessel was lured by the Allies into a trap. A total of fifty-five torpedoes fired at the target. Eleven hit the *Scharnhorst*. From a crew of 1,968, only thirty-six survived. Allied destroyers picked up survivors. In 1940 the *Scharnhorst* and her sister-ship the *Gneisnau* had sunk aircraft carrier *HMS Glorious* and her escort destroyers *Acasta* and *Ardent*. 1,519 men were lost. Thirty-eight survived, but none were saved by German warships.

4. David Kenyon's *Bletchley Park and D-day*, accessed late 2019, where he describes Hut 3's message processing path. This would be the same for the Naval section. p76-79.

5. Clarke's Professor Tropp letter, October 1993, Courtesy of Kerry Howard, with additions from the author's childhood memory.

6. Compares to Daisy's pay of £3.16s.8d. at the end of her Bletchley employment. In 2019 this equates to £174 per week.

Chapter 17: Intelligence Triumphs

1. ASDIC. In 1917. To maintain the project's secrecy no mention of sound experimentation or quartz was made. Instead 'Supersonics' a word describing early work was changed to 'ASD'ics, and quartz material became 'ASD'ivite: 'ASD' meant 'Anti-Submarine Division,' hence the British acronym ASDIC. In 1939, in response to a question from the Oxford English Dictionary, the Admiralty invented a story saying it stood for 'Allied Submarine Detection Investigation Committee.' This is still widely believed, though no committee reference to this has been found in Admiralty archives. Sonar Wikipedia, July 2020.

2. Newsday.com obituaries – 29 May 2016. *The Week*, June 2016.

3. *Bradford Plumer New Republic.com* article 47572/how-lichens-won-world-war-ii

4. Adapted from BP Roll of Honour.

5. Named after Grand Admiral Alfred von Tirpitz, the battleship was built and launched 1936-1939 for the Nazi Kriegsmarine (Navy). A sister-ship to the Bismarck, the *Tirpitz* was one of the most modern battleships in the Second World War. Ironically, however, she never saw action against a convoy or a naval battle group.

6. 'Heavy water' is the chemical compound ingredient hydrogen isotope deuterium needed to make an Atom Bomb. *They Listened in Secret* by Gwendoline Page, pp 41-42.

Chapter 18: Rationing and Writing

1. http://www.evelynwaugh.org.uk/styled-48/index.html
2. George Orwell, As I Please, Tribune, *20 October 1944*

Chapter 19: From SW17 to PO Box 111

1. August 13th, 1943 – Captives' Mail Lost. The BOAC (British Overseas Airways Corporation) flying boat which crashed in Eire on July 28 carried mail from British prisoners of War. *Daisy Lawrence Newspaper cuttings.*
2. August 13th, 1943: Grunts of Satisfaction. *Daisy Lawrence Newspaper cuttings.*
3. August 14th, 1943: WANT NEWS OF 60,000 BRITONS. *Daisy Lawrence Newspaper cutting.*
4. https://en.wikipedia.org/wiki/Du_Cane_Court.

Chapter 20: Block E, Typex Communications

1. During the Second World War an American version of the Typex machine was invented, 'Sigaba.' Its existence is attributed to William and Elisabeth Friedman and it's encrypted codes are still immune to attacks today. N*SA National Cryptological Museum, Fort Meade, Maryland, USA.*
2. Caroline Johnson 2015, Granddaughter of A.S. White.

Chapter 21: Culture or Intellect?

1. BP Roll of Honour: Stan Sedgwick 1/16/2017.

Chapter 23: The Listeners

1. From Peggy Johnson's letter, 1 February 2006. *Daisy Lawrence Archive.*
2. Peggy Johnson, ATS Royal Signals confirmed in a conversation with Daisy and Dot in 1996, that she was in 'the Y,' as a radio operative listening to German messages, at Beaumanor, Leicestershire.
3. *They Listened in Secret*, Gwendoline Page, p.161
4. One of the first confirmations of the successful Operation Chastise mission was received at Beaumanor. Rumour also suggests this Y group, or WOYG, knew details of the Katyn Forest massacre by Soviet Secret Police of 22,000 Polish nationals, as early as 1941. *Gordon Welchman: Bletchley Park's Architect of Ultra Intelligence*, Joel Greenberg, p.20.
5. *They Listened in Secret*, Gwendoline Page, pp.vii, and *Gordon Welchman: Bletchley Park's Architect of Ultra Intelligence*, Joel Greenberg, p.49 and p.83.
6. Pat Davies (née Owtram). WRNS, Y-Service. Bletchley Park website.
7. Pauline Sperring (née Tanner) WRNS driver, aged eighteen, bringing daily dispatch boxes to Bletchley Park from Portsmouth Dockyard, approximately 120 miles south. Bletchley Park website.

ENDNOTES

8. From Betty Law's daughter, referencing her mother's photograph published in *Between Silk and Cyanide: A Codemakers War 1941-1945* by Leo Marks. And Jean Argles SOE, FANY, co-author of *1000 Days on the River Kwai - Colonel Cary Owtram OBE* by sisters Pat Owtram Davies/Jean Argles.

9. The Double-Cross, or XX, System was a Second World War anti-espionage and deception operation of the British Security Service, domestic counterintelligence, usually referred to by its cover title MI5.

10. Winterbotham's book aimed to set the record straight after American author David Kahn published (Macmillan 1967) *The Codebreakers: The Story of Secret Writing*. Prime Minister Harold Wilson and the British government banned Kahn from mentioning Bletchley Park and its methods. Yale University (USA) then published John Masterman's *The Double Cross System*, an exposé of the British spy organization. In 1972, the British government conceded Masterman's US publication was far enough from The Official Secrets Act but ruled sixty paragraphs of classified information be removed. Some referred to Ultra. The publishing director agreed to remove twelve, buy still no UK publisher would touch it. Instead Weidenfield & Nicholson took the risk to release *The Ultra Secret*, by Frederick W. Winterbotham in 1974.

11. RAF Sergeant, Stanley Clegg, Bletchley Park records, permission granted 2016.

12. C-36 Hagelin was invented by Swedish Cryptographer, Boris Hagelin, in the 1930s. Originally designed to fit in a pocket the prototype was adapted for America, via William Friedman. The basic design, using a pin and lug mechanism, was offered to other agencies before the Second World War. German and Italian military also enciphered messages using Hagelin. Smith-Corona's factory in Groton, New York, manufactured C-36 and later the M-209, and produced 600 olive-drab machines per day. Hagelin received a royalty and is probably the only cryptographer to have become a millionaire. *David Kahn, The Codebreakers: The Story of Secret Writing 1967 First Edition, 4th printing 1968, Chapter 13, pp426-7. Wikipedia 2019: Torbjorn Andersson, The Hagelin C-35/C-36, Boris CW Hagelin - The Story of Hagelin Cryptos, Cryptologia 18(3) July 1994, pp204-242.*

13. The one-time pad or OTP was an early encryption technique from the 1900s, considered one of the most secure methods available. During the Second World War, a pad of printed sheets was used where the key for the Typex machine was known. To read the code an identical pad was used by the receiver who had the pre-arranged key. Messages were set and sent to the Admiralty and field commands. The OTP was then destroyed.

14. *Bletchley Park and D-Day*, David Kenyon, 2019, p.96; F. Winterbotham's Imperial War Museum interview, reel 30.

15. Bletchley Park website.

Chapter 24: Speaking of Japanese

1. *Bletchley Park and D-Day*, by David Kenyon, 2019 p.64. Reproduced with permission of The Licensor through PLSClear.
2. *ibid* p.67-68
3. *ibid* p.66
4. Docent, Mike Chapman, at Bletchley Park, 2014, who interviewed Michael Loewe
5. As stated in the Holden Agreement 1942 which gave the USA responsibility over all Japanese codes. The 1943 BRUSA Agreement overturned the ruling, where information was shared.
6. FRUMEL Ref: Erskine and Smith p.122 *The Bletchley Park Codebreakers.*
7. Introduction quote in Christopher Grey's Decoding Organization, Cambridge Press 2012.

Chapter 25: Hut 7 and Top Secret Ultra

1. Hut 7 interactive map; Bletchley Park's Director of Learning and Collections May 2014.
2. TNA HW 8/146, Major H. E. Martin report, first access by the author September 2018. 'Naval General Purpose System JN XI Bookbuilding & Translation.'
3. Maru means 'circle' or 'round' and is often a suffix to the names of Japanese ships, as in *Nippon Maru.* It implies the good omen of defensiveness or circles of protection, or a complete and safe round trip.
4. Adapted from an Air Force Hut 3 description, *Bletchley Park and D-Day*, 2019 by David Kenyon, p.77. Reproduced with permission of The Licensor through PLSClear.
5. TNA HW 8/146, Major H. E. Martin report p.18: A subtractor cipher is a system in which figure codes are disguised by subtracting figures obtained from a subtractor table.
6. TNA HW 8/146, Major H. E. Martin report p.18: the indicating system shows at what point in the subtractor tables a message starts.
7. TNA HW 8/146, Major H. E. Martin report p.18: Secret call-signs concealed the originator and addressees of signals. If the meaning of these were known it was a great help to the book-builder.
8. TNA HW 8/146, Major H. E. Martin report p.19: 'De-garbling was the correction of corruption which occurred, either in wireless transmission or in cipher processes applied by the Japanese, or by ourselves.'
9. Christine Slimming (née Drummond) 1996. Teacher at Prince Rupert School, Wilhelmshaven, Germany.

Chapter 26: Lonely Girl

1. Adapted extracts from *The Girl from Station X* by Elisa Segrave, p.160.
2. Topee - a lightweight helmet or sun hat made from the pith of the sola plant.
3. Adapted extracts from *The Girl from Station X* by Elisa Segrave, p181.

ENDNOTES

Chapter 27: Fun and Games

1. *Daily Express* article and BP's Iain Standen speaking on the *One Show.*
2. Air Raid Precautions (ARP) was established after German aircraft in the First World War terrified British civilians. *Histclo.com Dec.2015.*
3. At 83, Pamela Rose returned to the stage after her husband's death in 1999. *BBC Desert Island Discs* interview aged 97, June 5th, 2015.
4. Jean Campbell-Harris Barker, The Right Honorable Baroness Trumpington, The enigmatic life of Lady Trumpington, *The Guardian,* 27 April 2014. *Accessed July 5th 2016*
5. https://bspittle.wordpress.com/2009/07/04/rice-polishings/Accessed October 2019

Chapter 28: Lead up to D-Day

1. Operation OVERLORD and subsidiary plans are chronicled in histories and films, with the names of the Normandy beaches – Omaha, Utah, Juno, Gold and Sword. Young soldiers faced heavy fire and exerted extreme bravery when as part of a staggering number of Allied troops, 130,000 men crossed the English Channel, preceded by 23,000 airborne troops. 10,000 Allied soldiers died the first day. The invasion was the largest amphibious assault in history. *Bletchley Park and D-Day*, David Kenyon, p.ix and p.xii.
2. *They Listened in Secret* by Gwendoline Page.

Chapter 29: Letters from Home

1. Texts provided by Ronald Collingridge 2018.
2. Maurice Webb, Labour Party, was a well-known political journalist, including for the *Daily Herald*. A broadcast commentator and member of the National Union of Journalists, toward the end of the war he was elected MP for Bradford Central. In 1946 he became Chairman of the Parliamentary Labour Party and appointed Minister of Food in 1950, overseeing the continued and often more stringent previous rationing program of Lord Woolton.

Chapter 31: War's End

1. *The Last Lion* by Paul Reid, p.924 – p.927
2. ibid
3. ibid
4. ibid
5. ibid

Chapter 32: 'We Also Served'

1. The Siegfried Line, a system of strong points built along the German western frontier in the 1930s, was expanded in 1944. German troops retreating from

France found it an effective barrier for respite against pursuing Americans. A popular morale booster song for Allied troops marching in France was 'We're going to hang our washing on the Siegfried Line.' An earlier French version by Ray Ventura during the Phoney War (*Drôle de Guerre*), was '*On ira pendre notre ligne sur la ligne Siegfried*. When asked about the Siegfried Line, General Patton reportedly said, 'Fixed fortifications are monuments to man's stupidity.' Ref: *The World War II Bookshelf,* James F Dunnigan, Citadel Press, 2005, p.110.

Chapter 33: Rain of Ruin, Rain of Tears

1. BP Roll of Honour.
2. Valerie Glassborow, was a FO Civilian at CMY, at Bletchley Park with her twin, Mary Glassborow. She was paternal grandmother to Kate Middleton, Duchess of Cambridge. Ref: *Bletchley Park Website VJ Day*.
3. Mary Goddard left Bletchley on 6 October 1945. Her pay was £2.11.0, considerably less than Daisy, five years older (b. January 14th, 1922), but London Weighting may also have affected pay rates. Daisy was a Temporary Assistant; Mary was a Temporary Woman Clerk Grade II, BP ref 1944. When Dot left in May 1945, she was a Temporary Assistant with pay of £3.10.0., BP ref 599. Mary Goddard's ID card shows addresses at: Wilton Avenue, Bletchley; 5 Queen Street, Leighton Buzzard, and later 48 Storforth Lane, Chesterfield. Her brother-in-law, Jack Dart, helped explain the confusion with Mary Pilgrim. This was not Mary Goddard; she never married. Mary Pilgrim was at Bletchley – Daisy had a newspaper cutting for her wedding – but she also became a neighbour of Mary Goddard's after the war, at 4 Storforth Lane.
4. Barbara Abernethy joined British Joint Services Mission in Washington DC (BJSM). In 1947 she married Dr Joseph J. Eachus, the first U.S. Naval Officer to be assigned long term to Bletchley.

Chapter 34: After the War

1. Roosevelt took secret advice from senior Canadian-British intelligence official, William Stephenson to draft a plan for an American intelligence service based on Britain's MI6 and the SOE. Stephenson's wartime intelligence codename was *Intrepid*. His spymaster story became famous when another William Stevenson (no relation) wrote *A Man Called Intrepid* in 1976. Ian Fleming once wrote 'James Bond is a highly romanticized version of a true spy. The real thing…is William Stephenson.'"Col. William J. Donovan coordinated OSS/SSU from July 1941 assisted by British equipment, instructors and training, including short-wave broadcasting capabilities to Europe, Africa and the Far East. Up to Pearl Harbor, the bulk of intelligence came from OSS, which was fully established by 13 June 1942. Sources: OSS/SSU and www.intrepid-society.org.htm – from *Room 3603* by Harford Montgomery Hyde.

2. The India Office Records is an archive repository of the East India Company (1600–1858), the Board of Control or Board of Commissioners for the Affairs of British India (1784–1858), the India Office (1858–1947), the Burma Office (1937–1948) and other related British agencies overseas linked to the main office. The archive is complemented by over 300 collections and over 3,000 smaller deposits of Private Papers relating to the British experience in India. Previously in the India Office Library, the department is now part of the Asia, Pacific and Africa Collections of the British Library, London, and part of the Public Records of the United Kingdom.

Chapter 38: Mental Health

1. Many therapies have helped people with mental health problems, but the wider use of modern ECT using computers is returning. Banned in some countries, ECT treatment is well-established for adults with severe life-threatening depression. It is not recommended for people under 18 years old. Memory loss remains a controversially acknowledged side-effect, but the scale of memory loss is disputed. Studies by ECT doctors suggest lapses are mostly short-term and that memory function soon returns to normal. Opponents say 50%+ of their patients suffer serious long-term memory loss. Who is right? Other modern researchers suggest ECT reverses brain problems instead of simply eradicating psychiatric illness. Doctors in favour are convinced that new neural imaging treatment is effective and safe. Treatment is carried out under general anaesthetic with muscle relaxants to prevent violent convulsions. An amp of electric current is administered in a series of short pulses which induces a mild seizure lasting about 30 seconds. Specialists believe this may 'reset' the brain malfunction. Some believe this method is less barbaric than surgery. Campaigners against ECT say the treatment causes traumatic brain injury, as currents not only travel through the frontal lobes – the sea of intelligence, thoughtfulness, creativity and judgment – but also through the temporal lobes where the seat of memory, personality, character and individuality of the patient is damaged. The Royal College of Psychiatrists say ECT is safe but acknowledges those who disagree. Medics observe ECT relieves severe depressive illness where other treatment has failed, citing benefits that outweigh the risks and that ECT saves lives, particularly if you consider that 15% of people with severe depression will kill themselves. Some patients agree and ask for the treatment again if they start to feel depressed. Some say the experience makes them more creative. Others see ECT as a treatment of the past and that its severe side-effects are accidentally or deliberately ignored. *Adapted from Modern ECT* www.bbc.com/news/magazine-39961472, *by Chris Rogers and Marshall Corwin BBC News, New York.*

2. http://warriorcare.dodlive.mil/2015/02/18/combat-stress-vs-ptsd-how-to-tell-the-difference

Chapter 39: Believe

1. Designed by government architect William C. Clifford-Smith of London County Council, West Park, on Horton Estate close to Epsom Common and South London, was the last in the Epsom Cluster of five mental institutions. Mental hospitals were Clifford-Smith's specialty. His compact arrow "colony" design featured a central hall with connecting hallways to external villas. Constructed 1906-1917, its use as a mental hospital was delayed until after the First World War. From 1921 to late 1990, it became the last psychiatric and epilepsy hospital to serve London's home counties. At its peak the site could hold two thousand patients. It was a research lab, nurses' training centre and a cottage hospital, but lack of government funding and changing attitudes to mental health led to the hospital's closure and the buildings becoming derelict.

Chapter 41: The Seventies

1. Glossary of Names ©Jan Slimming 2015. Both sides of signed SGM Message 8th May 1945 ©Sally More 2015. Cannot be reproduced without the exclusive permission of the copyright holders.
2. P. B. Cow & Co. manufactured tough linens and industrial rubber as well as sports equipment in London SW16. They acquired St Helens Cable and Rubber Co., Warrington, Lancashire, and after moving to Slough, the company was acquired by Allied Polymer in 1971. During the Second World War, PBC designed and produced protective electrical wire casings and rubberized equipment for the armed forces—lifeboats and life jackets, as well as the airbed, Lilo. The company's life jackets and dinghies saved many lives and prompted C. A. Robertson, one of PCB's chief draughtsman, to start the Goldfish Club after he heard airmen's stories about ditching their aircraft in the sea. This exclusive club enabled survivors to meet and exchange experiences. *Grace's Guide to British Industrial History.*
3. **Arthur Raymond Cooper** died a few weeks later, on 31 March 1975. These Cooper brothers are not connected to Arthur R. V. Cooper and Joshua Edward Synge Cooper, as far as can be established. Cooper's son confirms his father was in Kashmir and his uncle's name was William. He and his cousin have no knowledge of their fathers' connections to Bletchley. However, the elder **William Percy Cooper** appears on the BP Roll of Honour as a RAF Cpl. Bombe Maintenance Technician at Eastcote (no dates). The other set of Cooper brothers: **Arthur R. V. Cooper** was a Foreign Office Civilian January 1939 to 1945 (BP Roll of Honor) and part of FECB, Signals Intelligence; first in Hong Kong, then he escaped from Singapore, February 1942, followed by a short spell in Australia with FRUMEL. From March 1942, he decrypted non-Enigma

signals from German, Italian and Japanese air forces producing intelligence reports. He was ten years younger than his brother **Joshua Edward Synge Cooper,** born in Fulham, London, April 3rd, 1901. One of the first to Bletchley Park's Mansion in 1939, his Air Section expanded to Hut 10, Block A, then Block F. By March 1942 he was Chief Cryptographer for Service Sections, and appointed Deputy Director Air Section. With a high reputation as Cryptanalyst, his GC&CS team grew to around 500, of which 200 were mostly WAAF dealing with German, Italian and Japanese codes, and meteorological problems. He continued to work for GCHQ until 1961. *Bletchley Park Trust.*

Chapter 42: Reunion and the Sales Time

1. Similar machine found in Stanley Moore's garage in the 1980s. www.onlineonly. christies.com/s/code-breakers/a-british-typex-cipher-machine-4/12499 and Crypto Museum.
2. https://en.wikipedia.org/wiki/Tony_Sale

Chapter 43: Still No Recognition

1. The National Archive, Kew. November 2018.
2. *Bletchley Park and D-Day*, by David Kenyon, 2019. Chapter 4, p.99.
3. *Saving Bletchley Park* by Dr. Sue Black and Stevyn Colgan.

Chapter 44: Conclusion

1. GCHQ was due to release more information at the end of 2019.
2. September 1st, 1943, eight Wren Typex operators were killed when the SS *Khedive Ismail* was sunk while sailing from Kenya to Ceylon by a Japanese submarine.
3. *Bletchley Park and D-Day* David Kenyon. p.248 and Bill Williams', note 11.
4. Depersonalization Disorder is a little-discussed mental-health condition. One senses a form of disconnect from the world around and your body—everything appears "in a haze or fog, or 2D." It is believed to be a defence of acute anxiety or trauma by switching off from reality. The condition is not rare: one in a hundred people are estimated to have this according to some channels of study over several decades. Experts agree it is as widespread as other medical disorders such as OCD and schizophrenia and, if left untreated, can affected people's entire lives. However, doctors do not learn about this at medical school. Though mental health is supposed to be a key part of an extensive training curriculum, knowledge of the condition needs to improve. Poor diagnoses and lack of adequate access to treatment contribute to the problem. In the UK there is only one specialist clinic, with limited resources. Fewer than eighty patients a year are seen compared to an estimated 650,000 living with the condition.

Epilogue

1. Helpful services for PTSD and CSR. https://allcallsigns.org; https://www.ptsduk.org/about-ptsd-uk; https://www.ptsd.va.gov/professional/consult.

2. The term Codebreaker today refers to the many involved with this operation during the war. As of 2020 over 13,618 people are listed as being connected to Bletchley Park, but there will be more to add no doubt. So far this number is made up approximately of the following groups, in descending order by number: FOREIGN OFFICE CIVILIANS 4,206, WRNS (Navy) 2619, ARMY 2412, ATS 1096, WAAF 968, RAF 567, USA MILITARY 548, ROYAL NAVY (men) 493, GENERAL POST OFFICE 216, CANADIAN MILITARY 80, AUSTRALIAN MILITARY 62, WAR OFFICE CIVILIANS 30, ADMIRALTY CIVILIANS 21, FRENCH NAVY 10. According to the *Bletchley Park Roll of Honour January 2020.*

Index

* Indicates codebreakers

*ABERNETHY, Barbara, 66, 240
*ADCOCK, Frank, 76-9
Air raids, 23-31, 38, 69, 91, 150, 210, 329
*ALEXANDER, Hugh, 92
Atomb bomb, xiii, 234-7, 325

Barrage Balloons, 25, 69, 292
Battle of the Atlantic, 39, 84, 135
BBC, 17, 27, 128, 225
Billets/billet office, 72, 91, 98, 171, 186,
    191, 198, 211, 239, 253
*BIRCH, Frank, 76, 107, 110, 128,
    182, 198
BLACK, Dr. Sue, 296, 310, 333
*BLACKER, Carmen, 177
BLETCHLEY PARK,
    History, 36, 66, 70, 73, 91, 103, 115,
        130, 156, 197, 202, 218, 236, 293,
        306, 333
    Transport, 59, 65, 71, 149, 160, 215
Battle of Britain, 31, 112
Blitz, The, 28, 43, 91, 128, 252
*BONSALL, William 'Tip', 112-13
*BUDD Family, 72, 101, 158

*CAMPBELL-HARRIS, Jean (Barker),
    199-201, 329
Canada, 39-42, 147, 206, 246
CHAMBERLAIN, Neville, 23, 28, 32
Chess Players, 90, 92, 154, 203
Christmas, 34, 44, 53-8, 145, 154, 204,
    241, 263, 283, 289
CHURCHILL, Winston, xi, 28, 31, 35, 41,
    44, 50, 55, 68, 76, 85, 90, 96, 99, 105,

122, 135-7, 155, 169, 181, 206, 221,
    225, 232, 237, 244, 275, 283, 312, 322
*CLARKE, William "Nobby", 78, 34, 174
*CLEGG, Stanley (SLU), 170, 327
CODES & CIPHERS PROCESSING,
    Banburismus netz, 92, 111, 116, 131
    Bookbuilding & Translation Party, 79,
        89, 113, 183-7, 196, 230, 328
    "Blisters", 112
    "Cribs and Kisses", 85, 97, 111, 116,
        123, 127, 192
    Emending, 115, 195
    Gibberish and Gobbledygook, viii, 76,
        100, 151, 192, 308
    Google/"Googol", 122, 125, 130, 310, 324
    Hub and Spoke system, 103, 193
    Message Conveyor Hydraulic pipe
        system, ix, 95, 171, 193
    Message sorting, 184
    "Parkerismus", 112
    "Stopping" and "Stoppers", 114, 151
COLLINGRIDGE Family, 24, 64, 210,
    270-7, 303
Colombo Trincomalee Ceylon, 168, 178,
    184-90, 234, 298, 333
Communications, ix, x, 89, 99, 106, 112,
    117, 120, 129, 151-3, 168, 170-3, 180,
    182, 188, 195, 229, 282
*COOPER, Ray and Peggy, 262, 266,
    283-87
Cow, P. B. (Inflatables), 283, 332
*COTTRELL, Shirley (Wheeldon), 161

D-Day, 104, 121, 138, 162, 167, 169, 175,
    177, 206-8
*DE GREY, Nigel, 77, 94, 104

*DENNISTON, Alastair, 75, 78, 84, 88, 93, 197, 240, 295
Devonshire House, 56, 200
Double Cross System (XX), 169, 327

Eastcote (HMS Pembroke V), 117, 122, 161, 239, 332
*EDNEY, Dorothy, 51, 56, 69, 71, 88, 101, 149, 156, 163, 173, 198, 201, 215-19, 224-7, 229-32, 275, 281-6, 290, 302-4, 307-17, 326, 33
Elmer's School, 68, 97, 176, 302
English Channel, The 22, 29, 55, 69, 109, 164, 206, 325, 329
Evacuees, 210, 231, 329

FANY, 43, 167, 215, 327
FAR EAST,
    18th Infantry Division, 27, 38, 50, 59, 67, 147, 305
    Capitulation, 44-9, 53, 98, 127, 174-6, 182, 203
    Formosa (Taiwan), 51, 67, 202, 321
    Hong Kong, 41, 47, 51, 178, 189, 203, 304, 332
    Tokyo, 175, 203, 234, 255
*FAUTLEY, Ray, 167
FECB, 168, 178, 189, 332
*FLEMING, Ian, 109, 169, 283, 323, 330
* FLOWERS, Tommy, 120
*FOSS, Hugh, 79, 84, 107, 112, 116, 151, 156, 174, 181, 186, 189, 322
France/Belgium, 23, 28, 29, 35, 55, 79, 83, 128, 167, 171, 177, 205, 207, 209, 294, 321, 329, 330
*FRIEDMAN, William, 93, 99, 114, 175, 281, 295, 324, 326
FRUMEL/FRUPAC, 178, 328, 332

Games, 3, 16, 19, 60, 80, 90, 130, 187, 202, 241, 251-57, 270, 275, 302, 304
GC&CS, xii, 298
GERMANY
    Abwehr, 108, 116, 132, 169
    Axis Powers (Tripartite), ix, 41, 69, 175, 244
    Berlin, 81, 119, 175, 221, 322

Bismarck, 136
Concentration camps, 222
Dönitz, Karl, 86, 135, 224
High Command, 105, 113, 119, 169, 294
Luftwaffe, 29, 31, 36, 112, 136, 298, 324
Munich Agreement, 23, 32, 81, 200
*GIBSON, Pamela Rose, 128, 200, 324, 329
*GLASSBOROW, Valerie and Mary, 235, 330
*GODDARD, Mary, 98, 199, 224, 240, 312, 330
GOTZHEIM Family, 98, 191, 240, 253

HALL, Reginald 'Blinker', xi, 78
*HAMILTON-GRACE, Anne, 193
*HANCOCK, John ("The Hankey Pankey"), 112
Hawaii HYPO, 41, 178, 324
HEALTH, 11, 18, 78, 92, 138-47, 160, 197, 203, 226, 310-12, 331
    Combat Stress Reaction (CSR), 269
    Depersonalisation Disorder, 302, 333, 272, 277, 279
    Electro-convulsion (ECT), 269, 278, 303, 331
    Hair loss, 264, 265, 278, 308
    Nervous Breakdown, 152, 175, 268, 275, 303
    PTSD, 331, 334
    Sanatorium/West Park Hosp., 260, 268-77, 303, 332
*HENRY, Ruth (Bourne), 72, 161, 245, 322
*HERIVEL Tip, John, 132
HODGSON Family, 232, 275
*HUMBLE, Olive, 186, 188, 199, 240

India, 16, 41, 45, 74, 79, 109, 114, 148, 151, 187, 214, 247, 259, 275, 278, 291, 300, 331

Jafo, 106, 157, 202
Japanese codes, 93, 94, 107, 113-15, 174-77, 180, 182-85, 187-89, 195, 328
*JEFFREYS', John, 89, 92, 111, 115, 324
Jewish people, 24, 105, 118, 124, 164, 262
*JOHNSON, Peggy (Skinner), 20, 51, 149, 163, 240, 307, 326

Kilindini (Allidina) Kenya, 178, 188
*KNOX, Dilwyn "Dilly", 76, 79, 84, 90, 92, 108, 111, 115, 132, 322

*LADD, C. A., 183
LAWRENCE Family,
Annie, 2-7, 12, 24, 26, 31, 34, 210, 219
Ciss, (Ann Collingridge), 3-9, 14-17, 24, 31-37, 47, 53-56, 140, 191, 204, 210, 258-64, 266-70, 274-77, 305
Harry 3-10, 16, 24, 31-37, 45, 57, 140, 204, 231, 247, 293
'Lawrie/Pat', 45, 69, 189, 301, 309
Oswald (Mister), 2-9, 13, 24, 33, 59, 231
Lend Lease Act (Destroyers for Bases), 35, 181, 321
*LEVER, Mavis (Batey), 108, 116, 133, 322
LISTENERS, 43, 51, 55, 106, 150, 163-73, 171, 206, 221, 298, 313, 324, 325, 326, 334
SIGINT, 78, 93, 172, 281, 323
*LOEWE, Michael, 178, 328
LONDON,
Balham, 19, 150, 261, 326
Blackshaw Rd 20, 24, 34, 39
Camberwell SE17, 18, 167
Clapham Common, 10, 58, 60, 130, 251
Collier's Wood SW18, 8, 30, 51
Euston, 56, 58, 61, 130, 200, 224, 227
Kenlor Rd, 2, 5-11, 24, 26, 34, 39, 146, 204, 210, 240, 259
Longley Rd, 11, 13, 20, 39, 60, 241
Southmead, 163
Streatham, 10, 19, 51, 218, 283
Tooting SW17, xi, 2-17, 20, 26, 30, 56, 58, 61, 69, 101, 124, 146, 149, 154, 204, 211, 221, 231, 240, 251, 258, 276, 300
Waterloo, 30, 58, 60 Westminster, 225, 247, 251, 296
Wimbledon Technical College, 8, 10, 16, 30, 163, 168, 276

MACHINES,
Bomba (Polish), 3, 82-84, 108, 116, 118, 22
Bombe, vii, xi, 72, 82, 86, 92, 104, 106, 108, 112, 115-18, 120, 127, 132,

154, 159-62, 177, 180, 193, 217, 234, 238, 282, 332
British Tunny and Heath Robinson: 118-21, 162, 283
Colossus, 106, 118, 120, 138, 159, 162, 193, 207, 215, 238, 283, 291, 293
Enigma, xi, xii, 79-87, 90-95, 104-13, 115-19, 121, 127, 131-36, 151, 157, 165, 168-71, 175, 180, 193, 282, 291, 322-32
Hagelin C-36, 172, 327
Hollerith, 92, 105, 123, 130, 150, 162, 181, 187, 190
Lorenz, xii, 113, 118-21, 168, 172, 207, 283
Sigaba, 115, 326
Typex, 91, 106, 115, 139, 149, 151-68, 171, 180, 207, 238, 282, 289, 299, 326, 333
*MARTIN, Major (Capt.), H.E., 107, 114, 183-38, 195, 239, 328
*McINTYRE, Cdr. J. P., 188, 196
*MENZIES, Col., Stewart, 84, 92, 227, 282, 322
*MILNER-BARRY, Stuart, 92, 111
MITCHAM, 18, 34, 101, 168, 172, 245, 248, 251, 265, 267, 270, 275-76, 284
MOORE Family,
Emma, 19, 51, 72, 102, 146, 259, 266
Doris, 18, 102, 252, 266
Frank, Snr., 18, 19, 102
Frank, Jnr., 18, 34, 102, 221, 261, 266
Stanley Albert William, 18-20, 27, 33, 38-40, 98, 204, 251-56, 260-68, 277, 286

National Service, xii, 27, 42, 55-57, 72, 231
Naval Intelligence (NID), xi, 77-79, 106, 118, 195, 230, 310, 323
*NAVE, Eric, 174, 179
*NEWMAN, Max, 106, 118-21, 162, 207, 215
Newspaper Reports, 49, 54, 98, 102, 146, 205, 212, 215, 241, 326

Office of Strategic Services (OSS), 246, 330
Official Secrets Act, xii, xiii, 66, 71, 95, 103, 112, 122, 153, 161, 164, 168, 178, 186, 230, 265, 280-83, 287, 299, 327

Parliament, 22, 55, 70, 105, 201, 225, 251, 296, 329
Pearl Harbor, 41, 49, 176, 184, 330
*PETERS, G. A., 183
*PICKLES, Leonard, 174, 248
Poland, 28, 83, 84
    ZYGALSKI, Henryki/Netz sheets, 80-84, 92, 108, 111, 116, 118, 175, 295, 326
Portsmouth, 33, 78, 208, 326
Public Records, 96, 244, 288, 294, 331

Radar, 9, 55, 112, 118, 159, 172, 297, 324
Radio, ix, 16, 24, 82, 95, 104, 113, 120, 159-67, 171, 224, 247, 268, 310, 328
Rationing, 26, 40, 53, 68, 73, 101, 140-45, 149, 231, 329
Recognition, 245, 297, 311
Red Cross, 47-51, 147, 203, 213, 309
REPORTS:
    BJ Telegrams (Blue Jackets), 77, 96
    BMP, 113
    Most Secret, 30, 91, 94, 171
    Top Secret ULTRA: xiii, 30, 40, 66, 91, 94-6, 99, 121, 129, 136, 160, 168-72, 176, 180, 281, 299, 322-27
Reunions, 246, 288-91, 307
*ROBERTS, Capt. Jerry, 118, 137
ROBERTSTON, Christopher, 291-2, 312
ROBERTSON, Jill, x, 249, 253, 254, 256, 257, 258, 266, 271, 272, 276, 308, 312
Room 40, xi, 74 -9, 88, 115, 174, 295, 322
Royal Arsenal Co-operative Society (RACS), 7-11, 14-27, 31, 42, 51-6, 69, 102, 124, 130, 149-55, 163, 202, 267, 282, 284

*SALE, Tony, 197, 293, 310, 333
Schools,
*SEDGWICK, Stan, 155, 236, 326
*SINCLAIR, Admiral Hugh, xii, 70, 78, 84, 170, 322
SOE, 167, 170, 317, 327

Special Liaison/Communications Units (SLU/SCU), 170-3, 207, 209, 299
*STRACHEY, Oliver, 89, 93, 169, 176

*TANDY, Geoffrey, 138
Telephone Lists, 94, 180
*TESTER, Ralph, 118, 121, 137
*TILTMAN, John, 79, 84, 89, 113-20, 174, 177, 197, 324
TIZARD, Henry, 30, 31, 118
*TOCHER, Jean Agnes, 138, 206
*TRAVIS, Edward, 36, 90, 92, 99, 117, 119, 153, 165, 197, 240
*TURING, Alan, xi, 82, 89, 92, 107-11, 115-20, 131-35, 200, 283, 287, 322
*TUTTE, William "Bill", 118-121
*TWINN, Peter, 110, 115, 132

U-boats, 39, 85, 118, 135
USA, 29, 35, 42, 69, 93, 99, 136, 206-07, 221, 2312-2
    Army/Navy Intelligence, 31, 36, 73, 94, 99, 112, 156, 174, 180, 211, 246
    BRUSA Agreement, 99, 117
    Liberty Ships, 86, 217
    Washington DC: Op-20-G Naval Intelligence, 41, 86, 93, 100, 115, 118, 175-88, 227, 246, 281, 294
USSR, 22, 36, 79, 137, 206, 221, 227, 232, 233

VE Day, 223-24, 231-5
VJ Day, 235, 236, 245
*VALENTINE, Jean, 160

WAAF, 43, 51, 153, 163, 189, 193, 333
WALTER Family, 6-14, 24, 33, 140, 231, 258, 260, 266, 276
*WELCHMAN, Gordon, 88-90, 92, 94, 103, 116, 122, 131, 165, 181, 202, 215, 287, 322
*WESTON, Peggy (Hill), 101, 224, 240, 245, 248, 309
*WHELAN, Ronald, 123, 181
*WHITE, Alfred Sidney, 153
WRNS, 43, 72, 82, 93, 103, 117, 119, 154, 159-63, 186, 217, 282